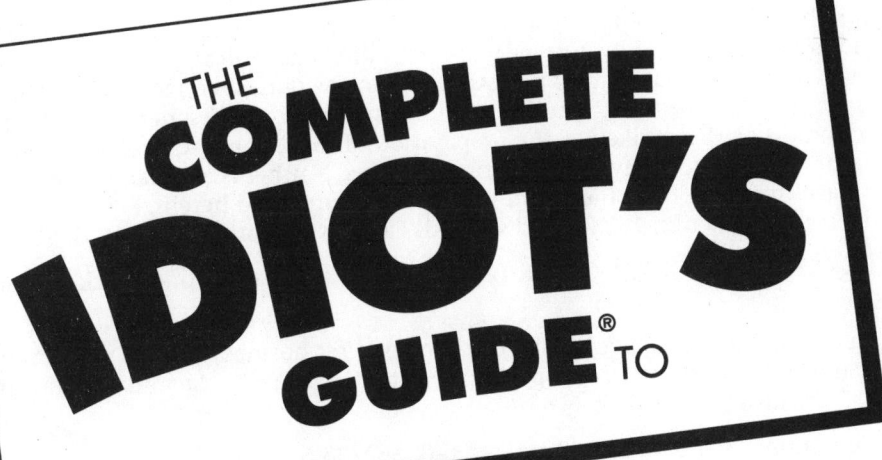

THE COMPLETE IDIOT'S GUIDE® TO

the Art of Seduction

by Janet O'Neal

D0430018

alpha books

A Division of Macmillan General Reference
A Simon & Schuster Macmillan Company
1633 Broadway, New York, NY 10019-6785

Macmillan Publishing books may be purchased for business or sales promotional use. For information please write: Special Markets Department, Macmillan Publishing USA, 1633 Broadway, New York, NY 10019.

International Standard Book Number: 0-02862738-5
Library of Congress Catalog Card Number: 98-88313

00 99 98   8 7 6 5 4 3 2 1

Interpretation of the printing code: The rightmost number of the first series of numbers is the year of the book's printing; the rightmost number of the second series of numbers is the number of the book's printing. For example, a printing code of 98-1 shows that the first printing occurred in 1998.

Printed in the United States of America

Note: This publication contains the opinions and ideas of its author. It is intended to provide helpful and informative material on the subject matter covered. It is sold with the understanding that the author and publisher are not engaged in rendering professional services in the book. If the reader requires personal assistance or advice, a competent professional should be consulted.

The author and publisher specifically disclaim any responsibility for any liability, loss or risk, personal or otherwise, which is incurred as a consequence, directly or indirectly, of the use and application of any of the contents of this book.

Alpha Development Team

Publisher
Kathy Nebenhaus

Editorial Director
Gary M. Krebs

Managing Editor
Bob Shuman

Marketing Brand Manager
Felice Primeau

Editor
Jessica Faust

Development Editors
Phil Kitchel
Amy Zavatto

Production Team

Development Editor
Amy Zavatto

Production Editor
Carol Sheehan

Copy Editor
Susan Aufheimer

Cover Designer
Mike Freeland

Illustrator
Jody P. Schaeffer

Designer
Nathan Clement

Indexer
Chris Cleveland

Layout/Proofreading
Angela Calvert
Mary Hunt
Cheryl Moore
Julie Trippetti

Contents at a Glance

Contents

4 Intellectual Magnetism: Your Brain Is the Most Erogenous Part of Your Body 39

5 Emotional Seductiveness: Creating Those Warm, Fuzzy Feelings 53

xi

Foreword

Seductively speaking, you're a pretty hot commodity. Don't look over your shoulder. I'm talking to you, Mr. or Ms. Average. Seduction isn't some mysterious power that only a select few have. It's a human quality. It's not a question of whether you've got it or not—you do—it's how you're going to draw out the tempter or temptress that lies within.

This is something I have made it my business to know all about. Although my most recent book, *Just Between Us Girls: Secrets About Men from the Mayflower Madam,* and my 4-hour seminar of the same name are directed toward women, I know the need to keep things intriguing is one that concerns both genders. How can you become irresistible? How do you get someone's attention, or keep the attention of the person you're with? How do you discover your sexual personality and how can you make it work with the object of your desire? Good questions. And in *The Complete Idiot's Guide to the Art of Seduction* you'll find good answers. Author Janet "The Love Coach" O'Neal takes you step by step through all the phases of seduction—from attracting someone's attention, to pre-date jitters, to setting the stage for a seduction scene that will knock the socks off of your lover-to-be (or long-time companion, for that matter). O'Neal's expertise will help bring out the ultimate seductress or seducer in you, but with only the most positive (and healthy) results.

Seduction isn't a matter of genetics—it's an *art*. And like any art that's worth appreciating, you'll need to put a little work into your finished product. The great thing is, it's going to be more fun than toil. You won't just walk away from these pages feeling sexy, you'll feel self-confident. What's sexier than that? Hmmm...why not crack open this book and find out?

Happy seducing,

—Sydney Biddle Barrows

Sydney Biddle Barrows is the author of the international bestseller Mayflower Madam, *which was translated into several languages and is in its 15th printing, as well as the book* Mayflower Manners. *A&E has done a biography on her, which airs periodically, and a film was made from* Mayflower Madam, *starring Candice Bergen. Sydney maintains a busy speaking schedule, and is a favorite guest of the top talk shows. She is currently working on a fourth book on cosmetic surgery and its effects on those who undergo it. She lives in New York City with her husband, attorney Darnay Hoffman.*

Introduction

Mention the word "seduction," and you have most people's immediate and undivided attention. Just about everybody is interested in learning more about how to be seductive—whether they are just starting out in the dating game, or they've been married for 25 years and are longing to put some of the sparks back into their relationship.

This book will tell you everything you need to know about becoming the sizzling seductress or seducer you've always wanted to be. And, as I hope will become abundantly clear while you're reading, when I talk about seduction, I am not talking about the archaic, manipulative act with which many of us have come to associate the word. The seduction you're going to learn about in this book is the art of enticing your partner and creating an exquisitely pleasurable experience for both of you.

In fact, it's far more appropriate to think of seduction as a process rather than an act. And it is a process that you must undertake with the purest of intentions. If there's one theme that will show up again and again in this book, it is that the most powerful element in any seduction is the intent of the seducer. In order for you to be able to seduce another person in a positive way, your desires must be grounded in a concern for the well-being of both you and your partner.

So who is this book for? Just about everybody! Never make the mistake of thinking that seduction is only for the young and starry-eyed, or for people in the beginning stages of a relationship. Two other points I hope to make clear in this book are that seduction is for everyone, and seduction is forever. If some of the chapters seem more focused on people who are going out and seducing somebody for the first time, this is only because I know how intimidating that "first time" with someone can be—no matter how experienced you are. Even so, nearly all of the advice in this book can be applied to bringing elements of seductiveness into a long-term relationship as well. To me, the best relationships are those in which both parties keep the seduction alive continuously. (And if you don't think perpetual seduction is possible...well, just read this book!)

In the final analysis, seduction is a true art form. Some people believe that artists are born, rather than made, and others believe that anyone who has the benefit of sufficient training in technique can become an artist. I firmly believe the latter is true. Of course, just as with any other art form, seduction is about more than technique. A genuinely delicious seduction is a combination of feelings, intentions *and* techniques, with the end result truly being greater than the sum of its parts. If this sounds hopelessly abstract, it's not. Being seductive is really quite simple if you follow the concrete guidelines in this book.

Before We Go Any Further...

Before I give you a breakdown of the book's organization, I want to say a few words about its focus. First of all, this book covers sexual topics, and I am sensitive to the fact that many people still believe sex should not take place outside of marriage (or at least outside of a committed relationship).

While I respect everybody's beliefs, I feel it is my responsibility to offer advice that reflects contemporary reality. I do not advocate promiscuity, and I do believe that the most fulfilling sex takes place within the context of a loving relationship. However, most couples in our society have sex before marriage, and many have it even before there's any thought of commitment. How you handle the sequence of events in your own relationship is up to you, but in any case, the advice in this book can be applied whether or not you are married or in some other type of committed relationship. And one principle I feel strongly about is that of safe sex. (See Chapter 14.)

How This Book Is Organized

This book is divided into four parts that take you through the process of becoming—and remaining—seductive.

Part 1, "Becoming A Modern-Day Seductress or Seducer," begins with a new definition of seduction, as befits the new millennium we're about to enter. Next we'll discuss how you can use the process of goal setting to become seductive and attract the person, or persons, you want in your life. And then we'll analyze the individual elements of seductiveness—physical, intellectual, and emotional attractiveness—and we'll discover how these elements combine to create your unique essence or spirit. I'll give you lots of tips on how you can develop your seductiveness in all of these areas.

Now it's time to go out and begin field testing these theories on seductiveness. In Part 2, "Attracting Dates: Casting Your Spell," we'll begin by taking a closer look at what men and women find seductive in the opposite sex. Then we'll explore some of the places you can go to meet attractive people. After that, I'll share tips on how to approach that enticing someone, and how to give and read romantic signals. I've even devoted an entire chapter to the varieties of flirting—the harmless, the harmful, and the frankly seductive. I'll end Part 2 with a seductive guide to the "Big D"—the date itself—and I'll show you how you can use the date to get to know your partner and help plan a most delicious seduction.

In Part 3, "A Night To Remember," things really start heating up. Following a cautionary chapter about safe, responsible sex, we'll discuss how you can set the stage for seduction, and take advantage of the exquisite sexual tension that is building between the two of you. We'll also discuss those "pre-game jitters." And then I'll devote two chapters to tips on how to make the most of the delicious chemistry that has led you to this point—in other words, how to create a completely seductive experience that will leave you both smiling, and make you just want more.

Since seduction is not just a single act, Part 4 is all about the rest of the process. How do you keep a good thing going? We'll begin with a survival guide to the first "morning after," and what to do whether you know this is going to be the first and *last* morning after, or it knocked your socks off and you want more! Next we'll discuss how to keep the relationship intriguing indefinitely, by continuing to meet your partner's needs outside of the bedroom as well as in it. Then we'll take a delightful look at sexual fantasies, and how you can use them to add spice to your relationship and bring the two of you closer together. And finally, because no book on seduction would be complete without mentioning love, we'll explore this complex emotion, looking at the interplay of love and seduction throughout the course of your relationship. I'll give you some advice on making the seduction last forever.

Extras

Throughout the chapters in this book, you'll find information boxes that help clarify some of the points in the text, or are just useful facts. Herewith, a guide to the information tidbits sprinkled throughout this book:

Heart Brakes

These boxes have advice about things to watch out for. They will help you steer clear of seduction pitfalls.

Wordplay

These boxes have definitions or clarifications of words and terms related to the subject matter in the chapter.

For HIS Eyes Only

These boxes contain tips, tricks, and secrets just for men. (Of course, I won't say anything if you take a peek at the women's boxes.)

For HER Eyes Only

These boxes contain tips, tricks, and secrets just for women. (Fair is fair— I won't say anything if you take a peek at the men's boxes.)

Ask the Love Coach

These boxes serve one of two purposes: either to give you tips and secrets that are interesting, important, and/or just fun to know; or to relate true stories of other people's experiences, and share advice on what to do if you're faced with a similar situation.

And don't forget the crib sheet at the beginning of the book. You'll find a handy list of men's and women's biggest sexual turn ons and turn-offs, and a seductive what's hot/what's not list. You'll also find little cards you can fill out, cut out, and put in your wallet, their purpose being to encourage you to set goals and create affirmations—both of which are powerful tools for transforming yourself into a seductress or seducer.

Disclaimer

Throughout this book I have included anecdotes to illustrate points. Except where noted, all such stories are from my client files or personal experiences. All names, except for those of public figures, have been changed to protect confidentiality.

This book is intended to provide helpful and informative advice, but it is not intended to replace consultation with a competent professional counselor or therapist where needed.

Acknowledgments

My gratitude goes out to the thousands of clients and callers whose insights and wisdom have taught me so much. A special thanks to those who were my coaching clients during the writing of this book; your patience and understanding when I had to shift appointments and juggle sessions have been most appreciated.

Thank you to all of the radio hosts, throughout the U.S., Canada, and Europe, who have given me an opportunity to speak with thousands of callers over the years. Thanks, too, to the producers and hosts of the TV shows, both local and national, who invited me into their studios.

I am deeply grateful to my original role models: my mother, Hazel Crowe, who taught me compassion and love for all people, and who encourages me daily; and my father, Ray Meader, who introduced me to the love of books, gave me the intelligence to write them, and the discipline to promote them. My sincere appreciation to Robert Meader, my brother by blood, and my trusted and cherished friend by choice. And a special thanks to B.C., for taking care of my mother, and to Helen, for taking care of my dad.

There are some members of my extended family who deserve pages, if not books, of their own. Dr. Bob and Dr. Leah Schwartz are two of those people. Thank you for being in my life and letting me know I can count on you, no matter what.

Special thanks also to Robert A. Knowlton for your superb advice, encouragement, and support.

I'm also grateful to Nancy Neill, my "shadow self."

My gratitude also goes out to Joe Vitale, who can always be counted on to give me his candid and valued opinion.

Thanks, too, to special friends and guardians: D.R., Morey W., Beau T, Patricia, Roz, and my joy, Prize and his bride, Chris. Of course, then there are the Blue Wolf, the Panther, and the Bear.

Much appreciation to Megan, Russell, and Jason for keeping me from ever having a dull moment.

Thank you to Dr. Marty and Horty Kaplan—I love you! You are so kind, intelligent, and loving.

Warm thanks to Jake, for loyally attending every meeting and writing session, and for keeping me warm at night.

And, of course, many thanks to Moose, for being my best friend, and teaching me that I have an untapped reservoir of strength, and lessons still to be learned.

I am especially grateful to Jane Dystel, the perfect literary agent for me; I always think of you as the iron fist in a velvet glove. Thanks also to Lauren Marino and everyone at Broadway Books for letting me do this project.

My gratitude to the team at Macmillan...I thank Nancy Mikhail for originating the idea for this book and encouraging me to do it. I am especially thankful for Amy Zavatto, my developing editor, who gave me the consistent, clear-cut direction a writer dreams of getting from an editor. Yea, Amy! And mention also needs to go to Susan Aufheimer, for her copy-editing suggestions.

I thank Connie Schmidt and Ron Kaye, "the Love Coach Literary Support Team," who went above and beyond the call of duty to help bring this book to life. The book truly would not have been possible without you.

And, as always, my profound gratitude to God, who has never given me more than I can handle (although these last few months have come close!).

Get in Touch with Me

I always love to hear from my readers. If you have any questions, comments, or anecdotes, or are interested in personal relationship coaching sessions, please send a self-addressed stamped envelope to: Love Coach, P.O. Box 570333, Houston, TX 77257-0333. I'd love to hear from you!

Trademarks

All items mentioned in this book that are known to be, or are suspected of being, registered trademarks or service marks, have been appropriately capitalized. Alpha Books and Macmillan General Reference cannot attest to the accuracy of this information. Use of a term in the book should not be regarded as affecting the validity of any trademark or service mark.

Part 1

Becoming a Modern-Day Seductress or Seducer

Seduction—what a titillating topic. The very word holds a promise of tantalizing pleasures, sensual indulgence, or, perhaps, forbidden delights. If you're like most of today's women and men, however, you're not hungering for forbidden fruit; you simply want a pragmatic, honest, and mutually pleasurable path to enticing a lover.

Over the years, I've worked with thousands of couples and individuals—first through owning the video dating service Friend Connection, and now through my relationship coaching. I've learned that many people have misconceptions about seduction and what it takes to be seductive. The good news is that anyone can master the art of seduction—yes, this means you, too—and you don't have to look like Cindy Crawford or Brad Pitt to be positively irresistible to a lover.

In this part we're going to set the stage for your transformation into a modern-day seductress or seducer. After learning a new definition of seduction—as befits the new era we're approaching—you'll learn how to take a proactive approach to your love life by setting goals. You'll discover the elements of seductiveness—all those facets of you that make up the alluring whole—and you'll learn how you can enhance them in order to create your captivating new self. So...let the magic begin!

Chapter 1

Savage!

Redefining Seduction

In This Chapter

➤ What is seduction? A new definition for a new millennium

➤ Good seduction versus bad seduction

➤ What makes a person seductive

So you want to be seductive. Hmmmm…where to begin? Just by virtue of having the desire to be so, you're already on the path to seductiveness. And you've definitely come to the right book.

Before we begin the how-to, though, I want to make sure we're all in agreement about what seduction means. There are easily as many negative as positive connotations for this word. For example, seduction can imply coercion and abuse of power. Over the years, the news media has assailed us with various high-profile cases, though in some instances it was difficult to tell just who was seducing whom.

On the other hand, we have hopelessly sweet and romantic images of seduction, many of which are fictional (the movie *Don Juan de Marco* comes to mind, for example). There are, however, countless true-life cases in which people are seduced in a delightful manner by someone who really has their best interests in mind. These cases just don't make the headlines.

The point is that there is bad seduction and good seduction—or, you might say, malicious and delicious seduction. Too often in the past, seduction has implied the harmful variety. With this in mind, I think it's time for the entire concept of seduction to get an overhaul.

Wordplay

Millennium has several definitions in the dictionary. The first is simply "a period of 1,000 years." The term also refers to the 1,000-year reign of Christ on Earth, as prophesied in the Bible. The third meaning (and more to our point here) is a period of general happiness and good living. No matter what your frame of reference, there's something about this approaching new millennium that is genuinely exciting—much more so than just any old New Year.

Wordplay

The word **seduce** has been in use at least since the 15th century. It comes from the Latin *seducere,* which is made up of the prefix *se* (without, apart) and *ducere* (to lead)—in other words, "to lead apart (or away)." In its earliest uses, seduce meant "to divert from allegiance or service," or "to induce [a woman] to surrender her chastity." The negative connotation lingers today, but the new seduction we're focusing on in this book is a positive, exhilarating experience for both parties.

Our aim here is to define, or redefine, seduction for real life (as opposed to reel life). We're going to look at seduction as a way to:

➤ Be alluring

➤ Be charismatic

➤ Be enticing

I want to make it clear that the focus of this book is the new seduction—seduction for the new *millennium,* if you will. For many of us, this new millennium that everyone's talking about holds the promise of being a more joyous, happy time; a time when people will become more conscious of, and motivated toward, a general state of well-being. It follows that the shift in emphasis of seduction would be toward actions that would have a positive effect on a person's spirit and life in general. The seduction we're going to talk about in this book is seduction that goes beyond purely selfish intent, and results in the benefit of all involved.

A Thousand Years of Good Intent

English is a flexible language. As linguists and other scholars continue to remind us, we have always changed the meanings of words according to time, place, and circumstance.

Seduction is certainly one of those words whose meaning has changed with the times. Originally, to *seduce* someone or to be seductive meant to *do something to* the person, or to entice a person to do something that was generally not in his or her best interest.

Over the years, however, the definition has expanded to include actions taken to win over or attract another person. The context may or may not be sexual, and the results may be beneficial or harmful. In just a little while, we'll explore examples of the varieties of seduction—nonsexual and sexual, beneficial and hurtful.

How Do You Tell the "Good" From the "Bad"?

What's the difference between the archaic, negative seduction and the new, enlightened sort of seduction we'll be exploring in this book? The distinction lies in two factors:

> ➤ *The intent or purpose:* You can judge whether your actions represent the new seduction or the old, based upon your motives. Are you just after a momentary thrill, with no regard for the welfare of the person you're seducing (or for how you'll feel about yourself when it's all over)? Or do you truly want to create a pleasurable experience for both of you?

> ➤ *The results:* For better or worse, the effects of seduction almost always outlast "the act." The ultimate results are as significant as the intent (and we all know what they say about the road to hell). Consider the residuals of your act: Will it leave one or both of you with feelings of guilt or regret, or with smiles on your faces?

If your intent is benevolent *and* your actions bring no harm to that person—or to yourself—then it's safe to say you are practicing the "new" seduction. Just to make sure we're clear on the distinctions between the various types of seduction, we'll look at a few examples.

Nonsexual Seduction: The Good, the Bad, and the Downright Ugly

Seduction comes in many forms; it isn't always about sex. In fact, sometimes it isn't even about you and another person.

Something to Which We Can All Relate: Food

Let's say you get hold of a big red apple, and it looks so fresh that you just know it's going to be crisp and juicy and sweet. Your mouth begins watering at the mere thought of that first bite. That apple is calling to you—yes, seducing you—until you simply can't resist anymore. You close your eyes, almost as if in prayer, open your mouth wide, and take that first, tantalizing bite.

Exactly as you had imagined, it has just the right crunch and it is bursting with sweet juiciness. When you separate yourself from the rapture of that first taste, your intellectual side tells you that

Heart Brakes

Seduction doesn't always have to involve another person; you can also be seduced by an inanimate object or a situation. If you're prone to self-sabotage, it's easy to fall prey to bad seduction of this type. One powerful antidote is to focus on the negative consequences you'll face if you yield to temptation.

it's nutritious—certainly not a symbol of original sin, but simply a piece of delicious fruit. As you eat it, your body feels better, and you seem to have more energy. Afterwards, you are filled with a sense of having been both nourished and delighted. There are no regrets; your body and your mind seem to smile in unison.

On the other hand, imagine that you're on a diet, and you're being tempted by a piece of pecan pie. That pie calls to you, sings to you. Though you know the pie is full of fat, calories, and artery-clogging cholesterol, its sweetness has an almost hypnotic appeal. Throwing caution and moderation to the wind, you eat the pie. After all, you've been depriving yourself for weeks now. But somehow when you're finished, you don't feel rewarded; you immediately feel heavy and guilt ridden. You feel bad about yourself, and your self-image has taken a minor nosedive.

For the purpose of this example, then, we can say the act of eating the pie represents bad seduction, whereas eating the apple represents good seduction.

Seducers on Two Legs

In the food examples we just listed, there really wasn't the factor of intent or purpose —at least not from the objects that seduced us. Obviously, apples and slices of pecan pie are not sentient beings. You could, however, consider these examples to be cases of *self*-seduction, in which case the pie incident would constitute self-sabotage.

Ask the Love Coach

What's the difference between seduction and manipulation? Is the latter necessarily "good" or "bad," or are there shades of gray? Bill and Louise had a spirited discussion about this very matter when they rented the vintage movie *Breakfast at Tiffany's*. Louise found the movie charming, and Audrey Hepburn's Holly Golightly character waifishly appealing. Bill liked the movie too, but had this comment about the character: "What a manipulator. No guy with any sense would tolerate that kind of behavior today."

Many people of *both* genders use manipulation of some sort when they're afraid to ask directly for what they want. Watching this movie led Bill and Louise into a discussion about their own relationship. They were both able to cite examples when they used manipulative tactics with each other. This behavior wasn't always overtly destructive, but it often led to misunderstandings and frustration. They each made a pact to be more careful about this in the future.

Now let's look at some examples involving other people. Imagine you're at a party and a woman you know comes up to you and says, "Michael, you're so good with children. You're so funny; kids think you're just like a clown. I would just love for you to dress up as a clown on Christmas Eve and spend a couple of hours in the burn section of the Children's Hospital, just giving the kids gifts and talking to them...you know, generally lifting their spirits."

Almost without your realizing it, she seduces you into taking time out of your frantic holiday schedule to visit the hospital. It's easy to understand why. The person making the request is someone who likes you and holds you in high esteem, and you feel the same about her. She has appealed to your higher self, enmeshing you in the holiday spirit and the natural glow that comes from doing good deeds.

Afterwards, of course, you feel wonderful. You think of how fortunate you are to be healthy, and you're glad you have brought some joy into these children's lives. You even promise yourself, "This is something that I will do every year from now on, because not only did I bring joy to the kids, it made me feel good."

Did the person who originally seduced you into going to the hospital and becoming a clown practice negative or positive seduction? Obviously, this is a case of the latter.

Picture yourself at another party. A woman you know who's a stockbroker comes up to you and says, "Michael, I have the greatest deal for you. I have some inside information no one else has about a stock that's about to split. You're going to make so much money if you buy it. Just think how great you'd look in that new Porsche you've been wanting." Glossing over that phrase "inside information," you let yourself be talked into buying the stock.

Why? This woman has appealed to your greedy side and your vanity. You want to make money, and besides, you really like the broker's implication that you would be more attractive with an expensive new car. So you purchase the stock—and then it doesn't split, after all. In the end, you lose a lot of money.

Heart Brakes

Malicious seducers often try to appeal to your baser emotions such as greed, vanity, or fear.

The woman did, indeed, seduce you, but not in a good way, and you ended up feeling used. She made a huge commission, and what did you get? Nothing but a big dose of what avarice will do to you. That's the negative form of seduction.

Sexual Seduction: The Sublime and the Squalid

For most of us, the word "seduction" has sexual connotations above all else. After all, that's why you're reading this book, isn't it?

Sexual energy is a powerful force, and when the factor of seduction is added, it can either move your soul or shatter you to your very core. Again, it all depends on how it is used—the intent and purpose, and the results.

Delicious Seduction: A Little Slice of Heaven

Imagine that you're coming home from a hard day's work, and you haven't had a very good day with the boss. You're cranky and tired. As you pull into the driveway, you see your husband's car. He's home early. That's curious; he's not normally home before you. Half suspicious, half worried, you fumble for your keys and push open the front door—only to look across the foyer to the stairs, where you see a rose petal on each step, beckoning you up the stairway.

What's this? you wonder. Following the trail of rose petals you are led into the bathroom, where you see a tiny envelope with your name on it. You open the envelope and read the note inside. The note says, *"My Love: The bubble bath is drawn for you. I hope it's the right temperature. I put in the rose scented bath salts you like so much. On the vanity you will find one champagne glass, and a chilled bottle in the bucket next to the tub. Please pour yourself a glass, slip into the tub, and just let the day fade away. I Love You."*

Wordplay

Delicious seduction is seduction that has a beneficial outcome for everyone involved.

You get into the tub, simply delighted. Your husband has never done anything like this before. You lie there in the gentle caress of the bubbles, sipping the champagne, and you begin to drift off and actually forget about how bad your day was.

Then you get out and find a brand-new, big, fluffy bath towel waiting there with another note pinned to it. The note says, *"This towel was made for one purpose: to pamper the most beautiful body that I have ever seen. After you are finished drying off, please come into the bedroom."* The softness of the towel delights you as you dry your body. You find that you're laughing now, your frustration washed away, replaced by the feeling that you really are beautiful.

You go into the bedroom and find another note. *"Lie down on the bed and put on this mask. Listen to the music I've selected on the stereo, and just relax. In a few moments, I'll come in and give you a massage. My hope is that my hands will speak clearly, and tell you just how much I adore you."*

You put the mask on and lie down, completely lost in a sense of sheer delight. The music begins softly, barely audible, then rises just loud enough for you to recognize and follow the melody. Strains of "Winter," from Vivaldi's *Four Seasons* begin to weave their unique spell. God, how long have you loved this piece? Your reverie is only slightly interrupted by the feel of warm oil, gently pressed into your skin by two strong, sensitive hands—hands that you know, and that know you, so very well.

Ask the Love Coach

Few things can add sizzle to a long-term relationship like a well-planned seduction scene. Pour all of your imagination and creativity into surprising and delighting the person you love, and even if everything doesn't go as you planned (the roses don't get delivered, the soufflé falls) your efforts will pay off because your intent will be clear. *That's* seduction for the new millennium.

The touch is soft but masculine upon your neck and shoulders, moving down your body, sweetly kneading away what little tension remains in your now supple flesh. He just keeps on, working those hands down the length of your body, all the way down to your toes. He isn't saying anything to you, yet you hear him well.

As you start to drift off, completely relaxed, you feel the slight tickle of a feather upon your skin, grazing lightly across your breasts and sending tingles, so familiar, yet brand new, through your body. Without even fully awakening, you reach out, drawing this wondrous man close against you, and the two of you make love passionately. And yes, my dear, you have just been delightfully and completely seduced.

Think about this scene (how can you *not*?). Was this a sweet seduction for the new millennium—delicious seduction, in other words—or an example of the old, "evil," *malicious seduction*?

Consider the intent. Your husband went to some trouble to put this entire scenario together and he did this out of adoration for you. Think of the results. During the next few days, you find your mind drifting back to that wonderful afternoon, thinking every day how loved you feel, and appreciating all of the work and thought that went into giving you such a delightful experience.

Wordplay

Malicious seduction is seduction that has harmful results.

Heart Brakes

Anyone who persists in trying to persuade you to do something after you've said "No" several times does not have your best interest in mind, and is clearly a malicious seducer.

This seduction left nothing in its wake but warm, tender emotions, increased feelings of self-worth, and the sense that the two of you are closer to each other than ever before.

Obviously, this was an example of delicious seduction.

Malicious Seduction: Devil on a Blue Bike

Now, let's take a look at another scenario. It's late at night and you go into a bar. You start dancing with a pretty good-looking guy in a motorcycle jacket. He's whispering something in your ear that you can't quite understand, and as you drink and dance and drink some more, things begin to get very sexy. Before you know it, it's getting late, but he keeps buying you drinks, and pretty soon your mind is a little foggy.

Then he invites you to take a ride on his motorcycle, and maybe come over to his place. That doesn't sound like such a great idea, mainly because you're in a committed relationship with a terrific boyfriend who's out of town, and because this leather-clad man is a complete stranger. But your new friend keeps up the pressure until you finally give in and go with him. When you get to his house, he opens up a bottle, and you have more to drink. Next thing you know, you're having some very rough sex. Afterwards, your head spinning from the booze, you fall asleep.

The next morning, you awaken early and find yourself next to someone you don't know at all, who is not nearly as sexy as he was the night before. He has a growth of beard on his face, and his breath reeks of stale beer.

You look around and really observe the way he lives, the place that you've put yourself in. To say that he's not very tidy would be an understatement, and you find that you want, more than anything in the world, just to be away—from him, from his filthy place, and, sadly, from yourself most of all. Your self-worth is about as low as it's ever been, and you feel very ashamed that you have been unfaithful to your trusting boyfriend.

Right now, you're experiencing what is known as "coyote love." A coyote, caught in a trap, will literally gnaw its own leg off to escape, and, at this moment, you would almost rather do the same thing than wake this guy up and ask him to drive you home.

This scenario, too, was a seduction, but what type was it? Was it delicious or malicious? The best way to tell is to ask yourself how you feel. Your self-worth is down, you don't even want to speak to this person, and God knows what horrible disease you might now carry. This clearly falls into the category of bad seduction.

For HER Eyes Only

Some "nice guys" complain that many women are attracted to "bad boys." They have a point. Whether from lack of self-esteem, fear of intimacy, or a desire to live "on the edge" (either directly or vicariously, through their tempestuous lovers) many women continually allow themselves to be seduced by men who are bad news. Apart from the obvious dangers—STDs, sexual assault, or worse—women who go for the bad guys are depriving themselves of true happiness. Learn to love and value yourself, and you will attract men who treat you accordingly.

There's No Such Thing As a One-Night Stand: Seduction Has Lasting Effects

When you engage in good seduction, you must have no harmful intent in mind for the person you're seducing. On the contrary, you must wish for this individual as much pleasure, both short and long term, as you desire for yourself.

As we just saw in the example above, a bad seduction inevitably has a toxic outcome. If your intent is clearly focused on your own selfish need, oblivious to the well-being of your partner, the outcome will always be less than joyous. After you've been on the receiving end of such a toxic seduction, you feel like you've been drained, as if the life force has just been sucked out of you. You're left feeling tired and not very pleased with who you are.

On the other hand, if you've been seduced by someone who holds your own well-being high on their priority list, life somehow seems better for you. And if you're the kind of sweet seducer who holds the pleasure and well-being of your partner as dearly as your own, the rewards you will reap go beyond those of a carnal nature.

In either case, seduction has effects that last long past the act itself. That's why it's always important to consider not just the intent, but the results.

For HIS Eyes Only

Some men, even in this era of safe-sex consciousness, are "serial seducers." Call it the Don Juan syndrome, the Casanova complex, or sex addiction—but whatever you call it, it's *not* seduction for the new millennium. No matter how benign their motives, serial seducers not only dehumanize the women they seduce, but they doom themselves to exist in what artist and writer Kent Nerburn calls "a misery of hopeless expectations." An enlightened seducer wants a more profound experience than the thrill of the chase, or the excitement of the next conquest.

General Seductiveness: The Elements of Allure

We've talked about seductive situations, but now it's time to get personal. Just what is it that makes a person seductive, and how do we recognize such a person?

On a recent promotional tour for my book, *Cracking the Love Code*, I had a fascinating conversation about this very topic with one of my escorts. An escort is a person who picks you up and drives you to and from radio and TV shows or book signings while you're in a city—your new best friend for a day.

My escort told me about the time she'd been an escort for General Norman Schwartzkopf. She described to me what a delightful day she had spent with him.

Ask the Love Coach

Being attracted to a person doesn't necessarily imply sexual attraction. If a person is truly charismatic, people of both sexes will be drawn to that person and will want to please and impress him or her. This sort of attractiveness, or universal appeal, is very seductive.

"He was so charismatic, so confident, so enjoyable to talk to, and so very funny," she said. She added that, while he certainly didn't fit her usual definition of sexy, there was something very sensuous and really quite sexual about him. She felt compelled, however, to fill her narrative with disclaimers. "Don't misunderstand," she said over and over, "I wasn't *attracted* to him."

To which I finally responded, "Oh, yes, you were. You were very much attracted to him. But just because you were attracted to him doesn't mean that you necessarily wanted to act on it in a sexual way." This was a very happily married woman, but she couldn't help noticing—and being affected by—a man with Schwartzkopf's obvious seductive qualities.

This only makes sense. After all, he was a phenomenal leader, and the ability to completely seduce is an essential quality of great leadership. In order to lead people into action, an individual must have more in his or her personal repertoire than the ability to bark orders. This type of person must be able to inspire and entice others to do his or her bidding, to obey—not just out of necessity, but out of a genuine willingness to please.

As a leader, Schwartzkopf had these qualities in abundance. He may not be a perfect reflection of our culture's masculine beauty ideal *du jour*, but he possesses that magical stuff from which seductive power springs: charisma.

Ingredients to Cast a Seductive Spell

What exactly does this magical substance consist of? It's not any single element or quality. It's certainly not anything that you can drape over you before walking out the door to greet the world. Rather, *charisma* is the essence of the person, the sum of all the person's other qualities and characteristics—and as such, it takes on its own energy.

This is one instance in which the whole is truly greater than the sum of its parts. It's much like a precious stone, which shines clearly with the reflected light of its many facets. Should one or more of the facets be flawed, the stone fails to shine and its value is diminished. However, with all facets polished to perfection, the gem exudes a light and splendor that is a source of awe and wonderment.

So, what are the magical ingredients of seductiveness?

➤ *A pinch of physical attraction*: The first important element is physical body and appearance. Physical presence is both an outgrowth of a person's attitude toward him- or herself and a factor in the shaping of that attitude. Obviously, a person tends to be happier and, thus, more attractive, if he or she is in good health. Grooming and hygiene are certainly factors in a pleasing physical appearance as well. And to a lesser, but still significant, extent, what a person wears can also enhance his or her self-image if the cut and fabrics are sensual, and signal approachability. Approachability is a key word here. A truly seductive person looks warm and real and touchable, unlike some of the stunning beauties or hunks we often see on TV and in the movies. We'll learn about physical attraction in Chapter 3.

Wordplay

The word **charisma** was originally a theological term meaning "free gift of God's grace." It is derived from the Greek *kharisma*, meaning "to show favor or grace." Though the word still has religious meanings, it is most commonly used these days to describe a person's power to inspire devotion and enthusiasm.

Ask the Love Coach

While a certain degree of mystery is intriguing, you have to be approachable to be seductive. It's important to look warm and touchable, but you also must smile, make eye contact, laugh, and generally seem interested in the people around you. Aloofness and disinterest are not seductive—receptivity *is*.

➤ *A dash of intellectual magnetism*: Another element of a person's essence is the mind. To be truly seductive, a person must be stimulating on an intellectual level. After all, it has been rightfully said that our primary erogenous zones are in our minds. What makes a person interesting? In general, a truly interesting person is one who has a keen sense of curiosity and is able to communicate that interest. This person expresses interest in you in a way that lets you know there are things he or she wants to learn from you, as well as teach you. Such a person has a hunger for knowledge about the surrounding world and about the person he or she is with. We'll talk about intellectual attractiveness in Chapter 4.

➤ *A touch of emotional seductiveness*: No less crucial than any of the other elements is the person's emotional being. By emotional being, we mean the ability to feel compassion, to open him- or herself to feelings for you, to have empathy with your plight or even the plight of someone he or she has never met, half a world away.

An emotionally attractive person experiences joy merely touching or being touched by you in a safe and tender way. And that is extraordinarily seductive. In Chapter 5, we'll discuss emotional seductiveness.

Heart Brakes

A person's intent is very much a part of his or her spirit. If someone's intent toward you is harmful, evil, malevolent, or just indifferent, it follows that he or she is not capable of what we referred to earlier as delicious seduction. By failing to seduce with gentle nurturing, the mal-intended rob themselves, and the people whose lives they affect, of the joy inherent in that sweet seduction we so crave.

➤ *Mix well, and you have…spirit*: Finally, we come to the person's spirit, or essence—and we're right back where we started. Spirit (to return to our original metaphor) is truly the luminescence of the precious gem, emanating from its many facets and shining its light out into the world. This essence includes how a person looks, thinks, and how he or she emotes, but it also includes factors that are less immediately discernible. Among these are a person's self-confidence and sense of self-worth, and intent toward others. We'll discuss spirit, and go into more detail about purpose and intent, in Chapter 6.

The good news is that by focusing on your own individual "elements"—the physical, intellectual, and emotional aspects that make up your essence—you can be seductive and charismatic yourself. Before we get into these elements of seductiveness, however, we need to talk about goal setting.

The Least You Need to Know

➤ There are other types of seduction besides sexual seduction, such as situations involving food, money, or other temptations.

➤ The difference between delicious seduction and malicious seduction lies in the intent of the seducer and the resulting feelings of the person being seduced.

➤ Whether the seduction is the good or bad variety, it can have long-lasting effects.

➤ Seductiveness is a combination of physical, emotional, and intellectual factors that comprise the person's spirit.

➤ You can learn to be seductive.

Chapter 2

Goal Setting: The Proactive Approach to Seduction

In This Chapter

➤ Taking control of your life

➤ The lessons of history: classic seductresses and seducers

➤ Deciding to become seductive

➤ Determining the type of people you want to attract

This chapter is about goal setting—deciding exactly what you want and beginning the process of getting it. If you're an incurable romantic, you may be wondering why we're talking about goal setting at all in a book about seduction. Perhaps you think any mention of goals in this context sounds too much like business and not enough like pleasure. Maybe you believe goal setting will rob seduction of its mystery and magic.

Relax! That's not the intent here at all. Being a romantic myself, I'm a great fan of mystery and magic—but I am also a firm believer in taking a proactive approach in all areas of life. In truth, goal setting is every bit as valid in your personal life as in your business dealings. Think of it this way: Most of us have experienced romances that ended in disaster, or perhaps just in disappointment. And why did this happen? More than likely it was because we set out blindly, with no idea of what we truly wanted and needed. We didn't have any goals; we just let things happen.

Whose Life Is It, Anyway?

You might not have thought about it, but you have already begun the process of setting goals. After all, you've decided you want to attract people, haven't you? That, in and of itself, is a goal. What have you done to achieve this goal? Well, you bought this book; that's a good first step. You're already on your way to becoming seductive.

In making the decision to become seductive, what you have really decided to do is to re-create yourself, which is not nearly as daunting as it may sound at first. After all, I'm not talking about turning yourself into something you're not. That would not only be destructive, it would be impossible. Instead, I am talking about becoming aware of and refining your dreams about yourself, and, through a focused, proactive effort, bringing those dreams to life.

Nobody else can do it for you, and it is going to take some effort on your part. The result, however, will be well worth it. You can and will transform yourself into the most desirable person you can be, and the people around you will most certainly sit up and take notice. To paraphrase a line from a popular move of a few years back, "If you build it, they will come."

It's your life, and you can make it as glorious as you want it to be.

Ask the Love Coach

Can anybody become seductive? Yes! This means you, too, and you don't have to be blessed with supermodel or superstar looks. You have your own unique form of allure, and once you zero in on your special qualities, you can learn to refine and accentuate them—and to project them so other people can see and appreciate them, as well. Seductresses and seducers are made, not born.

Maybe S/he's Born with It...But Probably Not

Some people just seem to be naturally seductive. In truth, however, very few people are born knowing how to be a great seductress or seducer. A look at some classic examples of alluring seductresses and irresistible playboys illustrates the point that seductive people are not born, but made (in more ways than one!).

Classic Seductresses: Geishas and Courtesans

Arthur Golden's fascinating and well-researched novel *Memoirs of a Geisha* describes in delicious detail the life, training, and mindset of a *Geisha*. A Geisha is trained from her childhood to attract, please, and entertain men, particularly wealthy businessmen. Although we may look upon it as servitude, becoming a Geisha was, and is, considered a very noble and revered calling in Japan. Girls chosen for this training are selected not just for their physical beauty, but also for their ability and motivation to learn the required skills.

Training begins early with a highly organized apprenticeship. The young girl receives extensive instruction in skills and traits valued by men of power: music, the arts, voice, make-up, and hair. She learns to converse about everything from history to current events to the gossip of the day. Her objective is to become ever more desirable, more alluring, and more intoxicating to the men she will entertain.

Indeed, the ability of the Geisha to absolutely enthrall her charges is legendary. And the book *Memoirs of a Geisha* is an extraordinary story of how an ordinary girl transforms herself into an incredible seductress.

A similar transformation takes place in a movie called *Dangerous Beauty*. This is a splendid (though admittedly somewhat idyllic) presentation of the life of a *courtesan*. The film shows how a common girl is transformed into a courtesan, and becomes so phenomenally seductive that the citizens of an entire city are ready to lay down their lives for her. In Europe of the 16th and 17th centuries, a courtesan was a woman who was thoroughly and painstakingly trained in all aspects of seduction and allure: education, wit, entertainment, and beauty.

Far from being a common prostitute, the courtesan was placed in a position of respect and power to a degree far beyond that of her female contemporaries. She frequently stood beside her man of the moment at important social and political functions. This position was not bestowed haphazardly; the courtesan had to learn well the skills that would inspire others to look upon her with respect.

In the examples above, neither the Geisha nor the courtesan was born knowing the ropes. They learned to become seductive. And the lesson for us

Wordplay

A **Geisha** is not a prostitute, but is a professional female entertainer trained in singing, dancing, playing a musical instrument, and practicing the art of conversation. In fact, the word Geisha means, "art person." This profession began in Japan in the 18th century and still exists today.

Wordplay

A **courtesan** was, for all practical purposes, a prostitute, but one who was highly trained and educated, and who catered to only the most wealthy and powerful men. In many cases, she wielded considerable power herself.

For HER Eyes Only

Women, for inspiration and entertainment, read up on what made the courtesans and Geishas so desirable. Check out some movies too; I've already cited *Dangerous Beauty*, which is a very seductive film. For a change of pace, rent *My Fair Lady*, the story of a woman who became the best that she could be. If Eliza Doolittle could do it, so can you.

For HIS Eyes Only

Guys, rent the movie *Don Juan de Marco*. The character played by Johnny Depp is no James Bond; he probably doesn't even drink martinis—but oh, does he know how to shake and stir a woman to her very soul. Of course, I'm not suggesting you seduce hordes of women into your bed—just that you check out what it is about this character that women found so entrancing. (The Marlon Brando character is no slouch in the romance department himself.)

modern, enlightened Western women is that we, too, can transform ourselves into enthralling creatures.

Naturally, I am not suggesting that you have to become a Geisha or a courtesan in order to be seductive. However, if the women of these more repressive societies could use their allure to rise above many of the limitations placed upon them, just imagine how empowered an independent, modern woman could become if armed with the basic talents and wisdom of courtesans and Geishas. The good news is that, unlike the Geisha and the courtesan, the woman of today needn't spend years in training to become seductive. Make the decision, apply yourself to the process, and you'll see positive results in only a few months.

Bond...James Bond: Seducer Extraordinaire

A seductive man with whom we are all familiar is the character of 007, James Bond. Granted, Bond is fictional, but I cite him because, fictional or not, he is a reflection of our culture's ideals of masculine allure.

Just what is it about this character that makes him so appealing to women? Is it his looks? That's only part of the story. While the actors who have played the British secret agent in the many Bond movies have all been attractive, their attractiveness was not based solely on the actors' physical appearance.

The truth is, James Bond wouldn't be nearly as sexy if he didn't know all of the things he knows. He comes across as being completely comfortable in circumstances that most of us will never face, and his repertoire of knowledge includes areas that, while exciting, are completely foreign to most people. After all, he's a spy, he's an incredible marksman with any kind of weapon, he can drive a race car, and he knows martial arts. It is obvious that he's in great physical condition, as he routinely performs acts that would leave the average man, at best, sore for weeks, and at worst, in the hospital or dead. With all those qualities at his disposal, it's almost inconsequential that he's good looking.

The point is that the things that make James Bond so attractive are virtually all things that he has learned, as opposed to naturally inborn qualities.

And Now, Back to Reality: What About You?

All of these people who were so phenomenally attractive started off as ordinary people. Yet, by acquiring skills and knowledge, which they applied to their lives, they transformed themselves into objects of near-worship. It isn't stretching the truth at all to tell you that you, too, are capable of transforming yourself into an alluring, desirable person. It takes some work, and it definitely takes a real commitment, but you can do it. You simply have to...

➤ Realize that wherever you are right now is the perfect place to start.

➤ Determine what you have to work with.

➤ Compare what you are with what you would like to be.

➤ Figure out the straightest path between the two.

In the following chapters, we will go into more detail about the different aspects of ourselves—those elements of seductiveness we talked about briefly in Chapter 1—and we'll discuss how to develop them into truly seductive assets. But now it's time to get to work on setting goals.

Short-Term Goals: The First Person You Must Seduce Is Yourself

Becoming seductive is just like any other desire you may have; you must define the desire before you can hope to realize it. Therefore, the first step toward becoming more seductive is to establish a picture in your mind of just what a seductive "you" would look like, sound like, feel like, and even smell like. In short, you need to determine just how a sexy "you" would appear in your own mind.

Ask the Love Coach

Goal setting is important, but it's not enough to just "think" your goal. To make it real, put it in writing. Having it there in black and white is a constant reminder of the promise you've made to yourself. This will help provide an extra boost when you get discouraged.

As I've said before, the image you hold of yourself is the one that others around you are most likely to perceive. Thus, the focus of this short-term goal is really upon seducing yourself. That's the first step in seducing someone else.

Your short-term goal, then, is to make a commitment to become the sexiest, most alluring, most charismatic being you possibly can. Here's how to do it:

1. *State your goal to yourself.* Make it very basic: "I want to become a seductress," or "I want to become a seducer." Don't worry about concrete definitions of what that means; for now, it is important only that you acknowledge that you want to achieve something.

2. *Write down your goal.* You'd be surprised what a difference that will make in turning your future goal into a reality.

Heart Brakes

When setting goals, don't become so involved in the process that you lose sight of the result. Some people are compulsive list makers, and they expend so much time and energy making and refining their lists that they never get around to actually doing anything on the lists. Your goals should be a prediction of your future, not just words on paper.

3. *Decide on a period of time in which to reach your goal.* But here's the trick: Make the time period short enough that you will have to actually work toward your goal, but make it long enough to be realistic (so you won't give up before you've even begun). Like Goldilocks and the three bears, you need to find a time period that's "just right."

A good rule of thumb for short-term goals is to allow yourself between 30 and 90 days. That way, you will see your goal as something you can realistically complete within the time allowed, yet there will be enough time pressure to get you moving, working toward making it happen.

4. *Be sure to write the time frame down alongside the goal.* Now it's official: You've made a commitment to yourself, so keep that commitment!

Long-Term Goals: Attracting Who You Want

Once you're on the way to becoming that new you, it's time to begin focusing on your second, more long-term goal. You will commit, in the next 6 to 12 months—however long you think is reasonable—to attracting the caliber of people you're interested in getting to know.

While this may seem like its own independent exercise, remember that this goal is closely related to your short-term goal of becoming more alluring. For one thing, you will have little luck attracting someone if you haven't honed your own attractiveness quotient. Conversely, you will want to enhance those qualities in yourself that will be desirable to the kind of people you are looking for.

For example, what if you are really hoping to meet and begin a relationship with a very basic, salt-of-the-earth-type person? You probably don't need to worry about learning the sociopolitical statements that are woven throughout Shakespeare's plays, but you will want to focus on more fundamental knowledge, like the best place in town to go for a steak. The flip side of this is that, if you focus your development on learning these more fundamental tidbits of knowledge, you aren't going to have much luck attracting a devoted academician.

Ask the Love Coach

When you're making your wish list for the type of people you want to attract, you need to determine which traits are negotiable and which are nonnegotiable. Characteristics such as hair color or height may be negotiable; but others, such as smoking or drinking habits, may not be negotiable. Being clear on the differences from the beginning will make it easier on you and the people you attract.

A good fisherman learns what bait works best for each kind of fish he or she wishes to catch, and uses the bait most likely to attract the fish being sought. Granted, attracting a romantic partner isn't as rudimentary as catching fish, and seductiveness should be much more than bait; but the basic principle is the same for both activities.

Here's how to create your long-term goals for attracting people:

1. Form a general picture in your mind of the kinds of people you want to attract. At this point, don't get too specific, such as listing each physical attribute you find attractive and eliminating everyone who lacks any of those attributes. (Such a practice will pretty well ensure that you will remain alone, and most people who engage in this practice *do* remain alone—not because they are too picky, but because they are afraid to get close to someone. The "pickiness" is, in the final analysis, just an excuse.)

2. Sit down and write out a list of the characteristics you find attractive, and by which you rate someone's seductiveness quotient. It's often difficult to do this at first, but once you start writing, you will probably find that you can't write fast enough to list the elements.

3. After you've made your list, set it down for awhile. Get away from it long enough for it to "cool."

4. When the list has "cooled" enough, read it over, and ask yourself which elements on your list are really critical to you, and which are less important or even inconsequential. Put a star beside the most important items. This is your "pass/fail" list.

Heart Brakes

Remember: Excessive selectivity takes the worry out of being close. Actually, it takes the *being close* out of being close. If you find yourself continually rejecting people because they don't measure up to the exacting list of standards you've created, perhaps it is time to re-evaluate your standards—and your own motives. How many of the criteria on your list are really necessary for your happiness in a relationship, and how many reflect arbitrary standards that few people could ever live up to?

5. Imagine a type of person who passes all your critical criteria. When you get a good picture of that type in your mind, expand your mental picture a little, and imagine what that person would be doing in his or her spare time.

6. Expand that mental picture a little more, and imagine where the person would be pursuing that favored activity. You now have a clearer picture in your mind of where to go to find these attractive folks. We'll go into that in a later chapter, but for now, know that you've taken the important first steps.

7. Finally, write down your goal. For example, "Within the next 90 days, I am going to meet six attractive new people. To accomplish this, I will do the following...." Follow with a short list of action items such as, "Beginning this Friday, I will start going to the weekly Singles Night at the local bookstore-coffee bar." Once again, you've made a commitment to yourself. Keep it.

You *Can* Get There From Here: Putting Your Best Self Forward All the Time

As you begin to develop your seductive new self, you are bound to face a few setbacks. I mentioned earlier in the chapter that the thought of reinventing yourself can be pretty daunting. It can seem even more so when you first begin to "try your wings" with your newly refined persona. Here are some guidelines to help you through the transition period.

➤ Don't get discouraged when you find the "old you" looking back at you from the mirror. That "you" is still a part of the new person you are creating; it's just improved.

➤ Remember that one of the biggest challenges to the newly emerging, alluring person you are becoming will arise when you come face to face with someone who is intimately familiar with the way you were before. Just as we have a tendency, as adults, to revert to our roles as children when we visit relatives, we also tend to allow our old attitudes to emerge when we reunite with old friends and lovers who knew us "then." Before we know it, the new, improved "me" evaporates, leaving only the person we have been trying so hard to outgrow. The good news is that just being aware of this tendency will help you overcome it.

Ask the Love Coach

How will your old friends react to the new, more seductive you? If they're true friends, they'll be delighted for you. If they're critical of you, consider their true motives. They may be uncomfortable with change, or simply insecure. You don't need to defend yourself to them. But be sure to examine your own behavior, and make sure you're not putting on airs. Not only is that distinctly *unseductive*, but arrogance leaves you particularly vulnerable to the scorn of others should you happen to "slip."

➤ If you have tried to change so much that the "old you" is completely hidden, you will naturally come across as being false, and your old friends will see it (and probably call you on it). Remember, if your true friends can see through your new persona, it isn't real for you, either. It is a mask you have put on to hide the "old you," and anyone you meet will eventually see through it, also. Don't try to become someone else; just become the most desirable *you* that you can be.

The Least You Need to Know

➤ You can become the seductive person you want to be.

➤ Becoming more alluring takes real commitment and a bit of work.

➤ People have been re-creating themselves for thousands of years, so you're not the first to try it.

➤ The most important person to seduce is yourself.

➤ Form a clear picture in your mind of the type of person you want to attract, but don't be so selective that you rule out everybody.

➤ Don't be discouraged by setbacks on the road to self-improvement; these are natural, and you can overcome them.

Physical Attraction: Looking Seductive

The first element of seductiveness is your physical self. Whatever those enlightened folks may say about how unimportant physical appearance is, let's face it: Your physical being is the first thing people notice when they meet you. Your appearance is going to make an impression, one way or another.

You may think you don't have a lot of control over your fundamental appearance, short of paying a visit to a plastic surgeon. In truth, however, there are plenty of things you can do to enhance the looks you were born with. Accentuating your good points, while minimizing those characteristics you consider flaws, is a common practice, not to mention the basis for a multibillion dollar cosmetics industry. So let's begin building that altar of desire you're going to be.

Is Your Presence a Sensual Delight or a Sensory Assault?

To become as physically alluring as possible, begin with an honest appraisal of your looks. Be thorough but don't be overly critical. The best way to start is to divide your physical presence into two distinct categories: what you like, and what you're not so fond of.

Start by rating your face. This is the first part of you that most people will notice. (In a little while we'll discuss body image and self-appraisal; just concentrate on your face for now.)

1. Stand in front of a mirror and really look at your face. Don't protest that this seems vain; you know very well that when nobody is around, you will gaze into the mirror, testing out new expressions, and making sure that the old ones look the same as they did the last time you checked. At least now you've been given permission, and you're doing it for a real purpose. Look at your eyes, nose, mouth, and the texture of the skin. Pretend the image you see in the mirror belongs to somebody else and that you're evaluating the elements to determine how they look to you.

Ask the Love Coach

The secret to looking seductive is part physical enhancement, part illusion, and a large measure of attitude. To be seductive, you don't have to have been born with designer genes; you just need to learn to work with what you have (which is more than you think!).

2. After you're done with the visual appraisal, make your list. Divide it into two columns: "Enhance," which are the features you like; and "Refine," the features you think need improvement. Perhaps your favorite feature is your mouth. You see a deliciously sensuous, sexy, kissable mouth. (And, yes, men and women can both have sensuous mouths, so lighten up, guys.) Your mouth definitely qualifies as an enhanceable element, so write it down on that side.

   On the "Refine" side, you might write down that you're not fond of your eyes because you wear glasses. Maybe you heard the term "four-eyes" a little too often while you were a kid, or maybe someone you didn't particularly like wore glasses, and you can't quite kick the association. For whatever reasons, the glasses are a bummer for you. So on one side of the list, you've got those eyes that just don't do much for you, but on the other side you have those gorgeous lips.

3. Decide what to do about the items on the "Refine" side of your list. (The features you like, of course, you'll just leave alone. If it works, don't fix it, right?) As was the case in your decision to become seductive, you'll probably find that goal setting will help you make the desired changes in your appearance. In some cases only a short-term goal is necessary, and long-term goal setting won't necessarily apply.

There are some things you can do one time that will make a significant difference. Suppose, for instance, that you don't like your glasses. The short-term goal here is a no-brainer: get contacts. If you can't wear contacts, you can simply buy a better-looking style of glasses. If, however, you want a long-term solution that involves neither contacts nor glasses, you might look into some of the newer and safer surgical techniques for correcting visual impairment. If you and your doctor decide this option is right for you, but you can't afford it now, this could be one of your long-term goals.

I want to share with you the stories of two people I've worked with in the past. We'll call the woman Julia, and the man Harold. Like most of us, Julia and Harold were not entirely happy with their appearances. But by being honest in their self-assessment, and making a series of short- and long-term goals, they were able to recreate themselves and increase their seductiveness quotient considerably.

Julia: Facing the Truth

Julia assessed her face and decided that her best feature was definitely her mouth. She had pouty, sensuous, Sophia Loren lips. Unfortunately, she wore thick glasses, and always felt self-conscious about them. Finally Julia decided she would break down and get contacts. She had always been afraid contacts would be difficult to put in, but her desire to become the sexiest woman she could be was strong, and getting stronger all the time. So she forced herself to overcome her trepidation over putting her fingers in her eyes, and got fitted with soft contact lenses. She decided to go for blue contacts— deep blue. Yum!

Julia didn't want to wear her contacts all the time, so she also invested in a pair of very attractive eyeglasses. This brings me to another point: Don't fret if you're one of those people who can't wear contacts; these days you can choose from an endless array of flattering lens and frame styles.

While Julia was analyzing her face, she decided her make-up needed an update. Off she went to a well-known department store, where she met with a make-up consultant who diplomatically let her know that her look was slightly dated. Julia had a complimentary make-up redo, and was delighted with the results. Yet she just couldn't justify spending hundreds of dollars on the upscale cosmetics for sale at the counter. She thanked the cosmetic consultant, and her next stop was the drugstore, where she bought many of the same textures and colors of make-up. Thus she was able to re-create the look at a significantly lower cost.

For HER Eyes Only

Don't hesitate to seek out expert advice on cosmetics; learn the basic principles of applying color and texture to enhance your looks. If you can't afford upscale-department-store prices, you can get the same look for much less at a drug or discount store. Or try some of the beauty supply stores that are popping up all over; these stores carry brand-name cosmetics at discount prices.

Harold: Right Hair, Right Now

Harold had a great face, with strong and even features, but his hair really wasn't that attractive. Actually, what was left of it was just fine, except he was losing it at a rapid rate. Lately he had resorted to the tried-but-not-so-true, "comb-it-over-the-shiny-spot" technique, which was highly unsatisfactory.

So, Harold made a short-term goal to get a different haircut. The other options were to invest in a toupee, spend a fortune on hair transplants, smear his head with minoxidil (which is far from 100 percent effective), or try some of that aerosol scalp coloring he'd seen on infomercials. None of these sounded at all appealing to him. Instead, he had his hair professionally styled in a way that didn't try to hide the fact that he was becoming bald. In short, he got a newer, snazzier look.

"Someday I may consider hair transplants, or maybe I'll try that new antibaldness pill that they've come out with," Harold says. "But for now, I think I've made the best choice, and I'm happy with it."

For HIS Eyes Only

Some of the sexiest guys in history, such as Yul Brynner, were bald. In fact, in recent years some of Hollywood's sexiest, such as Bruce Willis, Keenen Ivory Wayans, and Sean Connery, are balding (or bald) and not afraid to show it. Even Ted Danson has stopped wearing his toupee. These guys look great because they've found that getting a cut to flatter them (and not hide their baldness) is what works. Remember: confidence is *sexy!*

For HIS Eyes Only

If your thinning hair is getting you down despite what we've been saying about how sexy bald men can be, and minoxidil just isn't for you, check with your doctor about a new antibaldness pill called finasteride (marketed under the trade name Propecia). This is a weaker version of a drug used to treat an enlarged prostate. It's not a miracle potion, but preliminary results are promising.

Grooming and Hygiene

It's nearly impossible to come of age in our odor-conscious culture without knowing the basics about brushing, flossing, daily bathing, and using a good antiperspirant. I won't insult you by implying that you're other than fastidious in this area.

As for grooming, you're probably savvy about the essentials here too. If, however, you're well-groomed but still are not completely satisfied with your look, consider seeking assistance from someone whose profession it is to make people look good—a hairdresser or stylist, for example. These professionals deal with hundreds of different people, each of whom has a unique head shape, face, and hair texture. They can determine which hairstyle will work for you, and they can help devise the proper hair care routine for you.

Between your description of your lifestyle (including how much effort you want to expend on your hair) and the stylist's experience, you should be able to come up with a style that looks great all the time. A stylist might even save you from trying something that looks great on a magazine cover, but would look ridiculous on you. (And guys, more and more men are going to stylists these days, so don't feel self-conscious about it.)

Fitness and Health

Everybody has his or her own idea of what an ideal physical body looks like. Some people think anything short of Greek god/goddess perfection is completely unattractive. Other people, however, like the look of a few extra pounds on their love interests. So what level of fitness is right for you? The answer is, quite simply, whatever your personal best is.

Being healthy and fit doesn't necessarily mean being a gym junkie. What it does mean is the following:

➤ You are approximately the right weight for your height and body structure.

➤ You can function at your preferred activity level without tiring too quickly or hurting yourself.

➤ You feel comfortable with your body.

It is profoundly disturbing to hear about some lovely young woman who dies as a result of an extreme diet, all because her self-image was so distorted that she always felt that she was too fat. Yet in our culture, we tend to encourage this very scenario by perpetuating the image of the ideal woman as being svelte, even waiflike. In recent years, critics have lashed out at the "heroin-chic" look of runway models, who look to all the world like strung-out junkies. Equally heartbreaking is the person, be it a man or a woman, who wrecks his body, destroys his internal organs, and develops cancer at a young age, all as a result of taking steroids to "improve" the body's definition.

For HER Eyes Only

Many women spend a lot of time on their nails; but did you know that extra-long fingernails can be a big turn-off for men? Surveys taken during the time I owned my video dating service revealed that men really don't care for those brightly colored talons. Better to go for a more moderate look with well-manicured nails, and hands that look hold-able, not hazardous.

For HIS Eyes Only

Many women think beards and moustaches are very sexy, but remember that extra facial hair demands extra attention when it comes to grooming and hygiene. Keep beards and mustaches neatly trimmed, and consider investing in a mustache comb. And do take a few moments to give your face a once-over in a mirror after you've eaten (you really don't want your dinner companion to take one look at your beard and know exactly what you had for lunch, do you?).

It's far better to take an honest but kind look at your body as it is (more on *that* in a moment). Then work toward making it the best it was meant to be, rather than trying to change it drastically and force it into some completely unrealistic image.

Heart Brakes

All the medical reports tell us that dieting is not only ineffective; it is also counterproductive and even potentially dangerous. It's far better to eat sensibly and get the exercise you need to maintain a sense of vitality, than to starve and exercise yourself to death, just to reach some unattainable goal.

The key to making your body the best it can be lies in—you guessed it—sound nutrition and some form of exercise. It is beyond the scope of this book to delve into the particulars of your nutrition program or exercise routine, but there are many good books on health, fitness, and nutrition (including, of course, some great Idiot's Guides); check your bookstore. Meanwhile, be good to your body, and the result will be that you'll feel good about yourself.

It's Better than You Think: Adjusting Your Body Image

Let's check in on Harold and Julia again. In their own ways, each of them decided their body images needed some work. Both vowed to themselves to improve the way their bodies looked, but they were savvy enough to know they had to improve in their own eyes first, and then in the eyes of those around them.

Similarly, each of us has to arrive at an image of ourselves that *we* are pleased with. Like Harold and Julia, we can make a significant change in how we see our bodies by changing something simple and, to outward appearances, insignificant.

Apply the "Refine"/"Enhance" list and the goal setting process to your body image, just as you applied it earlier to your face.

1. Stand naked in front of a mirror. (You knew this was coming, didn't you?) Take a good honest look at your body, but remember that honest doesn't mean ruthless.

2. As you did earlier, make a list with two columns: "Enhance" (what you like) and "Refine" (what you don't like).

3. Look at the list and decide what you can do—now and in the long run—to minimize the effect of each item on the "Refine" side of the list. At the same time, take each item on the "Enhance" side, and figure out a way to accentuate it.

Even Cindy Crawford Doesn't Look Like Cindy Crawford...

Like so many women, Julia dreamt of looking like a supermodel—specifically, Cindy Crawford. Then one day Julia was fortunate enough to see Cindy, who is admired for her candor, on one of the model's many talk show appearances. Cindy made a comment that provided a near-epiphany for Julia, and which I think should be made into a bumper sticker or T-shirt and handed out to every female over the age of 10: *not even Cindy Crawford looks like Cindy Crawford.* Even though she acknowledges she's a beautiful woman, she admitted that many of her photos are re-touched to remove a little blemish she might have that day, or to otherwise smooth or enhance her image.

Cindy is not alone in her candor. In another example, actress Morgan Fairchild published a beauty book. This gutsy woman, who presents such a startlingly beautiful public image, included unretouched photographs of herself without make-up. The difference between the Morgan we see and the Morgan who wakes up in the morning is aston-ishing. Does this make her less beautiful? Hardly. But it does show us that her beauty is not the same as it's presented on the television screen or magazine covers.

The whole point is that you need to have an accurate, realistic image of yourself, and that you need to hold it up to realistic role models for comparison. If you continually strive to look like an image that's computer enhanced or airbrushed, you will always feel short-changed.

For HIS Eyes Only

We know women are continually faced with unrealistic ideals of beauty. But men don't have it much easier. They are bombarded with farfetched media images of the ideal man, and my work with clients has shown me that guys frequently attempt—unsuccessfully—to emulate these images. One client, Tom, groused, "If we're to believe the mass media, the 'ideal' guy is a combination James Bond/Brad Pitt/ *GQ* model. Eventually you figure out it's not possible to live up to all those ideals, and you find your own niche." Tom's right. Just like women, men need to be realistic in their expectations of themselves and their perceptions of their role models. Develop your own style; *real* women will love you for it.

Ask the Love Coach

If you envision your body image as a single entity that needs to be changed, the task can seem overwhelming. Instead, break the process down into individual goals to be achieved. Be patient with yourself, be kind to yourself, and you can accomplish more than you ever imagined.

Chiseled or Voluptuous? Achieving Your Personal Best Physique

When Harold and Julia began working on their goals to improve their bodies, one of the first goals they both set for themselves was to become more physically fit. I recommend you do this too. You needn't strive for a perfect body—if such a body even exists. Just aim to be healthy in whatever represents good shape for you.

Julia began to review the exercise programs she had followed in the past. She'd never been a big fan of the gym scene, so she decided to try something different. Since Julia had always been attracted to Latin music, she signed up for some dance classes and started learning the tango and salsa dancing. Now, instead of being an exercise drudge, she finds she is having a great time in the classes. Not only has she gotten in noticeably better shape, she finds that moving with the exotic rhythms and perfecting the steps makes her feel incredibly sensuous.

Julia has discovered another bonus to her new enthusiasm for Latin dancing. Having always been a bit on the voluptuous side, she used to lament that she would never be as thin and willowy as the models she saw in *Vogue*. Her attractive tango instructor, Raul, has helped change all that. Coming from a culture that appreciates curves on a woman, the flirtatious attention Raul pays her has given Julia a different perspective altogether, and a new appreciation for her own natural beauty.

Ask the Love Coach

If beauty is in the eye of the beholder, it is also in the eye of one's culture. Standards of attractiveness are arbitrary. For years our culture has presented the tall, willowy fashion model look as the ideal for women; but other cultures prefer the voluptuous, earth-mother type. Whether you're curvy, slender, or muscular, learn to love your own body, and it won't matter what the prevailing look is.

Harold had always been a jogger. He liked running, but he didn't really like having a runner's body. Though he was becoming more fit, his body kept getting thinner. He decided to cut down on his running program and chose to supplement it with weight training.

Harold started with an instructor to teach him how to handle the weights properly, and he began lifting a small amount of weight three days a week to improve his muscle definition. He soon found that the blood pumping into his biceps, along with their steady increase in size, made him feel very sexy.

It's Not How You Look; It's How You Feel

In no time, Harold found he didn't even think about the fact that he was losing his hair, and Julia discovered that, when she thought about her eyes at all, she thought of them as an asset instead of a flaw. And although Julia's and Harold's respective self-improvement regimens were certainly making them look better, what was most important—and what made them keep coming back for more—was that they felt better.

Ask the Love Coach

Time and again, I've seen people embark on self-improvement campaigns with the sole purpose of improving their appearance—losing a few pounds, gaining a bit of muscle mass, or some other specific but chiefly cosmetic goal. Often they do improve their appearance in the short run, but sometimes at the cost of their health. Even those who don't compromise their health rarely stick to their new way of life, because in some way their regimen is simply too grueling for them. You can avoid this scenario if your exercise routine makes you *feel* good as well as *look* good.

When you adopt a physical-fitness program, the secret to success is to focus on how it makes you feel. Sure, it's wonderful to experience the pleasure of knowing your endeavor is helping you to look great too; but if that's your only reinforcement, you probably won't stick with it in the long run. As Harold and Julia discovered, it's far more rewarding to find an activity that makes your body feel as wonderful as it's beginning to look.

Do What Makes You Feel Sexy and Vibrant

Can you see how Harold and Julia's examples can apply to you? As the two of them did, you can devise a regimen that will help you achieve your optimum physical condition but that will, at the same time, be a source of pleasure all its own.

There are countless activities from which to choose. If you need inspiration, the next time you're out and about, browse the free-publications bins in stores and restaurants. Check out some of the catalogs for community colleges or no-credit classes. In Houston, for example, we have Leisure Learning Unlimited, which offers classes in everything from samba lessons to sky diving. Your town or city probably has something similar. Or try your local Y; there's always something fun going on there.

When you are engaged in some activity you thoroughly enjoy, which also makes you feel better physically, your self-image and your overall sense of well-being will improve dramatically. And believe me, that is seductive. It is truly a win-win situation.

Doing a Double Take

If you've followed the suggestions in this chapter, you have already evaluated your physical attributes. But because you are, after all, a work in progress, and because your perceptions as well as your appearance will change as you continue on your journey, I recommend a periodic reevaluation. Take out your original "Enhance/Refine" list, if you still have it, or make a new one. Understand I'm not suggesting that you turn this into an obsession, but periodically reevaluating yourself is a wonderful way to gauge your progress.

Harold and Julia knew this. After working out for about six weeks, they each decided to zero in on their bodies again, and really take a look at their physical attributes.

Harold thought his growing biceps were definitely his best asset. Then he took a closer look at his face, and decided it was his other best asset. Julia still thought her pouty, sensuous mouth was her best asset, but now her long legs caught her attention too, and she was pleased. Her involvement with dancing had slimmed her thighs and toned her calves.

Just for the record, Harold never gave a second thought to his thinning hair. And Julia, having long since chucked the bottle-thick glasses, was seriously beginning to think her eyes were actually quite captivating. The "Enhance" side of each of their lists was growing, while the "Refine" side was dwindling.

You Wear It Well

The day came for Harold and Julia when they decided it was time to get to work on their wardrobes. They had gained confidence in their looks and felt they definitely deserved better "packaging." Both consulted experts to help them with their new looks.

For evaluating appearance and advising on changes, Harold and Julia had several types of experts to choose from:

➤ *Image consultants* advise clients on hair color, hairstyle, make-up, clothing, and accessories, and may advise on posture, general appearance, and demeanor. Some offer both personal and corporate image consulting services.

➤ *Make-up consultants* advise clients on type, color, and application of make-up.

➤ *Color consultants* advise clients on choice of colors for clothing that will complement their appearance.

Ask the Love Coach

Many image, make-up, and color consultants offer a combination of services. To find one, look in the Yellow Pages under "Image Consultants."

Harold was doing okay financially, but being in construction, he did not have a surplus of money. First he went to a quality department store and spent some time with a fashion consultant there, who guided him toward styles that would look good on him. With a little guidance, Harold got a feel for his correct style, and managed to stay within his budget at the same time.

Julia was a successful advertising executive, and she'd recently received a raise. So she decided to splurge and hire a personal wardrobe expert. This turned out to be a good investment for her. Unlike Harold, who put so little emphasis on clothes that he really didn't have any, Julia had a closet filled with clothes. However, too many of them were completely wrong for her desired image.

Ask the Love Coach

If you're on a limited budget (which most of us are), don't overlook the best-kept secret of celebrities and business people alike: resale shops. I am constantly amazed at the high-quality, good-as-new clothes that end up in resale shops because someone else simply grew tired of them. Such garments, unwanted by someone else, can become real treasures to you. Many famous people shop resale to remain stylish when they aren't rolling in money.

The first thing the wardrobe expert did was to clean out Julia's closets, leaving behind only a bare minimum of the best outfits. Anything that Julia hadn't worn in over a year, or that she truly didn't feel good in, was disposed of. The consultant divided the remaining outfits into three categories: work clothes, party clothes, and play clothes, and told Julia to keep at least three or four outfits in each category that she felt extremely good in. She also took a very good look at Julia's coloring and told her that, while her closet was full of neutral colors, she was an animated person and that brighter colors looked better on her.

What a difference this advice made. Julia found that simply changing from brown to red changed her entire look and color of her complexion. Her overall appearance changed from that of a mousy wallflower who was easily overlooked to that of a striking, dynamic woman who made a statement.

Whether you choose to consult an expert or decide to go it on your own, here are some guidelines for buying clothes:

➤ Buy clothes that fit you well and are comfortable. This is one cardinal rule that is every bit as important as style—perhaps even more important. While tight pants may be sexy on a man or a woman, the effect is completely diminished if you have to keep tugging and pulling because they don't feel right, and a "wedgie" isn't sexy on anyone. Better that you buy your clothes a size or two larger, so that you're comfortable in them and they hang properly without your constant attention.

➤ Select fabrics that feel good to you. I'm adamant about this point. A sensual person will have nothing touch the skin that doesn't feel delightful. It's better to wear a soft, cotton-blend sweater, than a wooly one that really itches, no matter how good the wooly one looks. You have to feel good in the fabrics.

➤ Opt for quality over quantity. Instead of trying to fill your closets, concentrate on buying clothes that fit well, are stylish but not faddish, and fill your senses with delight.

What the Sirens Knew

Have you ever met someone who, at first appearance, was breathtakingly gorgeous, only to have that image completely destroyed the first time he or she spoke? I bet most of us can name a few TV or film stars—male or female—who are extremely attractive physically, but when they speak, their voices are distinctly nonseductive. Of course, many "everyday people" have vocal challenges as well. Here are some common symptoms of an untrained voice:

➤ Some women take on a nagging, whiny, complaining tone. A man who hears such a voice will associate it with a woman who's impossible to please. This is definitely not seductive.

➤ Some men assume a staccato tone—an impatient, aggressive manner of speaking that can come across as domineering, condescending, or arrogant.

➤ Some men and women have a tendency to just drone on and on; their normal conversational tone is expressionless, flat, and dull. Either way, it's a turn-off.

➤ Some men and women may have problems with nervous or careless speech patterns: speaking too rapidly or too loudly, mumbling, and so on.

Ask the Love Coach

Voice or diction coaches aren't just for professional singers, actors, or public speakers. A good voice coach can help anybody refine tone and diction, and give general pointers on improving poise and overcoming shyness. Look in your Yellow Pages under "Voice Coaches."

After our physical appearance, our voice is the most predominant feature we bring into our exchanges with other people, so it's important that we learn to sound as attractive as we look.

Both Julia and Harold decided to work on their voices. Julia hired a voice coach. Her coach helped her modulate her voice, eliminating its slightly nasal quality. She also taught Julia various techniques to control her voice when she was nervous—techniques Julia was able to put to use right away when making presentations to clients on behalf of her ad agency.

Since Harold couldn't afford sessions with a personal voice coach, he simply started to record his own voice and play it back, really listening to how he sounded. He worked on playing down his Texas accent and on slightly lowering the timbre of his voice. He also worked on eliminating his monotone speech pattern by trying to add vitality to his voice.

Before long, both Harold and Julia found their voices had become more resonant, more animated, and generally much more pleasant to listen to. As a result, they also found that other people seemed more interested in what they had to say.

To evaluate your own voice, here's a simple exercise to try. Do this whether or not you plan to hire a voice coach.

1. Record and listen to your own voice. Use a tape recorder, or simply listen closely to your voice message on your phone answering machine.

2. Ask yourself if this is the voice of someone to whom you would like to listen. Make a list of the qualities you think you need to improve. If you're not sure, ask someone else whom you feel can give you constructive criticism.

3. Record your voice again...and then again...until you sound "right" to yourself or the friend you've enlisted to help.

You needn't be a supreme baritone or an exquisite soprano, poised to take the opera world by storm. You simply need to enhance the quality of your speaking voice so people will listen to what you have to say without being put off by the sound that carries your thoughts.

Ask the Love Coach

Most people with untrained voices would do well to heed these three words of wisdom from voice coaches: "lower and slower." When people are nervous, they often speak in a high-pitched tone, and/or they speak too rapidly. Voice coaches also say that the fastest way to change the sound of your voice is to change your physiology. A smile on your face puts a smile in your voice.

Knowing Your Style Requires Knowing Yourself

The whole point of all this effort, and all these exercises, is to help you discover and polish your own personal style. You aren't trying to be something you're not, but rather to enhance and improve what you already are. Observe the characteristics you admire in other people, allow them to metamorphose to fit your own persona, and thus consciously develop your own personal style.

Perhaps your style is basic and earthy, perhaps it's glamorous, and perhaps it is constantly changing; whatever your style is, it has to come from substance. It comes from knowing and being comfortable with yourself. Quite simply, you can't have a style of your own, you can't do things that are truly unique to you, until you have developed a level of confidence in and awareness of yourself.

The Least You Need to Know

➤ You have more to work with than you may have considered.

➤ Reality can be your best friend where self-image is concerned.

➤ You want every aspect of your persona to be part of a unified image.

➤ Even Cindy Crawford doesn't look like Cindy Crawford; strive to look like the best *you*, not like some retouched magazine photo.

➤ While physical appearance is important, your health and fitness program should focus more on how you feel than on how you look.

Chapter 4

Intellectual Magnetism: Your Brain Is the Most Erogenous Part of Your Body

> ### In This Chapter
>
> ➤ Using your brain to make you sexy
>
> ➤ Food for your hungry mind
>
> ➤ Being open to what others have to offer
>
> ➤ Choosing to be seduced by life

It is well documented that the mind is the primary erogenous zone. Indeed, if you want to be seductive, your mind is the most powerful tool you have at your disposal.

There are several ways to put this tool to good use. First, you can program your mind with positive *self-talk* to convince yourself of your desirability—and once *you're* convinced, it's a breeze to convince others. Second, you can create a powerful mental presence that will make you irresistible. The key to creating this presence lies in sharpening your curiosity, seeking out new experiences, and deepening your zest for life.

In fact, what this chapter is really about is being seduced by life and embracing all it has to offer. A person who truly embraces life is unquestionably seductive.

What Makes You Sexy? Your Thoughts

We've already talked about recognizing and accentuating your best physical qualities. Now, let's use that principal erogenous zone, your mind, and learn how to fully project those qualities. It's not enough just to be confident about that reflection you see in the mirror. Your entire attitude needs to be filled with the awareness of the glorious things you have to offer the world.

Let's look at some real-life examples.

Ask the Love Coach

A client of mine named Renee learned about positive self-talk recently when she volunteered to model a designer suit with a tight, short skirt for a charity fashion show. "I was afraid I'd be awkward, so I asked for some pointers from my friend Patrice, a runway model," said Renee. In addition to demonstrating how to stand, walk and pivot, Patrice gave Renee the ultimate confidence-boosting hint.

"Here's what I want you to do," Patrice advised. "Saunter down that runway, and when you come to the end, stop, turn around just so, take the jacket off, and sling it casually over your shoulder. At that moment, look at the audience—and with all your power, think these words, 'Don't you wish *you* had this tush?'"

The effect on the audience was electrifying. Now Renee uses a variation of this technique whenever she enters a room—and turns heads wherever she goes.

Wordplay

Self-talk is the little voice in your head that, for better or worse, is constantly making judgments about you. Constant negative self-talk eats away at your self-esteem. With conscious effort, however, you can redirect your negative thoughts into glowing affirmations of your wonderful qualities. Ask yourself what your self-talk is saying to you, and if it isn't serving you, change it!

Remember our friends Julia and Harold in Chapter 3? After Julia had been studying tango for awhile, she found that she could easily imagine herself entering a room, awash in the sensuous beat of some Latin band. Every step she took, she was aware of herself as a lithe, hot-blooded dancer, poised to spring into movement.

And when she entered a room, you had better believe that she was noticed. Of course, she didn't actually burst into a tango, but the effect the image had on her attitude and, indeed, on her physical presence, was actually palpable. She had truly *arrived*.

Like Julia, our old friend Harold set his own scene as well. Instead of being a slim, rather average-looking man who was losing his hair, he entered a room as someone who was physically powerful. He envisioned himself as being somewhere between Arnold Schwarzenegger in

Terminator II and Leonardo diCaprio in *Titanic*, someone whose shoulder a woman could cry on, yet who could protect her from the villains of the world. And when he entered a room, you can bet his presence was felt.

Ask the Love Coach

Have you ever walked up to someone who, on first glance, was quite average looking—but after talking to that person for awhile, you noticed he or she was actually a phenomenally attractive, profoundly sexual being? Assuming you remained sober throughout this process, what was the deal? Maybe it was the sound of the person's voice, or the fact that the person seemed genuinely interested in you. Then again, perhaps he or she simply exuded an *attitude* that you found irresistible.

Think of this the next time you are captivated by someone whose allure goes beyond physical appearance. If whatever it is this tempter or temptress has got affected you this much, isn't that reason enough to try applying the same mysterious magnetism to your own persona?

You say you don't know the tango from the bus stop, your arms aren't pumped, and strutting just isn't your style? No problem! Find the qualities in yourself that you would like to project, and fill your being with them until you can no longer contain them.

All it takes is a little imagination. Try this exercise:

1. Pick a physical feature you especially like, perhaps from the "Enhance" side of one of those lists you made in Chapter 3.

2. Imagine that this feature brings incredible joy to the people around you and makes you positively entrancing.

3. Write an affirmation reflecting this thought. For example: "My gorgeous brown eyes cast a spell on everyone I meet, leaving them feeling that they must get to know me better." Don't worry if this looks a little corny on paper; it's for your eyes only.

4. Beginning now, whenever you meet anybody, think about your chosen feature in the glowing terms you've created. You don't necessarily need to repeat your affirmation verbatim; condense it (for example, "Think eyes!").

This practice really works. Julia swears by it. Whenever she enters a room full of people, she repeats two words to herself: "Think lips!" As you begin to perceive yourself as more appealing, you begin to project that very appeal—and the people around you will respond to it.

Ask the Love Coach

How do you know if the positive self-talk you've been practicing is working? Pay attention to other people's reactions. If you notice people are responding more positively to you and seem more interested, it's reasonable to assume you already have a better image of your physical body and are projecting this awareness. Keep up the good work!

Your Intellectual Presence

Now that you've established an alluring physical presence, and have started to use the power of your mind to enhance it, the next step is to establish your intellectual presence. Sure, you look great, and, if you've been working on your voice (see Chapter 3), you're probably sounding better than ever—but that's not enough. To be truly seductive, you've got to have something interesting to *say*.

What *is* intellectual presence? It's a combination of several factors, including:

➤ *The way you think.* This is manifested in many ways, some of the most obvious being your opinions and your means of expressing those opinions.

➤ *The way you reason.* This is your ability to draw conclusions from the information at hand. Though this ability might vary depending on the situation, most of us are often at a middle ground between the cold and consummate logic of *Star Trek's* Mr. Spock and the artlessness of Forrest Gump.

➤ *How good you are at understanding other people's ideas.* Good listening skills are a must here; but beyond that, you should at least be capable of asking intelligent questions. A blank stare is not alluring.

These are all factors that make up your intellectual presence. But your powers of thinking, reasoning, and understanding simply do not develop in a vacuum. They have to be fed. Certainly they are nurtured by your self-talk, but in order to give them a truly balanced "diet," you need to learn about things that are outside your personal arena.

Ask the Love Coach

Jacqueline Kennedy Onassis was renowned for her ability to totally captivate every dinner partner who ever sat next to her. Her secret? Jackie knew the magic of eye contact. She would focus on her dinner partner as if that person were the only other individual at the table rather than trying to see what else was going on at the table. The lesson we can learn from Jackie O is if you want someone to be interested in you, let the object of your desire see that you are truly interested in him or her. You'll be amazed at the results.

Curiosity Livened Up the Cat

If you want to be an interesting person, you first must be *interested* in many things. It does no good to be beautiful and have an entrancing, sexy voice if you have nothing of interest to say. What's one of your best tools to sharpen the old intellect? Curiosity, pussy cat. Perpetually curious people are almost invariably fascinating, and never lack for interesting company.

A World of Things to Be Curious About

There are some folks (not you, I hope) who constantly complain of boredom. To tell the truth, I've always been stunned to hear people say they're bored. In my opinion, boredom is an outgrowth of fear or simple laziness, or perhaps it is nothing more than a failure of imagination. Unless you are locked up in solitary confinement, boredom is almost never a result of there being "nothing to do."

Heart Brakes

We all have a tendency to fall into habits and patterns that constrict our lives, but which we have trouble breaking nevertheless. If you stay sequestered in your own little world waiting for Prince or Princess Charming to come knocking at your door, you may be waiting until the day you die. Take that bold step out your front door (literally or meta-phorically), and be seduced by life!

Heart Brakes

Are you a person who insists, "I'd be bored if I couldn't work"? If you've let your job become all that you are, what's left when you punch out for the day? It's wonderful to love your work (I certainly love mine)—but don't forget that your job is something you *do*, not something you *are*. Make room in your life *for* a life. There's nothing seductive about being a workaholic.

To those who are chronically bored, I would ask you to consider this: There is a whole fabulous world just outside your door, and an infinite number of absolutely fascinating things to do.

Your task, then, is to allow yourself to be seduced by the world around you, to be overwhelmed by the siren song of new ideas, experiences, and people. In the final analysis, nothing is more seductive than a person who has been seduced by life. And as for boredom...well, the cure for that can be summed up in three words: *Look around you.*

Get Current

Simply broadening your perspective on current events makes a statement about your own level of interest, and shows the person you're talking to that you are truly enamored of the world around you.

Ask the Love Coach

You can expand your perspective on world events by exploring news media beyond the daily newspaper and local news channels. Short-wave radio, cable channels such as CNN International, and the Internet are all excellent sources of news with a worldwide perspective. Or visit a newsstand in your area; many of these have a large inventory of news magazines and journals, as well as newspapers from all over the world.

Although many of us get the fast-food version of the news from television networks, the "sound-bite" format of TV news reports just barely skims the surface of a story. For the most part, there's time for only the most sensational details of any given story. To really understand what is going on in any arena, it's necessary to read, listen to, and see any and every source you can get your hands on. And, yes, not only will you become truly seduced by life, but that seduction will be contagious, making you truly seductive to those around you ("Who *is* this interesting person?!").

Cultural Seduction

Before we even begin discussing culture, I think it is important to clearly define the word. In this context, the typical image that comes to mind is one of operas, classical music, Shakespeare, and those subtitled foreign films that many people pretend to understand, but don't. For many, even the thought of "culture" is off-putting. But the picture changes dramatically if you consider that culture is, by definition, any and all of the following:

➤ A particular civilization at a particular stage

➤ The tastes in art and manners that are favored by a social group

➤ All the knowledge and values shared by a society

➤ Refinement in tastes

"Okay, so culture is a lot more than snooty ladies with opera glasses," you may be saying, "but what does it have to do with seduction?" Well, as we discussed in Chapter 1, there are many ways to be seduced. And some of the most profoundly seductive experiences take place not in bedrooms, but in art galleries, museums, and even opera houses.

David is still in awe of what happened to him recently. He says, "I remember a time when I thought that to watch an opera was more boring than watching someone change a flat tire. You couldn't drag me to an opera for any amount of money. Then I started dating Rachel, who was somewhat of an opera buff.

"Of course I didn't hold it against her," he says, smiling, "but I was in no hurry to share any 'night at the opera' that didn't involve the Marx Brothers. Then Rachel got tickets to *Carmen*, and she really wanted me to go with her. I was reluctant, of course, even though she told me it's one of the most popular operas ever created. I protested, but Rachel refused to accept that as an excuse. She explained the story to me, and I have to admit it was starting to sound sort of interesting. Finally, she talked me into going."

To make a long story short, David was utterly blown away by this passionate tale of a Gypsy femme fatale who seduces an honorable young officer of the guard. "*Carmen*," explains David, "is all about seduction. The character Carmen is one of the most seductive women in any opera, film, or book. This is definitely a woman who's comfortable in her own skin, completely at ease with her sexuality."

Seeing his first opera was an eye-opening experience for David, and experiencing *Carmen* together was incredibly seductive for David and Rachel. David won't go into details, but his smile clearly states that the magic of that evening lasted long after the final curtain.

Ask the Love Coach

Shakespeare, opera, art films, Victorian novels...what's in them for you, the modern-day seductress or seducer? Although many of the works we associate with cultural literacy take place in a time and/or a society far removed from our own, nevertheless, the people in these times and societies shared many of the same hopes, dreams, fears, and pains we suffer today. (See, your high school English teachers were right.) To better understand others is to better understand yourself, and to better understand yourself is to be more seductive. The more hungry you are for life, and the more open you are to the feelings of others, *the more seductive you become.*

How about you? Even if you're not game for the opera, there are many ways to feed your hunger and broaden your cultural horizons. Treat yourself to these experiences:

➤ *Check out your local library or bookstore.* Walk into a library or bookstore, and really look around. Think about how many books there are that you would like to read, and how many you'll never read. Just for the fun of it, check out or buy a book by an author whose work you've never read, but whom you've been curious about. Or try a completely different genre than you usually read. If you normally read nothing but science fiction, pick up a mystery or a book of literary essays. If you're a self-help-book aficionado, read a humor book for a change. But no matter which genre you choose, just for good measure, pick up a collection of literary erotica as well, such as Anaïs Nin's *Delta of Venus.*

➤ *Lend an ear to your favorite music store.* Go into a music store and look around at all the different kinds of music you've never heard. Sit in one of the listening booths and experiment with different categories of music to which you don't ordinarily listen. If you're a classic-rock fan, try listening to some world music or something classical. If you're a jazz fanatic, check out some salsa or reggae. Then buy that "new" music, take it home, and listen to it. But don't just play the music; create a completely sensual experience for yourself. If you bought some hot Latin tracks, let loose with some sultry dance steps to match (and it doesn't matter if you don't know how to mambo; nobody's watching but your cat, right?). If you bought Yanni or Enya, light a few candles and some incense, step into a warm tub infused with aromatic oils, and lose yourself in the ethereal world created by the music.

➤ *Meander through a museum.* Pay a visit to an art museum and really *see* the paintings and sculptures. Indulge your sensual imagination. Guys, when you step in front of that Gauguin, don't just see a two-dimensional representation of a tropical scene; think of lovely and uninhibited Tahitian women slathering warm and fragrant oils all over your body. Women, when you look at that Rubens or Renoir, think of your own body being gazed upon by an artist, and then lovingly recreated on canvas. (Oh, and don't forget to notice that the women in these paintings are not anorexic fashion-model types.) Beyond focusing on the purely sensual aspects of the art works, make an effort to drink in the richness of the artists' experiences and feelings—and you will deepen the richness of your own persona.

Whenever you read a book, listen to music, or look at a work of art, try to feel the story behind it. Realize that behind every book is an author who had dreams, hopes, and hungers. Behind every musical score is a composer whose soul cried out for expression. And behind each of these creators was a full life, perhaps lived in a time and place foreign to you. Simply by absorbing some of the seductive elements of the artists, and all the passions of their cultures, believe me, your own level of seductiveness will increase a thousandfold.

Outside the Nine to Five

Body painting? Butterfly collecting? Tarot card reading? Tandem bike racing? It doesn't really matter what it is—everyone should have a hobby. They're wonderful things because, by simply finding something that sparks your interest and passion—and then acting on that interest and passion—you are adding dimensions and facets to your personality that will enrich your life. Most likely others will see and find your passion attractive, too.

Hobbies also give you confidence and increase your sense of self-worth. Rhonda, for example, had always been interested in painting, but thought it was one of those talents she just didn't possess. Then one summer, just for the heck of it, she took an art class, and ended up painting a startlingly beautiful red geranium. She hung the picture in her kitchen, and now every time she sees that lovely red geranium, she feels better about herself. "It's because I accomplished something I never would have imagined I could accomplish," she told me.

How about you? What's your hobby? If you don't have one, and don't have any overwhelming interest that you could turn into a hobby, think back to when you were a child. Recall some of the things you were interested in then. Often, as adults, we put aside the things that excited us as children, yet our interest remains somewhere below the surface. Just acknowledging and rekindling that long-forgotten passion can awaken in you the endearing qualities that will make you more desirable to other people.

Ask the Love Coach

There's a bonus to having a hobby: it gives you something to do on a Saturday night besides feel sorry for yourself if you don't have anyone to go out with. When you're thoroughly engrossed in organizing a collection of stamps, researching the value of a rare limited-edition print, or enjoying that sublimely illustrated collectors' edition of *Fanny Hill*, you'll find you don't have the time or the energy to wallow in self-pity, or to worry about what you *should* be doing on a Saturday night.

The Freewheeling (or Sky Diving or Sailing or Rock Climbing) New You

I had a client who took a vacation by himself because he decided that he wanted to learn to fly-fish. He went to Idaho, and for a couple of weeks, he fully immersed himself in fly-fishing. This man had gone through a difficult divorce, and when he left, he was very scattered and upset. He thought his life would never turn around. But when he came back, I barely recognized him. Looking more like Robert Redford than his old self, he was tan, he was happy, and he was incredibly sexy.

I asked him, "Something's very different about you. What's the change? Did you meet someone?"

He said, "No. That fly-fishing just blew me away. I know it sounds hokey, but I felt like I became one with the universe. When I caught a fish, I felt competent and self-reliant. When I ate the fish, I felt nourished.

"I feel better now than I've felt in years. Instead of feeling like there's nothing left for me, I feel there are so many choices of what to do with my life—so many things that I really don't know where to begin. I can't wait to start."

The changes in this man's life, and in the man himself, were dramatic. A year later, he had found a new love and remarried. From there, he had the confidence and strength to go out and build a whole new life.

How extraordinary it is that this man's solitary vacation, doing something he had always wanted to do, changed his entire life. Ask yourself what kind of experience could change *your* life like that. Then get going!

Soul Searching in Seoul

Robert Louis Stevenson wrote, "I travel not to go anywhere, but to go. I travel for travel's sake. The great affair is to move." And a great affair it is, indeed. Traveling to new places, experiencing new people and different cultures, will inevitably broaden your own perspective, making you a far more interesting person to be around. Just the fact that you are interested enough to seek out these new experiences adds to your personal appeal.

To me travel is synonymous with education, adventure, and some of the most enchanting experiences life has to offer. I have seen many of the world's most intriguing places. Yet there are so many wondrous spots I haven't seen yet, and want to (Australia and India are tops on the list).

When I meet someone who has traveled to these or other fascinating places, I feel immediately attracted to him. Why? If he has been someplace that I'm interested in, he has some new perspective that I want him to share with me. If we have traveled to the same places, there is a common experience that we share, which can create an immediate bond.

And the travel doesn't have to be some costly, extensive journey halfway around the world. You'd be surprised how much even little day trips around your home area can provide in the way of meeting and getting to know new people, and how different a culture can be, only a few miles down the road. So check the tour guides, call a travel agent, or just fill the car with gas and take off. There's a wonderful, exciting world out there, and maybe a whole new you, just waiting to be discovered.

Being Genius Enough to Admit to Ignorance

Think back to the most interesting people you've ever met. Remember, in particular, one who seemed especially confident and comfortable with him- or herself. Was this person spouting information and ideas, or enthusiastically listening to what you had to say? Did this person seem to have all the answers, or did he or she seem excited to hear what you had to say?

Heart Brakes

No matter how rich and varied your life experiences have been, don't make a habit of blurting out your whole life story to anyone who will listen. That's a real turn-off to most people. Don't ever feel compelled to give every bit of information about yourself all at once. Instead, exude confidence, wrap yourself in a bit of mystery, and you will be alluring, enticing...and seductive.

The plain truth is that we appreciate someone who has enough smarts to say "I don't know. Can you tell me?" This kind of person knows how to make the people around him or her feel important, and, by so doing, makes him- or herself more desirable to be around. Remember, sometimes the greatest conversationalists are the ones who know when to keep silent and listen. Think of yourself as a very flattering mirror. Let people see, in your eyes, an attractive reflection of themselves, and they will find *you* more attractive. Here are a few clues to follow when you're trying to inspire someone to be interested in you:

➤ *Nobody likes a know-it-all.* Few people are as annoying as those who feel compelled to dominate a conversation by showing how intelligent, wise, or learned they are. Such a person is clearly stating that what they have to say is more important than what anyone else has to say. Just as you would go out of your way to avoid such a person, make a real effort never to be one.

➤ *Everybody wants to be a teacher sometimes.* It makes people feel good to know they have something valuable to offer. Having the opportunity to broaden someone else's awareness is a real boost to the self-esteem.

➤ *Learning and self-respect are not mutually exclusive.* People who are insecure and doubt their self-worth will lie down and die before they admit, even to themselves, that they are ignorant about *anything*. People with a healthy self-image, however, are more concerned with learning something new than with appearing to know everything. Since self-confidence is a very important part of seductiveness (and an all-encompassing storehouse of knowledge is not), it makes more sense to admit that you don't know something than to pretend that you do. Besides, when it becomes apparent that you really don't know what you're talking about (and trust me, it will), any semblance of allure you might have established will fly out the window.

Look at the world as your oyster. It is waiting to share with you its many wonders. You have only to go looking for them. Treat every day as if it were the most important day—even the only day you have—and go out and learn as many things as you can possibly learn.

Ask the Love Coach

Seductive people listen and learn from others. Remember, there is nothing wrong with just listening and not having something to contribute to a conversation other than your inquisitiveness. (Besides, a little silence can make you quite intriguing.)

Many of the principles of becoming intellectually seductive are simple, but most people forget them. Therefore, if you use them, you will stand out from the crowd. With your desire to become more alluring, along with your ever-increasing understanding of these principles, you'll be attracting new and fascinating people in no time. Other people will want to be around you and will be eager to be seduced by you.

Ask the Love Coach

You can learn from everyone, even the people you might ordinarily overlook. Tom was working late one evening and got to talking with Max, a night janitor in his office building. He found out that Max was once a prize fighter. Tom had recently developed an interest in boxing, and soon he was making arrangements for Max to give him lessons. In return, Tom agreed to help Max improve his reading skills and prepare to take his high-school equivalency test. Now the two men have become friends.

"People don't come in packages that are labeled with all they know," Tom says. "You have to be willing to learn, and people will want to learn from you. Be interested in people, and they'll be interested in you." Take a lesson from Tom, and be open to the riches that other people have to offer.

Next, we'll dig a little deeper, and talk about those elusive emotional buttons that you need to push to make yourself more seductive. I think you'll be surprised: it's not as complicated as you might expect.

The Least You Need to Know

➤ Your mind is the most powerful seduction tool you possess.

➤ There is a world of things to engage you if you step outside yourself.

➤ To be interesting, you have to be interested.

➤ Sometimes it is more blessed to receive than to give. Be a good recipient of what people have to offer.

➤ Let your passion for life grow and shine, and people will be drawn to you.

Chapter 5

Emotional Seductiveness: Creating Those Warm, Fuzzy Feelings

In This Chapter

➤ Making people feel safe with you

➤ Being comfortable with your feelings

➤ Listening with your heart as well as your ears

➤ Making people like you by liking them

One of the most important parts of being seductive is the ability to make the person you're with feel warm, emotionally secure, and even joyful in your presence. Even if you're drop-dead gorgeous, if the object of your desire doesn't feel good around you—and doesn't feel a kinship with you that transcends physical attraction—you'll never develop a relationship beyond a short-lived and disappointing fantasy.

While making yourself more alluring on an emotional level is more difficult than changing your hairstyle or wardrobe, it is ultimately essential in your quest to become the most seductive person you can be.

Ask the Love Coach

It's emotionally seductive to feel safe with a person—not just in the physical sense, but in every way. Feeling safe emotionally means feeling at ease expressing your thoughts, and knowing the other person will treat you with respect. But it works both ways: To get respect from others, you have to give it. Learn to make other people feel safe in your presence, and your emotional seductiveness level will go through the roof.

What's Your Compassion Quotient?

If you're emotionally seductive, people feel comfortable showing their feelings around you, and vice versa. The key to emotional seductiveness is compassion, which does not mean pity. Rather, it means an ability to see into other people's hearts, and to put yourself in their shoes. But compassion involves more than lending a sympathetic ear when someone is down. Compassionate people have the capacity to find the sparkling thread of humor in everyday life—not laughing *at* people, but *with* them. They have a unique ability to infect others with their own sense of joy. Gauge your own compassion level by answering "yes" or "no" to the following questions:

1. When you ask someone, "How are you today?", do you really listen if the answer is something more than the automatic (and expected), "Fine, and you?" ____

2. When someone expresses frustration or talks about a problem they're having, do you listen with your full attention, not giving advice unless it's specifically requested? ____

3. When your neighbor regales you with an anecdote of his toddler's newest accomplishment, do you fully listen and really hear his story—refraining from interrupting with a "one-up" tale about your own child or the child of a sibling or friend? ____

4. Your best friend uncharacteristically calls you at four o'clock in the morning, devastated because she's just found out her husband is having an affair. Do you provide reassurance and make a commitment to get together with her later that day—without revealing irritation that your sleep was interrupted? ____

5. Do you take care to "be there" for a friend who's just lost a loved one, even if you feel a bit awkward because you don't know exactly what to say? ____

6. When someone tells you about his or her reaction to an experience, do you listen and genuinely try to empathize, even though you would have reacted quite differently in the same situation? ____

7. Are you easily able to find humor even in stressful situations—even if it means laughing at yourself? ____

8. When you meet someone new, do you avoid making rash negative judgments or critical conclusions? Do you try to focus on the traits about the person that you really like? ____

9. Can you have a spirited disagreement or conflict with a friend, and emerge with the friendship intact (perhaps even enhanced)? ____

If you can truthfully answer "yes" to all of the above questions, you have a healthy compassion quotient. If you hedged a bit on some of them, don't beat yourself up. There's no time like now to work on increasing your "CQ."

Ask the Love Coach

"Do you consider yourself to be strong or vulnerable?" That was the question of the day at a recent informal gathering of my friends and associates. Several people answered without hesitation, explaining their choice of one or the other trait.

Finally Lisa, a woman who had always exuded an air of supreme confidence, said, "I'm both strong *and* vulnerable." She went on to explain, "Most people assume you can be only one or the other, but true vulnerability can be a mark of strength. Both aspects are equally important." Lisa is a woman who can hold her own in the toughest business negotiations, but, as she says, "Kittens make me cry, babies make me cry, a work of art makes me cry. In order to be vulnerable, you have to have confidence and strength. If you lack that confidence, you're afraid to open up to new experiences—or to another person."

Lisa has the right idea. Strength and vulnerability are not mutually exclusive, and the sexiest, most confident, most dynamic people of both sexes usually are also gentle, soft, and vulnerable. That's definitely a seductive combination.

Feelings...Nothing More Than Feelings...

Before you can feel at ease showing your feelings or allowing someone else to share his or her own feelings with you, you must be comfortable having those feelings in the

For HER Eyes Only

I hear men complain, "Women say they like sensitive guys—'til a guy breaks down and cries around them." If you show discomfort when a man cries, that tells him you are not a "safe place" for him to express his feelings. Understanding the risk he's taking by showing his vulnerable side makes it easier for you to communicate empathy, not judgment.

For HIS Eyes Only

Men, how do you act when a woman disagrees with you? Do you listen to her opinion, withdraw in discomfort, or, worse, openly express contempt? You might not believe this, but even today many women are struggling to overcome their social conditioning to be acquiescent. Listening respectfully to a woman, even (or especially!) when she's expressing an opinion you don't agree with, can make you very seductive in her eyes.

first place. The truth is that virtually everyone experiences feelings with which they aren't comfortable, and that run contrary to their ideal image of themselves. For example:

➤ Men are taught from a young age that being a man means being able to withstand pain without being decimated by it—or even expressing it. Consequently, even after all that hoopla back in the 1970s about the sensitive Alan Alda type, it's still a common male belief that crying is unacceptable.

➤ Women are conditioned by our culture to be agreeable and to hide anger. For this reason, many women (yes, even in this post-feminist era) tend to shy away from expressing anger or even disagreeing with somebody's opinion.

➤ All of us, male and female, have our arbitrary lists of "shoulds" or "shouldn'ts" about feelings. These lists stem from a combination of factors, such as our upbringing, the social and political climate we live in, or even the people we're trying to impress.

You're on your way to becoming comfortable with your feelings when you realize that feelings in and of themselves are neither right nor wrong. (Of course, it's important that you *express* your feelings in ways that aren't hurtful to yourself or others.) As you become more at ease with your own emotions, you will create a climate in which other people are comfortable with their feelings when they're around you.

Learning to Listen: Using Your Ears and Your Heart

The single most critical element of emotional seductiveness is the ability to listen to others, not merely understanding their feelings on an intellectual level, but *empathizing* and "being there" with them. Emotionally seductive people are phenomenal listeners.

Kristin, a client of mine, understands this well. She has a dear friend who recently lost her husband. "Most people don't like to be around someone who has just lost a loved one," Kristin says. "It's very difficult. You want to offer comfort and support, but it seems that anything you say sounds trite and empty. Intellectual jargon or hypothetical platitudes are not going to make them feel any better. All I can really offer my friend is my complete presence with her. She knows that to the best of my ability I'm understanding how she feels, and I am actually sharing her pain."

Those are wise words. Of course, this principle doesn't apply only to talking with the bereaved. Practice the art of compassionate listening with everybody, every day. Learn to listen with your heart, not just your ears.

Wordplay

In order to be truly seductive to someone, you have to make the person feel that you share or can **empathize** with his or her feelings: pain, fear, anger, elation. No matter what the person is feeling, you need to be emotionally available.

Fools Rush In, But Seductive People *Listen*

Let's look more closely at the dynamics of seductive listening. When someone is sharing a personal story, seductive listeners are truly attentive, and don't immediately jump in with their own story, as if they were your opponent in a storytelling contest. Unfortunately, the latter method describes the way too many people "listen." All too frequently, when people get together and converse, whether in groups or one-on-one, the conversation is weighted with the participants' desire for one-upmanship.

A seductive listener refuses to play the one-upmanship game. Suppose, for example, that you have just related the trials of a recent move. Rather than jump in with an equally or more horrible story about moving, the seductive listener responds with empathy. For instance, what would be an example of a good listener's response to the above quandary? "That must have been very stressful for you, to be starting a new job, and have to move everything you own from New York to Tampa, with only two weeks to get settled. You must be exhausted. I would think that facing a major move like that would be overwhelming. You've come through it with more steam left than I would have had."

Such a response tells you this person has really listened to and empathized with you, and just as importantly, that he or she admires you. This one-two punch is more than most people can absorb without feeling very kindly toward the person who said it.

Ask the Love Coach

The conversation at the party had turned to "stupid pet tricks." Marian had just shared an amusing story about her cat that played "fetch" like a dog. But she hadn't even finished her last sentence before Jason jumped in with an "oh-that's-nothing" tale of his own about *his* cat, that not only played fetch, but was toilet-trained, came running like a dog when you called its name, and, to hear Jason tell it, could practically read at a fifth-grade level. In fact, Jason didn't really hear most of Marian's story. He was too busy planning what *he* was going to say, and waiting impatiently for a millisecond of silence so he could jump right in with his anecdote (sort of like a cat waiting to pounce on a mouse). Before this, Marian had been somewhat attracted to Jason, but her attraction level took a rapid nosedive after this incident.

Look at your own conversational habits. Do you really listen when someone else is speaking, or are you busy waiting for your chance to rush in and take over? Seductive conversationalists are more interested in listening to others than in thinking up ways to outshine them.

Wordplay

The best way to describe **resonance** is with an old metaphor. Imagine two pianos sitting side by side in a room. When a note is struck on one of the pianos, the same string begins to vibrate on the other piano, and the identical note rings out. In scientific terms, this is described as resonance, or the action of sympathetic frequencies. It's a great metaphor for empathetic communication as well.

Learning How to "Resonate" with Someone

Okay, I know; this business of "resonating" with another person sounds like more of that New Age hooey we hear all the time nowadays. Behind the trendy-sounding rhetoric, however, there's a sound and powerful principle.

Originally, *resonance* was a scientific term. In human terms, it simply means this: When you describe a feeling, experience, or idea, the person to whom you are describing it fully comprehends, and, to a degree, shares that feeling, experience, or idea.

A truly seductive person is one with whom the person speaking actually feels that resonance, which leads to the sense that the person is "with them" in the experience. Such a person validates his or her partner's ideas or feelings, and thus helps validate the person's worth. This is done not with feigned agreement, but rather via honest empathy and compassion.

The operative word in this concept is "honest." Since the perception of resonance takes place on a near-subliminal level, it cannot be faked. If you try to fake it, the other person will probably detect the insincerity—and that will effectively overshadow any other wonderful qualities you may have.

If you really think about it, you will realize that there's no need to fake it, anyway. All you have to do is really listen to the person and *imagine yourself experiencing a circumstance similar to that which he or she is describing to you.* There's no trickery involved, no deceit. All that is required is your willingness to be present with another person.

Laughter Is the Best Medicine (and the Best Aphrodisiac to Boot)

Cindy and Rick realized how in tune they were with each other almost from the moment they met. They happened to meet while standing in line at a Monty Python film festival, which led naturally to a conversation about their favorite comedians and humorous movies. It turned out that they liked all the same stand-up comedians and sketch performers, delighted in the same jokes and routines, could recite by heart the same favorite punch lines. They soon found they were compatible in many other ways as well, and have now been dating for six months. As you can imagine, this is one relationship that's infused with a healthy dose of humor and laughter.

Of course, you don't have to be a fan of British humor to appreciate the value of laughter. You may be asking, "What does this have to do with seduction?" Simply this: Humor and a sense of fun are not only healthy and healing, *but they are also some of the most powerful aphrodisiacs in the world.* Having fun, sharing laughter, or even just being silly together can add fuel to the fire of a new relationship, and can restore the passion in a relationship that has lost some of its sizzle.

Ask the Love Coach

Children delight in being silly, but for most adults silliness is a lost art. Rediscovering this art with your partner can put some "zing" into your relationship. Think of some completely silly things to do together. Blow bubbles. Go to the zoo and make faces at the monkeys. Play a kids' game such as Twister. Buy some face or body paints and paint each other. Have a food fight. Use your imagination; the idea is for the two of you to dissolve together in helpless laughter... and there's no telling where that might lead!

It's no exaggeration to say that laughter and joy can be more enticing to the opposite sex than a hard body or legs "up to there." And even if you can't tell a joke to save your life, it's easy to make humor a part of your life. Here are a few tips:

➤ *Learn to make yourself see the humor in everyday situations,* even those that you'd normally find aggravating. There's almost always a funny side. Laugh, and the world might not always laugh with you, but you'll feel better. And a person who's laughing, or at least smiling, is infinitely more seductive and attractive than someone who's throwing a temper tantrum or who's just a plain old stick in the mud.

➤ *Share your gift of laughter with others*—not in a way that they feel they are being ridiculed or laughed at, but in a manner that brings them into your personal circle of joy.

➤ *Never be afraid to laugh at yourself.* People who take themselves too seriously are not seductive. On the other hand, people who have the ability to find joy and humor in their lives, and to infect others with that joy and humor, are nearly irresistible.

To Make Others Like You, Like *Them*

This statement sounds so simple that it could be easily dismissed, but it describes the single most effective way to endear yourself to others: *Like them.* Think about how you react to people who really like you. It's difficult not to like them back, isn't it? Doesn't it make sense, then, to believe that another person would react similarly to being liked?

The key word in this idea is the word "really." You reacted positively to someone who *genuinely* liked you. On the other hand, you probably cringed when you perceived that someone was only pretending to like you, or liked you because he or she thought a relationship with you could be beneficial in some way. It is important to remember this distinction, because it can mean the difference between attracting others and sending them running.

For HIS Eyes Only

Guys, women value being able to tell you something that's very important to them and feeling that you truly understand. Unfortunately, a part of most men's wiring compels them to listen and then offer advice. *My* advice: Don't. Unless she specifically asks for suggestions, just listen to her with your full attention. *That's* seductive.

You might wonder how you can possibly make yourself like someone and not come across as being false. Well, you *can't* just make yourself like someone who doesn't have some characteristics that you find attractive, endearing, and intriguing in the first place. But sometimes you have to look for these traits. The following exercise will show you how you can "learn" to like someone.

Try this exercise with the next five people you meet:

1. *Really look at the person with the intention of finding qualities you like.* Don't focus on what you perceive as the person's flaws. When Joan first met Rob at a party, he was telling a deer-hunting story to a group of people. Joan was a vegetarian and an animal-rights activist who didn't believe in hunting. Had she focused on the fact that Rob was obviously a carnivore, and a hunting one at that, she would probably have decided she disliked him without even getting to know him. But because she made an effort to concentrate on positive characteristics, she was able to notice that he actually was quite witty and had a real flair for storytelling. These were traits she could admire.

2. *Practice thinking of the person in terms of the good qualities you've discovered.* Instead of thinking of Rob as "that redneck hunter," which she might have done in the old days, Joan looks at him as "that guy who tells the cool stories." And she has found she actually likes him. Now she looks forward to seeing him at parties and get-togethers.

For HER Eyes Only

A man feels safe with a woman when he feels he can tell her something about himself and trust her to keep it private. If you tell your friends and family the intimate details of your conversation with a man, he'll eventually get wind of it, and he'll never really trust you again. Bottom line: men value confidentiality, and women who value men need to respect that.

Ask the Love Coach

When you're looking for something to admire about someone, the quality or qualities you focus on shouldn't be just physical characteristics. It is too easy to like someone because of a physical attraction; more than likely, that person is probably tired of being valued primarily for his or her physical qualities.

And, guys, when you are talking to a woman and admiring her, be sure you are talking to her face and otherwise indicating that you are admiring her as a person. I've lost count of the times a woman has complained to me that a guy seemed to talk to her chest. I don't care if Dolly Parton could hide behind the woman you're talking to, look her in the *eye* when you're with her. A quick, occasional glance at her physical "assets" is all right, but leering is a definite turn-off.

3. *Let your "I-like-you" attitude shine through whenever you're talking to that person.* Even if she doesn't come right out and say it to him in so many words, Joan's enjoyment of Rob comes across to him whenever they're talking, and he feels good about himself in her presence. It would be nearly impossible for him not to like her in return.

There is something likable, even admirable, in virtually everybody you meet. You don't ever need to fake it and pretend you like someone. If you have to fake interest in a person, why are you trying to attract him or her in the first place?

Ask the Love Coach

Don't be dismayed when conflict comes up in your relationship. Remember that liking someone doesn't mean blindly agreeing with that person on everything. As a matter of fact, some of the people who are most dear to me are people with whom I've had pretty fundamental disagreements, even arguments. Being able to disagree with someone, yet still respect and admire him or her, is one of the highest compliments you can pay somebody. Just remember this: *You cannot be truly intimate with someone until you've had a conflict with that person.* Knowing how to handle conflict with honesty and compassion is truly seductive.

Emotional Seductiveness Creates a Win-Win Situation

The whole process of really listening to and empathizing, resonating, laughing, having fun with, and of genuinely liking another person, serves to validate his or her sense of self-worth. The most powerful—and the only positive—form of seduction is the kind that leaves the person being seduced feeling somehow enriched by the experience. To enhance another person's good feelings about him- or herself, and about the experiences he or she shares with you, is the ultimate goal in seduction.

Equally important is that the act of seduction be a positive, enriching experience for both parties. A true seduction is one that leaves both the seducer, and the person being seduced, smiling when they remember the experience.

The Least You Need to Know

➤ The first and most important thing you have to do to be seductive is to show up—not only physically, but intellectually and emotionally as well.

➤ To seduce someone, you need to make the person feel safe with you.

➤ To seduce someone, you need to make the object of your affection feel good about him- or herself.

➤ It is almost impossible not to like someone who genuinely likes you.

Chapter 6

Spirit or Essence: All the Elements of Seductiveness... and More

In This Chapter

➤ The intangible "something" that makes you who you are

➤ Building your self-confidence

➤ Character and intent: the components of integrity

➤ Self-worth: feeling you've got something of value to offer

In this chapter, we're going to discuss an intangible yet very powerful aspect of your persona: your spirit. Abstract though this quality may be, it is crucial to your seductiveness. For although it is difficult to quantify, spirit is the aspect of you that truly makes you sexy.

So, just what is *spirit*? Some people think of spirit as being synonymous with "soul," but for our purposes here, we're going to define it simply as your essence: The mystifying ingredient that is the sum total of all the other facets of your being. Your spirit is a blend of many ingredients:

➤ How you look

➤ How you move

➤ How you speak

➤ How you think

➤ How you feel

➤ How you express your feelings

➤ The presence you bring into a room

➤ Your intent—the motivation behind the other elements

But it is more than these. It is also the confidence you feel and the passion that drives you. Spirit, in short, is who you really *are*.

Though this elusive essence is comprised of all the other aspects of your being, it is also the core from which those aspects are drawn. Being as impalpable and abstract as it is, the spirit is also the most difficult element of your persona to work on. It can be touched only through one of its manifestations—one of the more obvious parts of your being—yet it responds to the elevation of other elements by being elevated itself as a by-product of your efforts. In other words, anything you do to upgrade one aspect of yourself will have a positive effect on your spirit.

Wordplay

The word **spirit** has several definitions in the dictionary, the first one being, "a person's mind or feelings, or animating principle, as distinct from his body." A more holistic way of looking at spirit is to think of it as encompassing the physical presence, rather than being distinct from it. Of course, "spirit" includes much more than the physical; it's the sum total of who you are.

Ask the Love Coach

Physical elements contribute to a person's appeal, but ultimately, *spirit* or *essence* is really what makes someone sexy. Your life experiences add luster to your spirit, so it's true that people really can get "better" as they get older. A shining spirit can give you seductive qualities that outlast physical beauty or youth.

What Color Is Your Aura?

According to some spiritual belief systems, the *aura* is an energy field around a person that shines with colors determined by their state of being—their emotional, physical, and spiritual condition. We won't go into whether or not this belief is valid, but the general concept is useful for *visualizing* what your spirit or essence projects to the people you meet.

That's what you're going to practice doing in the following exercise: Think of a color that describes your spirit, and then decide what that color means to you. (And it doesn't matter what the psychologists say or what the "aura experts" say; this is *your* exercise.)

So, pick a color, any color. If you're drawing a blank, here's a brief list to jog your imagination. Are you...

➤ *Red:* Does that mean you're passionate and sexy, or angry?

➤ *Yellow:* Do you have a cheerful, sunny nature, or are you "yellow" in the sense of fearful?

➤ *Blue:* Are you calm and steady, or melancholy?

➤ *Green:* Are you peaceful? Envious? Obsessed with money? Or concerned about the environment?

➤ *Purple:* Do you have a regal nature? Or is purple a spiritual color to you?

➤ *Pink:* Are you gentle and loving (traits usually considered to be feminine, but certainly present in men as well)? Or are you seeing the world through "rose-colored glasses"?

➤ *Gray:* Do you feel formless, or have a cloudy self-image? Or does gray spell dignity and strength to you?

➤ *Black:* Does black signify depression or mourning to you? Does it whisper of elegance? Or does it mean you're secretive, mysterious?

➤ *White:* Does this simply mean colorlessness, or does it signify purity to you? Or do you think of a white light as healing or soothing?

Wordplay

The dictionary defines **aura** as (1) the atmosphere surrounding a person or thing, and thought to come from him or it, and (2) a luminous radiation. While many people associate the concept of the *aura* with New Age beliefs, the idea is actually quite old. It's possible the halos surrounding holy figures in many of the Old Masters' paintings were actually supposed to represent auras.

Now try the following visualization exercise:

1. First, look over the list of colors above. Remember this is *your* exercise, so if the meanings of the colors listed don't ring true to you, make up your own meanings. If your color wasn't listed, add it to the list, and give it whichever meaning makes sense to you.

2. Find someplace quiet where you can sit down and concentrate. Turn on some soft meditative music, if that will enhance your concentration.

3. Close your eyes and imagine there is a radiant field emanating from your person. Its hue and intensity are shaped by your being and your mood. What color is it, and what does that color mean to you?

After you've found your color, think about what it means to you. If the meaning is negative, realize you can change either the color or its meaning to you. For example, do you see yourself as a "red," and does red signify anger to you? Then why not concentrate on changing to a neutral brown, or a harmonious green? Or why not focus on red as a color of passion?

Once you've found a meaningful, positive color, how can you use it? Simply think about your color at different times during the day—perhaps during your quiet time (or your meditation time, if you meditate)—and imagine yourself beaming that hue out into the world for everyone to see. It's really just another way of projecting your essence.

Spirit, Essence, or Whatever You Want to Call It: It's What Makes You *You*

We've discussed all the individual elements of your persona, describing how you can polish and improve them to make you more alluring and seductive. While each of these aspects is truly important, it's the sum total of all of them—the whole package—that actually comes across to the people you meet. Just as a chain is only as strong as its weakest link, that whole package that is you is only as seductive and desirable as the least desirable of the individual elements.

Ask the Love Coach

Camille is one of the most compellingly seductive women I know. Our youth-oriented culture notwithstanding, this 48-year-old siren can walk into a room and put all the nubile *Baywatch*-babe lookalikes to shame. She's not particularly beautiful in the conventional sense, but Camille exudes a radiance you can't help but notice.

You'd never believe she went through a real crisis when she turned 40. To get through it, she took an inventory of her life experiences—the traveling she'd done, what she'd learned about human nature, the perspective she had at 40 that she didn't have in her 20s—and she honestly began to be proud of her age.

To celebrate her 40th birthday, Camille went on an adventure trek to the Himalayas. She also went back to college and got her master's degree. And she's started an exercise and nutrition program that has given her a healthy glow. Now Camille is too busy to grouse about guys her age who ogle 20-year-olds (something that used to bother her)—but she's not too busy to notice that guys of all ages are ogling *her* these days.

When your physical, intellectual, and emotional parts are *all* working well, your intent is clear and your self-image is healthy. Such a balance feeds your essence—which, in turn, magnifies the attractiveness of your individual qualities.

It's like a perpetual-motion process, focused on making you a better, more desirable being. The more you elevate the separate aspects of your being, the more your spirit is uplifted, and the more it enhances the individual parts of your persona, which then... well, you get the point. A well-developed spirit is that special something that turns an apparently ordinary-looking woman into a ravishing beauty, or a marginally attractive man into a desirable hunk.

Self-Confidence: Where Does It Come From?

While your *self-confidence* is certainly influenced by events in the outside world, ultimately, it comes from within you. But just what is self-confidence? It is the belief that you can achieve your goals, perform well in completing the tasks you face, and deal with challenges without being overwhelmed. It is a freedom from fear, arising from the knowledge that you are a competent, capable person.

Self-confidence is also the awareness that the world is not filled with enemies and negative people. Those who lack self-confidence harbor the fear that each person or situation they face is a challenge to their safety or well-being, and that they, being less-than-capable, will probably be harmed or diminished by the encounter. The saddest part is that, by holding such a belief, you can actually make it come true.

Wordplay

Self-confidence means trust in your abilities and belief in your competence. It is fed by your accomplishments, such as learning a new procedure or solving a problem.

This may sound exaggerated, but if you approach all people as if they are your enemy, your defenses go up, and you don't let anyone get close enough to be your friend. If you perceive a situation as an attack, those same defenses go up, and you're so busy concentrating on protecting yourself that you completely miss anything positive the situation may offer. You need to realize that self-confidence doesn't grow in a vacuum. While some people seem to be supremely sure of themselves from birth, you can bet there were factors that shaped them and made them self-confident.

Increasing your self-confidence can help you overcome many of your fears. You can become more confident by learning or accomplishing something new, participating in appropriate support groups, or, paradoxically, by getting involved in activities that help you focus on something outside yourself. Consider:

Heart Brakes

Don't embark on any self-improvement program solely to please or impress somebody else. It's certainly all right if pleasing another person is part of your motivation; having someone else root for you can encourage you to keep up the good work. But whether you're losing weight, quitting drinking, or going back to school to finish your degree, do it first and foremost for yourself.

➤ *Participating in a sport.* Take a martial arts class or become an exercise enthusiast. Physical activity can make you more fit, healthy, and vibrant, which can increase your confidence dramatically.

➤ *Taking an adult education class.* Whether purely for the pleasure of learning or for professional advancement, continuing your education can make you much more self-confident. Taking classes also affords you a wonderful opportunity to meet new friends with interests similar to your own.

➤ *Attending a Toastmasters or similar group in your area.* These groups exist for one reason: to help people overcome their fear of public speaking, and help them polish their speaking skills. Even if you don't plan to do a great deal of public speaking, participating in a Toastmasters group can do wonders for your self-confidence.

➤ *Taking an acting course.* Whether or not you're interested in acting as a profession, an acting course can help rid you of your shyness and inhibitions, and, who knows, it just might bring out the "ham" in you.

➤ *Spending time in a supportive social setting.* There are many groups to choose from, such as religious community groups or, depending upon your situation, one of the multitudes of support groups available.

➤ *Getting involved in community organizations.* Consider a neighborhood watch group, a park committee, or a local board. Feeling that you are a vital part of your community can increase your self-confidence.

➤ *Getting involved in a cause.* Whether you choose an organization that is local, national, or international in scope, working for a cause you're passionate about will help make you feel that you're truly a part of the larger world, and that you're making a difference. That can be a real confidence builder.

As your skills increase, your self-confidence builds.

Essential Elements: Character and Intent

As long as we're focusing on the intangible elements of spirit or essence, we have to look at what are perhaps two of its most elusive facets: character and intent. *Character* is one of those qualities that whole libraries full of books have been written about, yet the definition remains incomplete. In its simplest form, good character means integrity. It means having a commitment to a set of values devoid of manipulation, and being rich with respect for yourself and for other people and things.

Ask the Love Coach

Doing good makes you feel good. Studies show that altruistic acts make us feel good emotionally and may even be good for our physical health. It's no exaggeration—and certainly no ill reflection on us—to say that we do good deeds as much for ourselves as for others. This doesn't mean you have to run out and become the next Mother Theresa. Acts of kindness can be very simple. For instance, next time you're on the bus or a subway, give up your seat to that person who looks to have had a really bad day. Or, instead of racing to merge ahead of another car on the highway and cutting it off, let the other person go first. You could even just give someone a nice smile and say "good morning." That person will feel great—and so will you.

Some people believe character is one of those "either you have it or you don't" qualities, but, like any other facet of yourself, it can be developed and enhanced. In the case of character, however, it's not so much a matter of specific exercises as commitment. It is a process, and stripped to its bare essentials it works like this:

1. You decide you want to act with integrity.
2. As you act on that decision, it begins to feel more and more natural, until that integrity is a part of your core.
3. When you become so accustomed to acting with integrity that you aren't even conscious of it, you have developed good character.

Intent is the conscious manifestation of your character. It is the definition of your desires toward other people and situations. Those with character will consciously choose to act in a way that is beneficial to those around them and, indeed, to their world. Such actions are guided, not by some desired response to the action (or fear of reprisal if one's actions are not beneficial), but rather by the desire to act well for its own sake.

There is a Jewish tradition known as the *mitzvah*, which, simply stated, is an obligatory good deed. The performance of mitzvahs is not contingent upon a system of punishments and rewards; rather, the idea is to do good and act with integrity simply because that is the right thing to do. I feel that no matter what our tradition or background is, this simple idea of acting with integrity for its own sake is something we would all do well to adopt.

Sometimes, we have to look closely at our intent before we act, to make sure we are striving for the highest good for all involved in a situation. It's easy to convince ourselves that we are acting for one reason, when our real motivations are completely different.

Ask the Love Coach

Thinking of doing a good deed? Here's a secret to give your altruistic act an extra edge: *Don't tell everyone about it.* That way, your good feelings about your deed will come from within you and won't be dependent on being "patted on the back" by others. This will deepen your sense of self-worth. It's subtle, but it really works.

About all we can directly and consciously do about our intent is to become aware of it. If our intent is less than noble, it's best to question our motives before we act at all. If our intent is benevolent, however, we—and those on the receiving end of our intentions—can be comforted by the knowledge that we are acting in good faith, without ulterior motives. And that level of comfort that you instill in others is a very powerful part of your seductiveness.

Self-Worth: The Reflection of Your Essence

There is frequently some confusion between the concepts of self-confidence and *self-worth*. Quite simply, where self-confidence is how you measure your own capabilities, self-worth is a measure of something much more intrinsic. It is your perception of your value as a human being. The two can either reinforce each other, or can be diametrically opposed.

The process of boosting your sense of self-worth is probably about 20 percent introspection and 80 percent action. Consider what it is you like and don't like about yourself; then go about the task of improving the things you don't like, and reinforcing the things you like.

A tool therapists frequently use to help clients increase their sense of self-worth is to ask them: "What have you done that you're most proud of, and why?" Quite often the answer is something the client did that brought joy to someone else. The more good you do for others, the more you'll have to feel good about. (Remember what we were saying about character earlier in this chapter!) A client of mine named Sondra has developed a routine with a couple of elderly neighbors who can no longer drive. These neighbors' children and other relatives live out of town, and their circle of friends and contacts is limited because they can't get around very well anymore. Once a week, Sondra takes them to the supermarket, and whenever possible she takes them to doctor's appointments or runs other errands for them. She also invites them to spend many holidays and other special occasions with her and her family. "In return," says Sondra, "I have gained two wonderful friends who have led long and fascinating lives. I really enjoy the company of both of these women. But what I enjoy more than anything is knowing I've helped make a difference in their lives. For me, few things can match that feeling of satisfaction."

How about you? What have you done that has made you feel good about yourself? Sit down and make a list. Then ask yourself, "What more can I do?" Just for starters, here are some ideas:

> ➤ Volunteer to work with children in the burn or cancer ward in the pediatric unit of your local hospital.

Wordplay

Self-worth is, in many ways, more profound and personal than self-confidence. It describes your concept of your merit and value as a human being. It is dependent to some degree on the opinions of others, but a healthy sense of self-worth comes from within.

Heart Brakes

Effective personal growth requires that you practice moderation. Too much self-examination can deteriorate quickly into an obsession, and too little action can drag you into depression.

➤ Help out with babies born to drug-addicted mothers.

➤ Give some of your free time to a soup kitchen (and not just at Thanksgiving or Christmas—these facilities often have a problem with too much volunteer help on holidays).

➤ Do some volunteer work for local AIDS organizations; help out at a hospice, take meals to AIDS patients, or help them care for their pets.

➤ Help out at a shelter for women who are abuse victims.

➤ Volunteer for a local literacy program.

➤ Run errands for elderly, housebound people, or volunteer at a nursing home. You don't necessarily need to find an organization that specializes in this—you probably have a neighbor on your street or in your building who could use a helping hand.

➤ Become a Big Brother or Big Sister.

➤ Get involved with a mentor program at your local high school or university.

In truth, there are many concrete actions you can take to improve your sense of self-worth. Everybody has something of value to offer, whether it be skills, information, or just encouragement. The simple act of smiling at someone who doesn't have much to smile about not only makes the object of your good intentions feel good, but makes you feel pretty good, too. And who doesn't love to be around someone who feels good? It's contagious!

Ask the Love Coach

Jeffrey, a client of mine, dropped out of college. Although he'd always planned to go back, he just never got around to it. The longer he waited, the easier it became *not* to do it. Without a degree, he sometimes didn't get jobs he applied for or was passed up for promotions. What was worse, though, was seeing his mother's disappointment. None of this added to Jeffrey's feelings of self-worth.

Finally, in his late 30s, Jeffrey began taking night classes while still keeping his full-time job. While his primary motivation for getting his degree was to increase his marketability, what really kept him going was knowing how pleased his mom would be. Jeffrey says, "Sometimes, focusing on the joy we're going to bring someone else really does provide that added impetus." He graduated with a 3.8 grade average, and his mom couldn't be prouder. He's pretty pleased, too.

Ultimately, your spirit or essence is just as obvious as a brightly lit neon sign that you carry with you everywhere you go. Only you can determine what your sign says to the people you meet. Carry a sign of confidence, of comfort, of good intent—and you will be remarkably alluring to the people around you.

The Least You Need to Know

➤ Your spirit, or essence, is the sum total of all of your other elements, and is really what makes you seductive.

➤ Your self-confidence is influenced by outside events, but it originates within you.

➤ Character and intent are important aspects of your essence, for they determine how comfortable others feel with you.

➤ You can increase your sense of self-worth by doing something good for others.

Part 2
Attracting Dates: Casting Your Spell

Now that we've laid the groundwork for seduction, it's time to go out and field-test your seductive powers. We'll begin by taking a close look at what men and women find seductive in the opposite sex. Next, because you have to get out and find the person of your dreams before you can seduce him or her, we'll discuss the pros and cons of the various "hunting grounds." No matter where you go, you need to know how to attract your "quarry" once you're there. Toward that end, we'll go into the how-to's of the initial approach, the nuances of body language and other romantic signals, and the perils and pleasures of flirting.

Sooner or later, someone is going to catch your eye, and vice versa—and you're going to actually go on a date with that person. You'll find a step-by-step "survival guide" to the date—and how to use it to your seductive advantage—as well as a basic evaluation system to help you decide if you should go out with this person again. After all, even if you're not looking for your soul mate right now, you certainly don't want to seduce (or be seduced by) someone who's not right for you at all.

Chapter 7

The Ultimate Seductress: A Man's Perspective

In This Chapter

➤ What looks sexy to a man

➤ Becoming a walking vision of allure

➤ How a true seductress acts

➤ The spirit of the seductress: making (or breaking) the allure

The debate about what constitutes seductiveness in a woman has raged for thousands of years. You would think that, after all this time, we would have reached some sort of consensus on the topic, but we have not for a number of reasons.

In this chapter, we will attempt to sort fact from fantasy, and to describe those attributes that men really desire and find appealing in a woman, as well as those that can instantaneously turn her from being a siren into a pariah in a man's eyes. The bad news is that women can sometimes do some of the things that turn guys off without even realizing they're doing them. The good news for women is that these behaviors or traits are easily avoided with a little awareness. Even better news is, despite what women have been led to believe, the traits men are genuinely attracted to aren't impossible fantasies or unachievable goals, nor are they confined to a physical appearance that only a few women can achieve.

You women can use this chapter to help you come up with your own personal assessment of your seductiveness. That way you can enhance the traits that make you more alluring, while minimizing (or even doing away with) those that can turn men off.

His Description of a Sexy Woman

One of the first questions a man asks about a woman he's never met is inevitably, "What does she look like?" The typical female response to having such a question asked about her is to bristle at the notion that so much of her perceived value is wrapped up in her physical appearance. Women who don't think they're attractive don't feel comfortable being compared to other women they believe are prettier. And really beautiful women are tired of men who can't seem to look past their exterior.

For HER Eyes Only

What constitutes a seductive woman?

➤ When a *pretty* woman walks into a room, young boys turn to stare.

➤ When a *beautiful* woman enters a room, grown men turn to stare.

➤ When a *seductive* woman enters a room, however, *other women* turn to stare.

When you add the fact that physical attractiveness is such a subjective value, differing from man to man, culture to culture, and even time period to time period, the very notion of defining physical beauty becomes somewhat ludicrous.

Our concern in this book, however, is not to perpetuate a long-running historical debate, but to provide the modern woman with some real clues about how to make herself more alluring to men in general. While individual men certainly have their own unique preferences, some feminine elements seem to carry an almost universal appeal. We will concentrate upon these elements.

So what is this "universal" standard of beauty, if such a thing exists? What are the common elements that are attractive to all men? And, most importantly, how many of those can the average woman, who is not a supermodel (more than 99 percent of the females in the world), manifest in herself? Heady questions, all, and the answers may well surprise (and encourage) you.

The Real Deal

Face it, very few of us have perfect, supermodel bodies or faces. While there may seem to be an overwhelming amount of evidence that falling short of such mythical levels of beauty is a real handicap, you needn't feel shortchanged. The women staring back at you from the pages of *Elle* and *Vogue* may be images of impassioned promises, but you, a living, breathing object of real beauty, are that promise, fulfilled.

Accentuating that promise, and that allure, is simply a matter of bringing your more appealing features into focus and drawing attention to them, while minimizing those features that you feel are less attractive. Here are some hints (also refer to Chapter 3, on the physical elements of seduction):

➤ *Pleasing parts:* Focus on a part of you that you really think is attractive ("think lips," "think legs"). If you are particularly proud of your legs, for example, you may want to wear dresses that draw attention to them. That doesn't mean you have to wear skirts so short that you can't sit down comfortably. The men I've talked to seem to actually prefer a skirt that is a bit above the knee, perhaps with a slit in the back. The quick glimpse of a little more thigh (and perhaps the hope of seeing a bit more) is frequently more tantalizing to a man than seeing everything all at once. Remember, men are visually oriented creatures, capable of intense fantasies. Inspiring those fantasies, even with a minimum of visual stimuli, can go a long way toward seducing a man.

➤ *Appealing apparel:* In all you wear, look for a proper fit and feel, so that the garment makes you feel as good as it makes you look. Your clothes must allow you to move naturally and comfortably, adding to your sense of confidence as you wear them. In addition, your clothes need to look "touchable" to a man. While a crisply pressed business suit may communicate competence and confidence, your overall look needs to be less harsh than the common dictates of business attire. Run your fingertips across the fabric of your favorite outfits, and ask yourself what the material is saying. Look at the cut of your clothes, and ask yourself what your overall impression is. Then ask yourself if these are the things you want to communicate to the men in your life. If the answer is no, it might be time to do some careful shopping.

➤ *Finishing touches—for maximum touchability:* The same approach applies to your hair and make-up. You want *everything* about you to look touchable, even inviting to a man's caress. Men have often told me that if a woman looks like the slightest touch would destroy her image, they simply won't want to touch her. In short, lose the shellac hairspray, ditch the three coats of industrial-strength mascara, and strip off a few layers of rouge. In addition, if you tend to trowel on the foundation, give the trowel to your favorite bricklayer. A man would much rather see a few real flaws than a perfectly applied coat of putty and paint.

For HER Eyes Only

When it comes to perfumes or colognes, quite simply, a little goes a long way. Many men actually tell me that a woman's natural scent (so long as her personal hygiene is good) is more attractive than some sweet, flowery fragrance from a bottle.

"Drop-Dead Gorgeous" Defined

While men are, as a rule, visually oriented, and are frequently quite verbal in describing what they find attractive in a woman, a little bit of probing reveals they are not as universally obsessed with specific parts of the female anatomy as one might think. When my male clients describe their image of a beautiful woman, they may well begin by describing a full, well-proportioned bust line, or a taut, toned bottom. Almost without exception, however, they go on to describe the woman's eyes, and how those eyes seemed to beckon with some hidden promise. Other times, they go into great detail, describing a smile that held laughter even in its silence, or soft, pouting lips that seemed to beg to be kissed.

When I press the men for specific details, such as the color of the woman's eyes or the actual physical shape of her mouth, the guys seem to falter a bit. It seems that they are enthralled not so much by the actual physical characteristics as by their own interpretation of what those characteristics represent. In short, they are describing the *spirit* behind the physical.

You may be thinking, "Great! I can work on the shape of my butt, and wear clothes that enhance my bust line, but how in the world can I change what the shape of my lips 'says' to a certain man, or what the color of my eyes communicates to him?"

Here's where the really good news comes in. While you can (and should) continue to work to keep your physical body in healthy condition, you can have an even greater effect by working on your attitude. Tell yourself what a mouth-watering morsel you are, and imagine every head in the room turning to admire you as you enter. Like Julia in Chapter 3, you can imagine your every move to be a sensuous dance. Imagine your mouth uttering some profoundly seductive promise to the ear of every man in the room. Imagine your eyes saying, "Perhaps..." to every gaze you meet.

And when you're actually with a man, focus all those promises of untold pleasures upon him alone, as if he were the only man in creation. Again, by seducing yourself you are seducing any man who comes in contact with you, even from across a crowded room.

Here is an exercise you can use to hone your self-image and prepare yourself for your "grand entrance":

1. Take a long, leisurely bubble bath, adding your favorite fragrance to the bath water. You might even want to light some candles and turn the light off. Put some sensuous music on the stereo, perhaps Sadé, Leonard Cohen, or some jazzy Billie Holiday. As you sink into the warm water, focus on the sensations it offers your skin. Feel how it literally draws the tension from your body, and allow yourself to sigh softly as you give yourself up to the experience. As you wash your body, luxuriate in your own touch, focusing on each sensation as your fingers glide across your skin.

2. When you are finished, emerge from the bath to a brand new, extra plush bath towel. Pat yourself dry as you would have a lover do it, relishing in the softness of the towel upon your skin, as well as the suppleness of your body beneath your fingertips. Imagine how glorious that body must feel to a man.

3. After you are dry, splash on some refreshing cologne, making sure to apply it to all those places where you would want your man's attention to be drawn.

Standing before the mirror, illuminated by candlelight, gaze appreciatively at each part of your body, imagining your man's pleasure if he could see through your eyes right now.

4. Now, as you dress, let each article of clothing you put on be a conscious attempt to amplify your seductiveness. The garments touching your skin must be soft and smooth as a lover's lips, and must be as beautiful as the woman you wish to be. The outfit you wear must serve as a subtle, but clear, reminder of the seductress upon which they are draped. They hint at pleasures just beyond his reach, on the fringes of his dreams.

5. Apply your make-up carefully, and conservatively. Imagine that your lips are the portrait of unspoken promise, adorned with the care of a Botticelli. Your eyes are their own deep pools of passion, and need only a subtle touch to draw his attention to them. Once there, he will be lost in their allure.

6. After you finish dressing and venture out into the presence of the object of your desire, remember the sight of your own nakedness as you stood before the mirror. Hold the image of that sexy, seductive, confident woman in your mind, remembering that this beauty was no air-brushed super model—it was *you*, in all your glory.

Seductive Is As Seductive Does

If you pay attention to the media nowadays, you probably assume that men think the most seductive women are 18 to 25 years old, wear as little clothing as possible, and have the inclination genetically implanted in their brains to hop into bed at the earliest possible opportunity. Such an assumption is not only frustrating and demeaning to most women, it is patently untrue.

For HER Eyes Only

Over and over again in surveys, men have told me they are really turned on by a feminine woman. I began to question what that means. Is it all about frills and froufrou? No, not really. A woman can be a carpenter in overalls and still be feminine. Femininity is at once more abstract and more profound than all the outer trappings with which we've come to associate it. The simplest way to put it is that *a feminine woman makes a man feel like a man in her presence.* And don't worry; we're not talking about old-fashioned, sexist role playing, but rather about the very essence of masculinity and femininity.

For HER Eyes Only

We've all heard the saying that a woman should be "a lady in the parlor and a whore in bed." The more modern version? A woman should be competent and sophisticated, with an element of the ultimate temptress lingering just below the surface. It isn't broadcast, but he always knows it's there.

For HER Eyes Only

There's an old joke in which a man states that the most important quality in his woman is that she be facing in his direction. Silly as this may seem, we women frequently forget that a man wants and needs our attention. Focus on him; let him know that, at this moment, he's the most important thing in your world.

Wordplay

Trust is an important element in seductiveness. It means knowing that how your partner behaves around you accurately reflects what he or she actually thinks or feels. It doesn't mean agreeing with everything the other person says or does, but it does mean letting that person know that his or her well-being is a priority to you.

So how does a woman have to behave in order to be considered alluring to men? Does her every action need to scream "yes" to everyone she's with? Hardly. Remember that a man, just like a woman, wants to feel valued and special. A woman who seems to be available to everybody she encounters may well be the object of his prurient fantasy, but not of his prolonged attention. A far more appropriate projection would be, "Perhaps...but only with you." To be truly seductive, such a statement would come from deep within her, rather than being tattooed across her forehead.

Focus, Focus, Focus!

The first element in female behavior that men consider alluring is the woman's ability (and desire) to focus her attention on him and him alone. I'm certain every woman knows what it's like to be talking with a man who seems to be paying as much attention to other women as he is to her: It doesn't feel very good. So why would we think that men like receiving the same treatment from us? Is it because they don't have the same feelings that we do? Of course not.

A Confidante...or the Town Tattler?

Another element important to a man is his need to be able to *trust* the woman he's with. He needs to know that she is being honest with him, and that the stories she tells her friends about him will be consistent with what she says to his face.

He needs to know that what he says to her in confidence will remain their shared secret. He wants to be sure that, if he shows her his more vulnerable side, it won't become an item for discussion around the coffee pot at the office.

This sounds simple enough, yet we women often damage that trust just by sharing someone else's confidence with him. We may think that we're letting him "inside" when we tell him about so-and-so's problems, but we're actually letting him know we can't keep a secret. So don't say anything that could be construed as gossip, or he will close up like a bear trap, and may never let you in again. Learn to be gentle and discreet in your descriptions of others, as gentle as you would want your man to be with you.

The Spirit of the Enchantress...Making It or Breaking It Without Lifting a Finger

In the exercise earlier in this chapter, we demonstrated how a woman's attitude and her internal dialog can dramatically affect her outward seductiveness, simply by making her feel more seductive. At an even deeper level, our attitudes affect the way we perceive the men in our lives, and thus, how we act toward them.

The key word in this whole process is *intent*. How we feel toward men in general, and the man we are with in particular, has a great effect upon our behavior, even in ways of which we are unaware. These attitudes may be the product of our past relationships, or may even be deeply ingrained into the very fabric of who we were at birth.

Your intent toward another person is comprised of all your hopes, fears, past joys, and past pains. Though intent makes up a significant portion of a person's attractiveness and allure, people frequently give little consideration to what that intent is. We want, without understanding *what* we want. We seek tokens for reasons we never consider. It follows, sadly, that if we are unable or unwilling to consider our own real needs, it becomes natural for us to not consider the needs of our partners. Our intent toward the other person becomes narcissistic and destructive.

For better or for worse, your intent will be projected to the men you want to attract, either adding to or subtracting from your seductiveness quotient. Without lifting a finger, you can make or break the enchantment. The good news is that if you're projecting a less than enchanting persona, you have the power to change it. It's all up to you.

In the final analysis, we women are real winners in the seduction game, because the better a man is at pleasing us, the happier he is. Just by enjoying ourselves when we're with a man, we go a long way toward ensuring that he is enjoying himself, as well. And by feeling more seductive, more alluring,

For HER Eyes Only

You need to remember that no single person is going to meet all of your needs. If a man suspects you are looking to him to have every one of your needs met, he will shy away from you and the impossible responsibility you are placing on him. Remember, to feel seductive, you must accept and be comfortable with yourself, faults and all—but you should apply the same principle to your partner as well.

For HER Eyes Only

If a man feels he is pleasing you, he will, himself, be pleased. If he believes he is making you happy, he will feel happy, too. This may sound like a sexist statement, but it's true. Ask yourself how many couples you know where the woman is miserable, yet the man is really happy. There just aren't any. So if you expect men to want to be with you, you'd better let them know that you enjoy being with *them*.

we actually *become* more alluring. No matter where you go, you aren't likely to find a better deal than that. So go out, have a wonderful time, and dazzle the men in your life in the process!

The Least You Need to Know

➤ Despite the media fantasies, a real woman, in the flesh, is much more appealing to a man than an airbrushed picture of a centerfold or supermodel.

➤ To be seductive from your very core, first you must seduce yourself.

➤ You will be enticing if you look and act sensual, real, and touchable.

➤ To be seductive to a particular man, you need to convey the message that he is truly special and not just an interchangeable partner.

➤ If a man feels he is pleasing you, *he* will be pleased.

Chapter 8

The Ultimate Seducer: A Woman's Perspective

In This Chapter

➤ Making her the only woman in your world (at least for tonight)

➤ Showing her you're truly interested

➤ Leaving the strong, silent type in the movies where he belongs

➤ Handsome is as handsome smells (and tastes and feels)

➤ Treating her as your equal, even though you want to jump her bones

Among the many surveys that I conducted with clients over the years, perhaps some of the most enlightening responses were to questions about what actually constituted attractiveness and allure. In Chapter 7, we presented a guy's-eye view of a seductive woman. Now it's your turn, guys, to find out the answers to the burning question: What makes a man seductive to women?

You might expect that the women I surveyed would have named qualities such as physical appearance, intelligence, and affluence as the most critical factors in defining a seductive man. To my surprise, however, these factors rarely appeared at—or even near—the top of most women's lists. The majority of the women who responded were more concerned with the fundamental qualities in a man's *attitude* than they were with his outward appearance or his accomplishments. Despite what the media would have us believe, substance really does take precedence over style where women are concerned.

Our primary objective in this chapter is to help you guys become more aware of your own unique substance, and polish those aspects that women seem to almost universally appreciate. At the same time, we'll concentrate on minimizing those behaviors that, even though they may seem insignificant to a man, are sure-fire ways to turn women off.

The Most Important Game You May Ever Play

Since a lot of you guys are into sports, let's make a game out of this. Imagine that there is a universal scoring system that women use to evaluate men. Every guy starts in the minor leagues, with every chance of making it to the majors. To make things fair, you all begin with a score of 0. Each foul a man commits results in points being deducted from his score—but on the other hand, every successful play earns him additional points in the game of love. As we review women's major turn ons and turnoffs, you guys will be able to get a better perspective on how well you play, and how you can improve your game. (And you women can determine how much value you place in each item.)

Focus Makes Her Heart Grow Fonder

Few things are more seductive to a woman than a man who focuses only on her. According to virtually all the women I spoke to, one of the biggest mistakes a man can make is *not* focusing on his date. It's easy to lose points here—but it's just as easy to gain them.

For HIS Eyes Only

Guys, nobody expects you to be blind or dead where other women are concerned. If a particularly attractive woman catches your eye, it's okay to look—but keep it brief and, above all, subtle. Whatever you do, don't let your attention be focused on another woman for very long. Your date will see it, and you'll have a hard row to hoe to make up for it.

Keep Your Eyes on the Prize—Her!

One of the best ways you can show you're focused on the woman you're with is to use good eye contact. Really look at her as you speak and listen to her. Don't let your eyes roam all over the room looking at other people (particularly other women); zoom in on *her*.

I'm certain that you've heard women complaining about being with a man who looks all around the room and focuses on everything (or, more accurately, every*one*) but his date. There's nothing worse than a man who jerks his head around to watch a pretty woman walk by.

Since the primary rule of being attractive and interesting to a woman is to *be* attracted and interested, this kind of behavior goes a long way toward keeping you out of the major leagues. I've even known women to get up and leave the table at a fine restaurant, rather than stay with a man who gawks at the other women in the room.

On the other hand, I've known men who seem to be completely oblivious to other women, and who give the impression that they wouldn't even give a naked supermodel a second glance when they're with a woman. This kind of man, sports fans, hits superstar status with the woman he's accompanying. It tells her that you appreciate beauty as much as the next guy, but that you find *her* more captivating than anyone else. You won't even have to say anything; your actions will speak loud and clear, and she will appreciate it more than you can imagine.

Making the Present Perfect (and Leaving History in the Classroom)

To be seductive to the woman you're with, you have to make her feel that, for now, she is the only woman who really matters to you. One of the quickest ways to shatter this feeling is to dwell on your past relationships in her presence.

Many women have told me that one of their greatest turn-offs is a man who talks too much about his ex-wife or former girlfriend. It doesn't even matter *what* he has to say about a past lover; simply talking about her is a losing proposition. If he gushes about how great she was, a woman will figure he's still hung up on her. If he grouses about how horrible she was, a woman will assume that he'll be saying the same thing about *her* in six months.

The time for discussing past relationships comes later in the relationship. For now, the woman you're with needs to feel as if she's the only woman in your world. There's no way to gain points by summoning ghosts from the past. Save the past for the future, and you'll prevent yourself from losing valuable points.

"But what do I do if my date *asks* me about a past relationship?" asked my client Rob. "Is she just setting me up?" Hardly. If your date asks you such a question, she's trying to get to know you better (and see how well you've handled yourself in other relationships). Here's how to handle questions about your past that not only won't lose you any points, but may even gain you a few:

➤ Relate some positive aspects of the old relationship, without sounding as if you're still carrying a torch.

➤ Even if the old relationship didn't end on the best of terms, find something positive that you can honestly say about it.

➤ If she wants to know why you broke up, focus on describing the things *you* could have done better, and don't provide a laundry list of your ex's shortcomings. You'll appear much more evolved in your new lady's eyes, and you might even gain a better understanding of your place in the old relationship in the process.

➤ If, on the other hand, her questions begin to seem like a cross-examination, and they're making you uncomfortable, you're not obligated to keep providing answers. (You might take note of her grilling as an early warning sign. Pay attention to your gut reaction.) Tactfully let her know you'd rather go on to other subjects—that you're much more interested in the present, and in her.

Whatever you say or don't say about the past, your goal is to make it clear to the woman you're with how glad you are that you *are* with her—right here, right now.

Ask the Love Coach

Throughout history, women have been won by fine words. The story of Cyrano de Bergerac illustrates this point. The truth is, everyone loves to hear words that reach deep inside and touch the soul, but few of us are skilled poets. No matter. What is important is that the words come from deep within, and that they reflect your honest thoughts and emotions. A simple "I like your smile," spoken from the heart, will be more powerfully seductive to a woman than all of Shakespeare's sonnets, repeated from memory.

Make Her Feel Fascinating

In all of the studies and surveys I conducted, the number-one biggest dating turn on for women was, "A man who shows genuine interest in me." A woman absolutely loves it when she senses that you find her fascinating. You can demonstrate your interest in several ways. Again, this is an excellent chance to win points. Beyond all thoughts of a game, however, you may well be setting the course for a whole new relationship here, so pay attention to details. Here's what you should do:

For HIS Eyes Only

Guys, a woman wants you to let her know where she stands with you. If you're out with her and you're genuinely interested in seeing her again, let her know. This *is not* the time to play games. After all, she probably has other pursuers, so you want to make sure you're in the running. If you're not interested in going out with her again, don't lead her on.

➤ *Listen to her and ask questions.* Ask her to tell you about everything from her greatest accomplishments or her best qualities to how her day was or what she did last weekend. As she's telling you about herself, listen closely, and ask more questions where appropriate. Not only will you be letting her know that you are really interested in her, you might even find more about her that you like and can relate to. Remember: To be interesting, be interested.

➤ *Be a gentleman.* First off, most women still like it when you open doors for them. In recent years, there's been some confusion about this. What it boils down to is this: *Good manners are never sexist.* Beyond the courtly gestures, being a gentleman means displaying consideration for her comfort and well-being. Pay attention to her physical comfort: Is she cold? Does she need something from the waiter?

➤ *Make her feel at ease.* She needs to feel that if she accidentally knocked over her water glass, or dropped her spoon on the waiter's foot, you wouldn't act as if she'd committed some terrible blunder. Remember, she may be every bit as nervous and self-conscious as you, particularly if you're in elegant or stuffy surroundings. Put her at ease, even make her laugh—and your score will go through the roof.

➤ *Touch her in a tender, caring way.* Touching can be a sticky topic to figure out. Is it okay to touch? How much touching is too much? Once you're on a date, it's not only okay, it's a turn on if you touch her occasionally. Touch her when you're talking to her, as you're walking to the car together, walking her to her door. Be careful not to touch in an overtly sexual or predatory manner; just be subtle and affectionate. (We'll go into this subject in more detail in later chapters.)

Heart Brakes

Never make a promise to a woman if you have no intention of keeping it. It's very disappointing when a man you like promises to call and he doesn't. If you're not interested in going out with her again, be polite, let her know you enjoyed the date—but don't lead her on. (And if you *are* interested, and promised her you'll call, do it, for goodness sake!)

Forget the "Strong, Silent" Approach—Open Up!

For many years, the ideal man was portrayed in movies and television shows as the strong, silent type. Men learned that they weren't supposed to show any feelings. Guys, it's time you taught that silent dude to talk! After all, a woman needs to know she's attractive and interesting to her date. In that respect, we're not that different from you men. And we're also every bit as curious about you as you are about us.

Of course, I realize you guys can feel pretty uncomfortable letting your date know what you're like below the surface. There's always that fear of rejection, and it's easier to face the rejection if you haven't put so much of yourself on the line. Unfortunately, if you don't put those feelings out there where your date can see them, you'll be ensuring that the rejection will happen.

So take a chance. You might get shot down sometimes, but eventually, your efforts will pay off. If you want to win, you've got to play. If you never play, you've already lost.

Ask the Love Coach

In the last 20 years or so, a new image of the ideal man has emerged. He isn't afraid to share his feelings, and he is strong enough to be a little vulnerable. Women know that everybody has fears, or things that make them uncomfortable. The man who can acknowledge that something makes him feel vulnerable is actually showing he is strong, whereas the man who hides his feelings is letting her know he is too afraid to take a risk. And if he's not willing or able to take a chance with her, why would she want to take a chance with him?

You don't have to tell her your whole life story on the first date. That's not only inappropriate, it's a turn-off to most women. But do let her know a little about the fascinating (and seductive) being who lives below that powerful exterior. Here are some suggestions to win points with her:

➤ Initiate a conversation about hopes or fears by sharing with her some of your own dreads or desires. Of course, don't pick any weird ones on the first date, such as your desire to loll around naked with the Miss Universe finalists in a vat of green gelatin, or your fear that a meteor will come crashing into your home and destroy your priceless collection of celebrity dentures.

➤ Tell her about a happy, amusing, or touching memory from your childhood. But save the dramas and the traumas for serious heart-to-hearts later on in the relationship. Remember, she's not a therapist or a talk show host; your goal is to give her some insight into you—but you want it to be the type of insight that will encourage her to like you and to be glad she's with you.

➤ It's okay to talk about some of your accomplishments, but don't cross the line into boasting. Women are generally turned off by bragging. You'll win more points if you focus more on what makes you passionate or enthusiastic, and talk about your accomplishments in that context.

The whole idea is to allow her a glimpse of who you really are. You'll be giving her the encouragement she needs to open up to you, and even to like you. And even if your time together doesn't turn into a seductive experience, she'll leave with a good impression of you.

Ask the Love Coach

Marguerite describes a recent blind date as "a legend in his own mind, an ugly memory in mine." Edward was an entrepreneur who had recently enjoyed a string of successes with his franchise companies, as well as considerable media attention.

"Unfortunately," Marguerite groaned, "his ego was easily as large as his bank account. Ed spent most of the night bragging about his awesome rags-to-riches story, his business 'conquests,' and his Machiavellian tactics for becoming number one in his field. Not once did he ask me anything about myself or my work."

To say this man lost points with Marguerite is an understatement. As far as she was concerned, he was out of the game permanently. Nearly all of the women I surveyed cited a boastful man as a major turn-off. If you spend your time listing all of your remarkable qualities and great achievements, you're telling a woman you have an ego so large you can focus only on yourself. No woman wants that. She wants to know about you—but she also wants you to show interest in her and ask her questions. A confident man doesn't need to shove all of his fine qualities in a woman's face—and confidence is a big part of seductiveness.

Cleanliness Is Next to, Well, Her!

I knew a man in college who, when preparing for a date, would actually sift through his dirty laundry until he found a shirt he wanted to wear. Upon finding it, he would sniff it—and should it be, shall we say, reminiscent of its last wearing, he would simply spray some cologne or deodorant on it and put it on. Maybe you were like my old friend when you were young and wild. Nowadays, of course, you're not guilty of any such hygiene-impaired behavior (right?). Since we're discussing seductiveness, however, there's a little more to know than the essentials about daily showers and brushing your teeth.

For our purposes, let's say there are two levels of hygiene. First there's basic hygiene, which is all the stuff you already know. Then there's the next level: seductive hygiene. Seductive hygiene involves going that extra mile to be extra appealing. Women being the sensitive creatures that we are (note that I didn't say *delicate*; I said sensitive, as in having acute senses), it's easy for a guy to lose points in this area. But it's not at all difficult to win them, either.

Before we go any further, don't think I'm picking on you men. I'm well aware that women, too, are sometimes less than impeccable with their grooming, although this occurs more frequently within the context of a long-term relationship (she wears the same old faded T-shirt around the house all the time, or she doesn't shave her legs quite as often as she did back when you were dating—but that's a topic for another book).

In the early stages of a relationship, however, women are, if anything, *too* self-conscious about grooming and hygiene. Okay, I know there are exceptions, and you guys can write your horror stories to me at the address you'll find at the front of the book. For now, let's concentrate on you. Even the most fastidious men sometimes forget that *when you want to be seductive, you have to make an extra effort to get to that next level.*

To illustrate this point, we'll look at a few examples. The names are fictional, of course, but every one of the situations below is based on feedback from my clients.

For HIS Eyes Only

Though many women think a neat, clean beard is sexy, keep in mind that the bristles of a two-day growth can feel like sandpaper.

Putting a Damper on the Situation

Situation: James has just completed his twice-weekly workout at the gym, and realizes he's running very late for his afternoon date with Stacy. There's no time for his usual shower, but he figures he'll just shower at Stacy's place, as he's done on a few other occasions. He quickly runs a comb through his hair and beard, and heads out into the 90-degree heat and 100-percent humidity of a Houston summer afternoon. He grabs an onion bagel with scallion cream cheese at the little shop next to the gym, jumps into his car and heads towards Stacy's townhouse. When Stacy welcomes him at the front door, he draws her toward him and tries to give her a big kiss on the mouth. He's somewhat hurt when she turns her face for a cheek kiss instead, and even more so when she extricates herself from the hug—a little too quickly, it seems.

Seductive Solution: There were a few very unseductive mistakes James made in his haste:

➤ He should have called Stacy from the gym and said, "Hon, I'm running a little late. I've just finished my workout, and I've gotta jump in the shower so I'll be presentable to you." And then he should have showered at the gym, using extra care to get the sweat out of his beard. Says Stacy, "I love beards and think they're very sexy, but, frankly, kissing a sweaty beard is like kissing a dirty wet mop. It's a real turn-off."

For HIS Eyes Only

Here's a little tip on the use of colognes and aftershaves: More is not necessarily better. Apply your favorite cologne as if you wanted it to whisper, not scream. Don't let anything that comes from a bottle interfere with the intricate workings of your own personal chemistry. And know that there are many women out there who prefer a good, clean, natural male smell to the most expensive designer fragrance.

➤ James should have taken a few minutes to brush his teeth, apply deodorant, and even put on a splash of that cologne Stacy likes so well.

➤ He would also have done well to leave out that onion bagel with the scallion cream cheese, too.

If James was in such a dead rush that he couldn't shower at the gym, he should have held off with the kiss and hug until after he'd showered and brushed his teeth at Stacy's place. Believe me, she would have understood. And she wouldn't have been so turned off.

Take My Breath Away

Situation: Rick and Toni are on their fifth date, and Rick has chosen an elegant new Italian restaurant in a trendy part of town. Toni is delighted with his choice (and is obviously delighted with Rick), and the evening is off to a wonderful beginning. The sexual tension between Rick and Toni is growing, and both wonder what the evening might bring. For now, it seems their main challenge is to get through dinner without disappearing under the table together!

But first things first; the waiter arrives and they order their meals. Rick, a real garlic lover, begins with a garlic-infused vegetable soup, and for his entrée chooses garlic-roasted chicken with penne pasta. He's also a spinach fan, so he has a big side order of sautéed spinach. Throughout the meal he consumes several pieces of garlic bread, while Toni just has a couple of plain rolls. Afterwards, as they're walking toward a coffee bar for an after-dinner cappuccino, Rick stops and draws Toni to him to kiss her. She cuts the kiss short, pulls away, and for the rest of the evening gently rebuffs any other effort he makes to get physically close. After he says good night to her at her door, he's left wondering, "What went wrong?" Later at home, he looks in the mirror and sees the big piece of green stuck between his teeth. When his roommate comes home later on, he comments, "Is someone having a garlic cook-off here?" Now Rick *knows* what the problem was with Toni.

Ask the Love Coach

While garlic adds a delicious flavor to the food we eat, its effect upon our breath is the stuff of legends. Be aware that once garlic is in your system, brushing, breath mints, and mouthwash are of limited effectiveness. The only real cure for garlic breath is the passage of time. So when you're trying to be seductive, it's best to forego the garlic, unless you're trying to ward off vampires.

Ask the Love Coach

We've all seen enough TV commercials to know that bad breath is caused by bacteria. Well, those nasty little critters like your tongue as much as, if not more than, they like your teeth, so don't neglect to brush your tongue during your oral-hygiene routine. Pay special attention to the back of your tongue, a favorite hangout for microbes; also brush the top, sides and underside. A little attention to detail will ensure that your tongue (and you) are well-prepared for whatever the evening brings.

Seductive Solution: How could Rick have kept this evening riding on its original momentum?

➤ Unless he could have persuaded Toni to consume as much garlic as he did, Rick should have been much more moderate in his garlic consumption—or better yet, skipped the garlic altogether. Yes, that's possible even in an Italian restaurant.

➤ Rick should have excused himself after the meal and ducked into the men's lounge for a brief oral-hygiene break. As he now knows, it's important to keep your breath as fresh as possible throughout the date. It would not have been out of line for Rick to sneak a travel toothbrush and some dental floss along on the date. Lacking that, he could have popped a few breath mints. And he should have checked himself out in a mirror after the meal—always a good idea, particularly after you've eaten something green!

Heart Brakes

Even though toothpicks were designed for use in public, let's face it—it's not at all erotic to watch someone picking their teeth, particularly at the table. So do try to duck into the restroom to perform this duty. At the very least, be discreet. And for gosh sakes, do your flossing in the restroom and not in the car. Some things really are better left for much later on in a relationship.

Smoke Gets in Her Nose

Situation: Wes is picking Brenda up for their first real date. They've been working together for a few months and have had lunch several times, but this is their first dinner date. Wes is a long-time smoker, but Brenda is an avid nonsmoker, and is allergic to cigarette smoke to boot. Wes has always been careful not to smoke in

Brenda's presence, because he knows she's a nonsmoker and is allergic as well. Arriving at Brenda's house, he takes a few last puffs from his cigarette before he gets out of his car, and walks up to her door. Brenda greets him at the door with a smile, which quickly fades as she catches a whiff of fresh smoke on him. Even though they normally greet each other with a friendly hug, she politely refuses to hug him this time, and instead begins walking toward his car. Wes is puzzled by her seeming aloofness.

Ask the Love Coach

Your mother taught you to wash your hands before meals, and your Love Coach is telling you to always wash your hands very well before you get intimate with a woman. Not only is this just good form, but many women are susceptible to irritation or infections under unhygienic conditions. Women on birth control pills are particularly vulnerable to infections. So take a few minutes with soap and water before you touch her intimately. After all, you want her to "itch" *for* you, not *because* of you.

Seductive Solution: How can a smoker and nonsmoker get off to a good start for a potentially seductive evening?

➤ Wes should know that even if he does not smoke in front of Brenda, the smell of fresh (or stale) smoke will be very apparent to her. It's on his breath, it's in his clothes, and it's in his car. Breath sprays or mints help a little, but they're only as effective as their most recent application. And they don't do anything to remove the smoke smell that lingers in the fabrics of Wes's clothes, or on his hands and fingers. Wes should have avoided smoking altogether before picking up Brenda.

➤ Before leaving home to pick up Brenda, Wes also should have practiced some good hygiene and brushed his teeth. It also wouldn't have hurt to use his little bottle of breath drops on the way over to her place.

➤ In addition, he also needs to carefully and thoroughly wash his hands. Tobacco odor on the hands is very noticeable to a nonsmoker, and can be a real turn-off.

Heart Brakes

Despite the recent trendiness of cigars, and the proliferation of cigar-smoking women, most women (and men, for that matter) still find the smell of stogies intensely distasteful. Use with caution.

Dangerous Digits

Situation: It's the middle of their first night together, and Hank's girlfriend, Rita, wakes up with a start. Her leg has been slashed by the toenails from hell. Hank, who had taken such pains with every other area of hygiene and grooming, had neglected to trim those talons of his.

Seductive Solution: Many women wish their fingernails would grow as rapidly and well as the average man's toenails. The solution to this one is a no-brainer. Hank should clip and file his toenails, and if he doesn't take the initiative, Rita should broach the subject. After all, long toenails are not only hazardous to your partner's tender skin, it's just good hygiene to keep one's toenails trimmed.

Ask the Love Coach

Many women notice men's hands—in fact, to some women, a man's hands are one of the sexiest parts of his body. A woman will notice not only the general appearance of your hands, but also the way they feel against her skin. So pay a little attention in this area. You don't need to go to a professional manicurist, but do keep your nails trimmed and clean and your cuticles pared, and if you have very dry skin, use an unscented moisturizer.

Well, we could go on and on, but you get the idea. When you do a good job of keeping up your standards of personal hygiene, your score in the game of love will undoubtedly go up. A little extra attention to your grooming tells a woman that you care what she thinks about you, and that you feel she is worth the effort it takes to be not just presentable, but seductive. She will appreciate the effort and the attitude, and will be much more receptive to your allure. In fact, she just may think you look and smell good enough to eat!

Romancing the "Little Woman" Ain't What It Used to Be

I begin this section with the assumption that you, as an enlightened man of the new millennium, know to treat the woman you're with as your intellectual equal. Even if she's breathtakingly gorgeous, even if you want to jump her bones, you know there's a human being beneath all that beauty. And you're savvy enough to let her know you see her as a peer.

For whatever reason, however, be it a byproduct of attitude or upbringing, some men still have a tendency to talk to a woman in a way that suggests she is either less sophisticated or less intelligent than they. While the old sitcoms may have frequently portrayed women in this light, these men need to realize that, just as television has evolved from black-and-white to high-definition color, women have emerged as powerful participants in every aspect of life.

Acting toward a woman in a patronizing manner is truly one of the cardinal sins. Women have long ago abandoned the "dumb and helpless" image, and a man who approaches a woman as if she were less capable than he will rarely get a second chance with her. So remember: *Never* talk down to a woman or patronize her—unless you just like being alone a lot.

If you're not sure how to win points here, and are not certain exactly how to act so a woman knows beyond a doubt that you're not a sexist pig, the first thing to know is that you really don't have to *act* at all. Just relax and remember:

➤ If you *perceive* the woman you're with as a capable peer and potential partner, your actions will take care of themselves. Your respect and regard will come through loud and clear, and you'll definitely gain points. Conversely, if you don't feel that respect and regard for her, there's no way you'll be able to fake it well enough to fool her.

➤ If you *care enough* to make an effort to take care of the simple details, and you hold women with respect, you will be the seductive winner you hope to be. If you don't care enough, or you hold women in disdain, there's no amount of things you could do to make you more seductive.

The choice, ultimately, is yours, and the stakes are high: Achieve success in attracting a woman who can enhance and enrich your life or ensure that you'll be alone until you get it right.

The great mystery of "what a woman wants" really isn't such a mystery after all. A women wants a man who can make her feel beautiful and significant, and who can be a friend as well as a lover—a man who eschews the stereotypes and isn't afraid to let his true, seductive self shine through. It's really not that difficult to win points in the seductiveness game. Follow the tips in this chapter, and you'll be playing at a championship level in no time.

The Least You Need to Know

➤ To be truly seductive to the woman you're with, focus on her rather than on every attractive female who comes within eyesight.

➤ Express interest in a woman by asking her questions, listening when she speaks, and looking out for her comfort and well-being.

➤ Don't be afraid to open up to a woman, but don't spend time bragging about your achievements.

➤ If you're interested in a woman, give her clear signs of your interest, but if you're not, don't lead her on.

➤ "Seductive hygiene" simply means making an extra effort to take care of cleaning and grooming details that many men overlook.

➤ Even if you're sexually attracted to a woman, remember that there's a human being underneath all that allure and dazzle, so treat her as the equal that she is.

Chapter 9

Meeting Attractive People: Matching Your Destination with Your Expectation

I want to congratulate you on making it to this point on your journey to becoming more seductive. We've spent the previous chapters getting you ready in body, mind, and soul. You're feeling better about who you are. You've gotten pretty clear on what you can, should, and do expect from another person in your life, as well as from yourself. Now, it's time to decide where to best apply your newly honed skills, and where to put the new you on display!

Where in the World

Though there are some places that spring immediately to mind as the ideal meeting grounds, you might want to give your destination some thought before you head out the door. Many of the places that are at the top of your hit list were probably picked before you figured out what you really wanted or needed. Maybe they even reflect an intent that is no longer consistent with that which fills you now.

So let's start by making a list of the five most likely places for you to practice being your seductive self:

1. _____
2. _____
3. _____
4. _____
5. _____

Ask the Love Coach

The first thing you want to keep in mind before venturing out is that you are in search of an enjoyable experience. Close your eyes and imagine a crowd of attractive people, all hanging out and having a great time. Look around and ask yourself where they are. Now open your eyes and go there. Simple, wasn't it?

Now, let's look at your list, and see if it matches with what you want and expect from a first meeting with someone. For example, if you're the type who likes to sit down and engage someone in quiet conversation when you first meet, you're not very likely to get an opportunity to do so at the boisterous new club that's always packed wall to wall. If you're the loud and boisterous type yourself, you might find the pickings pretty slim at the Friday night poetry reading sponsored by the local bookstore. On the other hand, if you're really into poetry and still like a raucous good time, you might try one of those anything-goes "poetry slams" that are occasionally held at some comedy clubs. The point is to figure out the type of person you want to attract, and then decide where you can go to meet such a person. Read on for some ideas.

Clubs and Bars: Keep Your Eyes Open, Your Head Clear, and Your Boots On

If you're like most people nowadays, clubs or bars are probably on your list, perhaps even at the top. After all, places like these are all about partying and meeting new people, right? Well, look a little closer at what the clubs have to offer.

For one thing, clubs are really geared toward first impressions and outward appearances. Especially in venues that have live music or a DJ, the noise level pretty well rules out in-depth conversation, except perhaps the occasional witty remarks that can be squeezed between songs. So you find yourself winging along on looks and one-liners, the mainstays of old-style seduction.

In an environment where even a simple "hello" has to be screamed to have a chance of being heard, how likely are you to get many clues as to the other person's basic personality, much less, his or her intent? Not very. And, speaking of intent, consider that the single factor common among clubs (and club-goers) is alcohol. While I am by no means a temperance worker—or even a teetotaler—it is important to realize that inhibitions and common sense are both soluble in alcohol.

What that means to you is that the people who spend a lot of time at a club are usually spending the time drinking, and they may be less than fully capable of making good decisions about their behavior or companions. You need to ask yourself if you are looking for someone who is an astute judge of character or one who is easily deluded—someone who can be fun on his own or who needs a little chemical incentive. Again, your intent, as well as that of the people you hope to meet, becomes a matter of prime importance. And the place where you go to meet them takes on a new dimension of significance.

This isn't to say that you'll never meet anyone worthwhile in a club, or that all clubs are devoted to the pursuit of collective mental impairment. There are many terrific places out there, such as jazz clubs and rock-and-roll bars, where some truly wonderful people go to have a good time. My point is that you need to remember the basic function of the clubs—to make a profit from their clientele's drinking. So enjoy the clubs, but keep your wits about you, and stick to your own game plan, not the club owners'.

Attention Shoppers! There's a Macarena Contest in the Produce Section in 15 Minutes!

Over the last few years, tales of romance that begin in the grocery store are increasingly common, and for good reason. If you think about it, you are in the grocery store, presumably, for one reason: to buy food to sustain and enhance your life. Even the foods you choose to purchase make statements about who you are. And since single people have to eat like everybody else, they will be in the store making their statements, as well.

Next time you're in the grocery store, really look at what you have in your basket, and ask yourself what kind of statement your choices make about you. Is your basket brimming with healthy foods that say you care about your body and don't mind going to some effort to prepare for its nourishment, or with frozen insta-meals, pork rinds, and beer that say you'd rather not be bothered? Look (discreetly, please) in the baskets of other shoppers, and play a little game of writing their life stories based on the items they've picked out. Then write your own story, based only upon clues obtained from your own basket's contents. You'd be surprised at how accurate the stories can be.

Ask the Love Coach

Murphy's Law: If you throw on your rattiest clothes to do errands, you will bump into the man or woman of your dreams. Well then, from now on when you go to the grocery store or the shopping center, dress as if you were about to meet the love of your life. Not "to the nines" in a silk suit or an evening gown, but in nice looking, casual clothes such as you might wear to a friend's house.

I have a friend who, upon visiting a new boyfriend's apartment for the first time, was overjoyed to find that he had a well-stocked spice cabinet and items such as artichoke hearts, capers, and feta cheese in his refrigerator. To her, these items were representative of a man who was a true sensualist, and who savored the many flavors of life. To him, the items were simply necessary condiments for the preparation of his daily meals. His basic attitude was communicated to her without any effort on his part. It's worthy to note that she discovered, months later, that he also had a deep fondness for hot dogs, but by then, she was already hooked!

If you see someone you find attractive, you can always find an excuse to approach him or her. Maybe you're not the world's greatest judge of what constitutes a good tomato, or maybe you notice something in his or her cart that you've been tempted to try, so ask for the person's help or an opinion. The number of approaches are almost infinite.

Singles Night at the Local Bookstore/Coffee Bar: Sometimes You Can Tell a Book by Its Cover

Bookstores and libraries aren't just for eggheads anymore. (Not that there's anything wrong with being an egghead; in fact, it's become rather stylish.) In case you haven't been in one of the big superstores lately, take a trip to one near you. No doubt you'll notice a significant number of interesting people hanging around, looking altogether literary.

You might even notice that the bookstore has lots of couches clustered around coffee tables, or, for that matter, that there is a painfully trendy coffee shop right there in the store. Why do you think they put all that stuff around? So people who were so devoted to their reading could have a place to nap or something to sustain them during their quest for knowledge? Nope. These little touches were added because people like you enjoy hanging around bookstores looking for people who are interesting (or at least attractive). So go back to the bookstore, grab yourself a cup of the latte du jour, and keep your eyes open this time. While you're at it, buy a few more copies of this book for your friends. My publisher will love you for it.

Ask the Love Coach

Bookstores are more than just a place to hang out. Many bookstores, big and small alike, play host to all sorts of organized events, such as singles get-togethers, poetry and short story readings of new and popular authors, open-mike nights for local, budding talent, book clubs, and discussion groups. These events are a good place for you to meet people with similar interests. This is also a great place to practice a little self-confidence boosting. Get up there at one of the open-mike nights and read a poem or story you wrote. Get involved in a discussion group about a book you just read and share your thoughts with others. Whatever it is, along with impressing yourself, you just may impress someone else!

No Matter How Weird It Is, There's Bound to Be a Group for It

No matter how obscure your interests, you may rest assured that there is an organization out there to fit it. Into Peruvian llama herding? Collecting stamps from countries that don't exist anymore? Or how about a '76 Pinto collectors' club? You can bet that such a group exists somewhere. And if it doesn't, you can start your own.

Heart Brakes

Play it safe if you're putting up a flyer in a public venue, and don't post your home address. Arrange to meet in a public place, away from your residence or work. Just as you'd do with a singles ad, get to know the people you're attracting before opening your door—and your life—to them.

There are a number of ways to find listings for groups that cater to your interests—event listings in your local newspaper, announcements on radio stations, or flyers posted on bulletin boards in the places you frequent (such as bookstores). And if you simply can't find anything, post your own flyers to see if anyone is interested in starting a group.

Religious Groups: Who's There to Pray and Who's There to Prey?

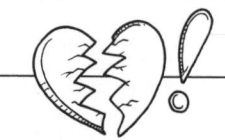

Heart Brakes

In the last 20 years, there has been tremendous growth in the number and type of recovery groups. While many people attend these groups purely to improve their lives or ease their pain, some people see these meetings as a target-rich environment, where they can find vulnerable people on which to prey. If one of these groups has a special appeal for you, then by all means, check it out. But be on the wary side toward any romantic dalliances that may originate there.

Before you start rolling your eyes and putting the book down, I need to tell you that church isn't the way you probably remember it from your childhood. Forget the fried chicken and potato salad, forget the hokey attempts to make gospel psalms sound like rock-and-roll, forget those dweeby church camp songs ("If you're happy and you know it, kum ba ya!"). Nope, churches have seen the light, so to speak, and many have responded by incorporating programs that actually are fun. Most churches, synagogues, and general places of community worship have what they call a singles ministry that, thankfully, doesn't go overboard on the ministry part. It's not unusual to have singles gatherings at museums and theaters, and even the occasional happy-hour get-together. Some even plan weekend outings at nearby tourist attractions, and a few really spirited ones put together singles cruises and international vacation packages.

If you really want the fried chicken and potato salad, I'm certain you'll be able to find it out there, but if you are game, you'll find a lot more, as well.

The Internet: Getting Lucky Online

With the quantum leaps in communications technology over the past decade or so, more and more people are making their presence known—and seeking out other people—on the Internet. The unchecked flow of information makes it easier than ever before to reach out and touch someone, whether they live on the next street or halfway around the world.

It's easy to get excited about the increased potential for meeting new people that the Internet offers, but you need to temper that excitement with good judgment and a stiff dose of reality.

For starters, the very lack of regulation over content online that makes it such a potential boon to users is also the source of its greatest potential for disappointment. Since an online presence is such an insulated and faceless thing, it is easy for individuals to present themselves as what they would like to be (or what they think you want them to be), rather than what they actually are. And herein lies the peril we've heard so much about.

We are mildly disappointed when the charming person we met in the chat group starts pressuring us to buy cookware or seminar tickets or the like. We are irritated when that "educated, sincere, professional male" in the description turns out to be toothless Melvin, who lives with his mother just north of Checotah, Oklahoma. We are outraged when we find that our 14-year-old daughter's online boyfriend is really a 42-year-old married man with a history of preying on children. And we are terrified when the sweet young woman we met in the *chat room* has chosen the psychopathic Glenn Close character from *Fatal Attraction* as her role model.

The sad truth is that we just don't know if the person we meet online bears even the slightest resemblance to the description they give of themselves. And, even if they're honest in their description, we need to remember that it's pretty easy to be on our best behavior when our contact is limited to a few lines (or even pages) of text. Things can be completely different when you spend any length of time face-to-face with each other.

Wordplay

A **chat room** allows you to have real-time "conversations" online with many people at once or just one person. There are chat groups for every conceivable interest. If someone in the chat room captures your interest, the two of you can transfer to a private chat room and continue your exchange, one-on-one. Online chat is as safe as you want it to be—since you use a nickname to identify yourself for the duration of your chat, you don't have to reveal your real name or even your e-mail address.

For instance, if you think that Internet sex predators frequent only the kinky newsgroups or sex chat rooms, think again. These folks can pop up even in the most benign cyber-environments. Take the case of a computer professional's e-mail list to which a client of mine subscribes. This list is similar to hundreds of special-interest online groups where members exchange ideas and tips, commiserate with each other, and form genuine friendships and business associations with other list members.

My client told me the saga of Darrell, a successful software entrepreneur who was one of the most frequent contributors to the list. His posts were often opinionated, and sometimes just this side of arrogant, but were usually very informative as well. Though he came across to the list as a dedicated professional, Darrell had a secret side. He had a habit of initiating private correspondences with new female list members. In fact, he aggressively pursued any new woman who sounded even vaguely interesting, and it didn't matter if she was married or not. (Darrell, by the way, *was* married, but, of course, his wife "didn't understand him.")

These personal correspondences always followed a pattern. At first Darrell would keep the messages on a professional level, and most of the women were thrilled to receive personal attention and savvy advice from such a successful colleague. But Darrell also wrote quite charmingly and persuasively, and before long, many of these exchanges would disintegrate into steamy cyber-affairs. When the affairs turned sour, as they inevitably did, Darrell would become viciously abusive to his partners. Most of the women ended up dropping off the mailing list.

107

If Darrell's affairs had been limited to cyberspace, they would have been bad enough, but Darrell was a traveling man. Throughout the year he attended trade shows and conferences all across the country, and he often arranged to meet female list-mates in person. He would always put a professional facade on the meeting, at least initially, but—you guessed it—more often than not, these meetings ended up in Darrell's hotel room. He went through woman after woman, and was instrumental in the breakup of two marriages and the near destruction of another. One of his lovers ended up under a psychiatrist's care, partly as a result of being "Darrelled." I'm not implying that these women were innocents who played no part in their own victimization. But I will say that most of them were fairly young and a bit naïve, or for some other reason were very susceptible to Darrell's charms (not to mention the expensive champagne, first-class restaurants and hotels, and limo rides he plied them with).

For these reasons, I recommend that online romances, while they can be beautiful, be approached with some degree of skepticism. Beyond the rules of common sense where personal safety is concerned, you also need to apply that same common sense when you're considering investing your emotional well-being in another person.

Now that we've got the scary part out of the way, I encourage you to look into chat or discussion groups whose focus is on a subject that interests you. Participate in group discussions, and, should someone involved in the discussion tickle your fancy, feel free to carry on the correspondence privately. If you go slowly and use good sense, you might meet someone whose presence in your life is a real treasure. If you get impatient, or throw your good sense out the window, you'll learn why some treasure is better left buried.

Personal Ads: Learning to Read Between the Lines

Just like the Internet, the personal ads in your local paper or magazine can provide you with an abundance of new people to meet. And, just like the Internet, the personal ads represent a faceless anonymity that some people perceive as license to reinvent themselves into someone quite different from their own real personalities.

Heart Brakes

Predators in cyberspace can sometimes wear the most benevolent of guises. If you think you're being victimized, stop responding to the predator's posts, and notify the owner of the mailing list.

The biggest difference between the Internet and the personal ads is one of geography. Where the Internet allows people to communicate with others in virtually any location on earth, the personal ads are generally confined to your own city or region. This makes it easier to physically meet the person, since you won't be required to update your passport and take a loan out for airfare; but there is still the potential for deceit inherent in a relationship that is largely based on one person's flattering self-description. For this reason, it is especially important to use caution in responding to an ad that catches your eye, and to retain a degree of anonymity until you have come to know the real person, as opposed to her prose.

Some of the periodicals that run personal ads also stage *mixers* where individuals can mingle in the safety of a large group while meeting the people who have placed ads. This is a great idea, since you are afforded an opportunity to get to know the people without even divulging your name, much less your home address or phone number, until you have determined that it is a good idea to do so.

Most people you meet through the personals will be in that expansive middle ground between soul mate and date from hell. You may have some disappointing experiences, but if you exercise all due caution, that's the worst that will happen. And who knows, you may meet some real gems.

Dating Services: A Viable Alternative

Another marriage of technology, commerce, and romance is evidenced by the number of dating services available today. What began hundreds of years ago with the neighborhood matchmaker has evolved into a multimillion-dollar industry. From computer-generated statistical analyses of relative compatibility to videotaped interviews of potential dates, dating services offer a modern-day method of matching people with kindred souls.

Perhaps the weakest link in the dating-service approach is our inherently unrealistic tendency to view technology as infallible, and to view an unsuccessful date as being the result of some personal shortcoming in ourselves or in the partner selected for us. We need to remember that successful human relationships hinge upon many variables that no computer program or compatibility index can even begin to address. If the computer says we're a perfect match, it means only that we share some common elements. Whether or not we make a good couple is ultimately based on criteria that the computer never considers.

Another caution: Watch out for the tendency to jump rapidly into (and out of) relationships with people you meet through the dating service. I've

Wordplay

Mixers are get-togethers that usually are geared toward specific groups of people (singles, MENSA members, computer enthusiasts, and the like). They provide a wonderful opportunity to meet other people in a fun, non-threatening environment. Particularly if you're newly single, keep a lookout for announcements about singles mixers that appeal to your particular interest.

For HER Eyes Only

It's safer to place your own personal ad than to respond to others' ads. This puts the screening process in your hands, because the newspaper or other publication where you place your ad will pass on responses to you. Usually you'll receive a letter (and a photo if you requested one). Of course, having this information is no guarantee that the person is as wonderful as he claims to be, but it's still safer than having your personal information passed on to someone who is, after all, a total stranger.

Heart Brakes

Relationships take time, patience, and clarity to develop. It's not easy to ward off impatience, but you need to make an effort to do so.

seen people become dating-service junkies, getting hooked on the process and never really developing a real relationship. Somewhere in our make-up is a desire to have it all right now. In some people, this tendency is very strong, and when they discover a person is different from their idealized image of a mate, they simply abandon the relationship. After all, they reason, there's an abundance of other candidates available, one of whom might well be "the one." Some people get so caught up in the process that they would probably prefer a lifetime membership in the service instead of a life-long, satisfying relationship.

This may sound as if I don't place much value in dating services, but that simply isn't the case. As the owner of the largest independent video dating service in the country for over 10 years, I saw firsthand just how effective such a service could be, so long as it was run properly and the clients had realistic expectations. The real power of the dating service is dependent upon the humanity of its operators and the commitment (and honesty) of its clientele. And, just like the relationship one seeks, the relationship between client and operator must be forthright and comfortable.

What Are Friends For!

Movies and TV shows are full of humorous tales about the well-meaning matchmaker with a compulsion to help single friends find their way to blissful couplehood. In most of these shows, the matchmaker is misguided, the matches a disaster, and it all makes for highly entertaining comedy. In real life, however, friends can be an excellent source of people to meet, if you clearly state what you are looking for. But you have to know how to "work" your pals if you're going to get the results you want. Here are some pointers:

➤ *Come right out and ask them.* Don't just beat around the bush, sighing wistfully that you wish you could meet someone. Ask a friend if he or she knows anyone who's suitable for you to go out with.

➤ *Be specific.* Don't assume your friend knows what sort of person you want to date. You don't have to write out a shopping list, but you should specify the major qualities you're looking for (or want to avoid). If you feel strongly that you don't want to go out with a smoker, for example, or you desire to date only people who are 45 or older, let your friend know at the outset.

➤ *Let them know you're serious.* The best way to let them know is to say it—"I'm really serious about this. I don't want to go out to bars and clubs, and I don't want to get into doing personal ads either. I trust *your* judgment, and I hope you'll help me out here."

➤ *If you feel so inclined, offer them an incentive.* Book clubs and video clubs do it all the time; they give you free merchandise if you sign up a friend. Similarly, you can offer your friend some sort of incentive if he finds a suitable date for you. I'm not suggesting you approach dating as a business transaction, but you might offer to do a friend a favor if she comes up with the goods—cook her a gourmet dinner, baby-sit her dog while she goes away for a weekend, or help her install that new graphics software in her computer. Or, hey, you could always try cash. Don't laugh; I've had friends and clients who have done this, and their friends have come up with some great matches for them. If nothing else, that offer of green stuff lets your friend know you're really serious about finding a suitable date.

➤ *Thank them for their efforts.* Once your friend starts fixing you up, be sure to say thank you and to make good on any favors you've promised. If things don't work out with your date(s), don't be too hard on your pal. He or she probably gave it a good shot, and besides, one true friend is more valuable than all the would-be dates in the world.

Unexpected Places: It's Not So Much Where You Go As What You Bring

If we were to list all the places where you could potentially meet someone interesting, we would fill a wall of books, and still be woefully incomplete. In the final analysis, the place really isn't that important. What does matter is your attitude, your intent, and, to put it simply, who you are.

A pleasant, confident person has a better chance of attracting someone in the dentist's waiting room than a dour person has of dazzling someone at an upscale cocktail party. You've probably heard the saying, "No matter where you go, there you are!" Keep this in mind as you go about your daily tasks. Enter every situation completely seduced by life, and you will draw to yourself people who want to be seduced, as well.

I don't care if you're in the Laundromat washing your underwear, or in the grand ballroom of a four-star hotel toasting foreign dignitaries. Be the fascinated—and therefore, fascinating—person you want to be. If you're standing in line at the movie theater, realize that your place in line is a potentially rich resource for life experiences, not just an inconvenience on the way *to* an experience.

Make your plans for your day, your week, or your *life,* but allow yourself the freedom to experience all the wonderful things that don't always fit into those plans. If you can truly embrace the experiences that come your way, and remain open to the ones that simply happen, you will find yourself

Wordplay

Remember: **Life** is what happens while you're making plans.

seduced by life. And when you are seduced by life, other people will be seduced by your very presence. They, too, will forget about the details such as place or schedule, and will seek to absorb the richness of life that you so obviously savor.

The Least You Need to Know

➤ When deciding where you want to go to meet attractive people, take into account who you are and what you want, and match your destination accordingly.

➤ Clubs and bars, though they are at the top of many people's hot list, are often not the best places to meet a date.

➤ Bookstores, special interest organizations, and religious groups are viable (and relatively safe) places to meet compatible people.

➤ If you are looking for a partner, the Internet and personal ads are two possible sources, but both hold lots of potential for deception or even danger.

➤ Dating services can be useful tools for finding compatible partners, but beware that you don't become hooked on the process.

➤ Friends can be an excellent resource for meeting people to date, but you must let your friends know you're serious, and be specific about what you want in a date.

➤ Your attitude and who you are ultimately matter more than *where* you are when looking for a compatible partner.

Chapter 10

The Approach: Putting All That Preparation to Work

In This Chapter

➤ What to say after you've said "hello"

➤ Looking approachable without looking needy

➤ Women approaching men: a new paradigm

➤ Nipping the buddy syndrome in the bud

➤ Setting the stage for the next step: asking for a date

As an author, I am painfully aware that a book, sitting on a shelf in a bookstore, has all of 15 seconds to sell itself to prospective buyers. Shoppers will glance at the cover, pick the book up if the cover catches the eye, and give the book a quick once-over. They might read the back cover text, and, if their interest is still piqued, scan the contents and foreword. Anything negative they encounter during this brief process will send the book back to its place on the shelf, and the process begins again with the next book that looks interesting.

Like it or not, the same process also applies to our method of selecting a prospective partner. If we're not attracted to the aspects of a person that are immediately apparent, we simply move on. Never mind that this person may have lots of wonderful qualities. Just as a book may have a marvelous story that goes unread due to poor packaging, many delightful people remain alone simply because they don't make a good first impression.

Ask the Love Coach

Have you ever tried to sell something? Whether it's Girl Scout cookies or raffle tickets, it's hard to sell anything that doesn't impress you or that you don't know that much about. The same goes for selling yourself: Learn to appreciate your own qualities before you try to sell them to someone else. Remember, self-confidence is one of the best aphrodisiacs around—for you *and* for the object of your desire. So, take some time and figure out what's great about *you*. The most important first impression is the one you make upon yourself.

You've spent a lot of time and devoted a lot of thought and energy to making yourself more appealing and more seductive. Now it's time to figure out the best way to present all that seductiveness in the all-too-brief seconds that occur just before—and immediately after—you meet.

Like, What's Your Sign? Probably "Stop!"

One of the most hideous artifacts of the '70s—second only to polyester leisure suits—was the emergence (if not refinement) of the pickup line. The widespread resurgence of interest in matters metaphysical gave rise to the use of the clichèd approach, "What's your sign?" By asking a prospective love interest "What's your sign?" the pursuer was attempting to identify him- or herself as a deep thinker, interested in much more than something as mundane as a simple date.

Ask the Love Coach

Before issuing your "opening statement," ask yourself if it applies uniquely to the person you're with, or could be used with just about anybody. If it's a generic statement, don't use it (unless your partner is particularly proud of being a generic person!).

Well, it may have worked for about three days, twenty-odd years ago, but the pat one-liner has completely lost its effectiveness in modern romance. Nowadays, men and women alike are looking for something more than shallow attempts at cleverness. We want someone who is observant enough to perceive our value as a whole person, secure enough to acknowledge that value, and intelligent enough to understand what we feel is important. In short, we want to be around people who are three-dimensional, whose personalities have more depth than a one-liner can encompass.

On the odd chance that you're unsure of what I mean by a "line," I've listed a few examples of the things you *never* want to say to someone you've just met:

➤ "What's your sign?"

➤ "You look just like my ex-_____."

➤ "God, I bet you look good in a swimsuit/naked!"

➤ "If I said you had a beautiful body, would you hold it against me?"

➤ "Hey, I like your outfit—I'd like it even more crumpled up on the floor next to my bed."

➤ He: "You look just like my third wife."
   She: "And how many times have you been married?"
   He: "Twice."

The whole point of avoiding such corny one-liners (or, in the case of that last example, two-liners) is that you want to be perceived as a person of substance, and that you see a prospective partner as such a person, as well. At this point, you may be wondering how, with only a few seconds available to you, you can communicate so much? It's really not that difficult. The secret, if you will, lies in something we've mentioned before in this book:

➤ Your intent

➤ How you express that intent

Assuming a benevolent intent on your part, how do you convey your intent in an enticing manner? I'll answer that question with another one: When you first notice a person, what is it about him or her that first catches your eye? No, forget that. We want to focus on the entire person, remember? Okay, what is the *second* thing? Maybe the way that person speaks is particularly entrancing to you. Perhaps he or she is talking about a subject that you find particularly interesting. Zero in on something that makes this person different from all the other people in the room.

And no matter how attracted you are to someone's looks, remember that you're not going to focus on

For HIS Eyes Only

No matter how drop-dead gorgeous she may be, and no matter how attractive some of her physical attributes might be to you, remember to focus on what makes her unique as a person. Whatever part of her you focus on will be the part you are telling her you want most.

physical anatomy. After all, no matter how appealing a person's physical attributes may be, those attributes are more or less common to half the world's population. If you approach someone focused on physical appearance alone, you are saying that any one of the billions of individuals who share his or her gender and some of those same physical traits would be just as attractive to you right now. Hardly the basis for a fulfilling relationship, is it?

Your task, then, is to find some extraordinary, not overtly sexual trait about that person, and *let him or her know you've noticed.*

When Silence Is Golden...and When to Break That Silence

So far, we've paid a lot of attention to what *not* to say, and how *not* to act when you approach someone, so it's probably time to give you some pointers on what you *should* say, and how to approach someone in a way that makes that person feel valued and special.

The first and most important rule in determining what to say is "Don't say anything!" That doesn't mean you should turn yourself into a silent bump on a log. What it does mean is that before you speak, you need to look and listen. Most people give a series of clues, both subtle and blatant, as to what they're about and what is important to them. A truly alluring person will actually pay attention to those clues, and structure his or her approach around them.

Ask the Love Coach

Frequently, the greatest command of the language is demonstrated by exercising *silence.*

Here's some general advice on how to approach someone you're attracted to, based on whether they're a *talker* or an *observer*.

The Talker

In many ways, talkers are easier to approach than observers, because they give out more blatant signals. Let's say you've walked up to someone who is engaged in a conversation. Listen carefully to what is being said and look for signs that he or she feels strongly about a topic. Then, ask yourself how your own feelings might be complementary or even challenging. It's not nearly as important to agree with what is being said as it is to show that the words of this individual have been thought-provoking to you.

As a matter of fact, you may find that, by sharing a different point of view, you have piqued the person's interest in you. You don't want to outright challenge the validity of the other person's ideas, but, by giving the person an opportunity to explain his or her opinions, you open the door to a truly meaningful exchange, which can be *very* exciting.

The Observer

What if the other person is, like yourself, observing silently? Do you just sit there, staring at each other?

Heart Brakes

Just because you don't completely agree with another's opinion doesn't mean you shouldn't engage that person in conversation. However, never provoke or argue for argument's sake. Good, healthy debate is one thing—but nobody likes to feel put on the spot.

Hardly. Try looking closely at the other person's body language, sense of style, and all those other subtle things that can serve as clues to what another person is all about. You don't have to be psychic to determine what a person's spirit is like. You just have to be willing to look past your own immediate desires and trust your own powers of observation. For example:

➤ *Notice the person's facial expressions* as he or she looks at the people around both of you. Does the person seem amused by other people's behavior or put off by it? This minute observation can tell you a lot about how an individual feels about others, and may give you ideas how to approach this person. Suppose, for example, you see your intended looking with amusement at a bickering couple across the room. You can sidle up to him or her and whisper something off-the-wall such as, "We'd better stand back. They're just warming up for their audition for the *Jerry Springer Show*."

➤ *Notice the person's body language and general demeanor.* You can tell a lot about a person just by his or her posture and general behavior. Does this person exude an aura of confidence, or does he or she seem shy, or perhaps defensive? Temper your approach accordingly. (We'll talk more about body language in Chapter 11.)

➤ *Notice the person's style of dress,* and how it correlates to his or her general demeanor. Let's say you see someone who is dressed very conservatively—in a business suit, for example—and he or she is acting silly and making funny gestures. Maybe this means that this individual is well-balanced and has a multi-faceted personality. You could approach such a person by showing appreciation for his or her silliness, or by sharing your own perspective on the need to keep a sense of balance between career and the other aspects of life.

Developing and using your powers of observation is not only a useful tool for tailoring your approach to someone; it's also an icebreaker in and of itself. One client of mine, Jeff, has been known to initiate conversations with women he's interested in by spontaneously describing a complete life story—fabricated on the spur of the moment—for people he doesn't even know, but who just happen to be walking by. The effect is often hilarious and quite endearing. Just ask Elizabeth, his current girlfriend.

"I was standing by myself at a reception," she says, "when suddenly Jeff, whom I'd never seen before, just walked up to me and struck up a conversation. He said, "See the guy over there in the blue suit? Why do you suppose he looks so irritable?' And then Jeff went into this long spiel about how the guy's girlfriend had dumped him for another woman, and the guy had also gotten fired from his job as a designer of computer-controlled pooper scoopers, because one of the models he'd designed had a tendency to consume small dogs. So he had to fall back on his multi-level-marketing gig selling edible underwear, but then the FDA discovered the underwear contained an additive that aggravates male pattern baldness, and now he's being sued by all of the friends, family members, and other relatives that he suckered into buying the product. It was a completely off-the-wall story that Jeff just made up as he went along." Elizabeth was so charmed by Jeff's crazy intro that she agreed to go out for coffee with him after the reception. They've been dating for three months now.

Ask the Love Coach

According to Neuro–Linguistic Programming (NLP), there are three principal ways in which people process information—visual, auditory, and kinesthetic or tactile. Everyone uses all three modes, but most people have one that's dominant. What does this mean to you, as a potential seductress or seducer? It means you can determine just how to push the right buttons on that person who's caught your eye. A *visual* person, for example, is likely to be attracted by your looks. An *auditory* person tends to be captivated by the sound of your voice and by what you *say*. A *kinesthetic* person is warmed or turned on by your touch.

You can determine which category your prospective lover falls into by noticing verbal and body language cues. For example, visual people tend to talk about how a situation "looks" to them, auditory folks discuss how it "sounds," and those of a kinesthetic nature speak of how it "feels." There are other cues, too (a kinesthetic person may like to touch others a lot during conversation; an auditory person might give clues that he or she is really into music).

What you're going to discover, as you begin to put these suggestions into practice, is that the list of acceptable approaches is as long as the list of people you may want to approach. We're not all cookie-cutter reproductions of each other—we are each unique individuals, and your approach must be individual too. There's no single "right" method. The real secret is in being observant and keeping your own intent clear and clean.

Looking Interested, Not Desperate

Remember back in Chapter 5, when we said the best way to get someone to like you was to like them? It follows that, if you want someone to be interested in you, you should express interest in that person first. There are any number of ways you can show interest in someone without looking desperate. The most important factor here is your intent.

If you are a reasonably happy person who enjoys life and who simply wants someone in your life with whom you can share that enjoyment, you will probably have little difficulty attracting someone. People like to be around other people who are happy. The old adage, "smile, and the world smiles with you," is a wonderful rule to follow in your efforts to become more seductive.

If you're not a very happy person, and you feel you simply must attract somebody in order for your life—or your self—to be complete, you will exude an aura of neediness that will turn off prospective partners in a heartbeat. Why? There are several reasons.

➤ You are placing the responsibility for your well-being on someone else's shoulders, and that is an awesome responsibility nobody can live up to.

➤ You are communicating an attitude that your need is so great that *anybody* can make you feel better about yourself. The person you're with will feel that his or her single greatest asset where you're concerned is merely proximity. That's hardly the way to make someone feel special—and if your partner doesn't feel special, he or she will not be open to being seduced.

➤ Finally, if you come across as someone who is generally unhappy, the people you really want to attract will avoid you in droves. The only people you will attract will be the ones who feel compelled to heal every "wounded bird" they encounter, and they will put all their energy into "fixing" you. Believe me, while therapy can be of great benefit, it has no place in a romantic relationship. It gets very old, very fast. To finish the old saying I mentioned earlier, "cry, and you cry alone."

Ask the Love Coach

A client of mine named Nick was attractive, witty, and charming, yet rarely went out on a date, even though he was a regular attendee of his church's large, active singles group. When he came to me for counseling, Nick insisted he was attentive to women, never made sexist remarks, and was always respectful, but that women routinely turned him down for dates. Those who did go out with him inevitably declined his subsequent invitations.

"There must be something wrong with women today," Nick declared, "if someone who has as much love to give as I do can't seem to get one to have a relationship with me."

Nick's problem was that he saw himself as a great repository of love, seeking someone on whom he could lavish it all. What came across to others was neediness: a black hole of human need who was seeking someone, anyone, to fill him up. He didn't make the women he met feel unique or special, no matter how hard he tried, because he was really thinking about only himself.

I coached Nick on his self-image. I helped him see that he didn't need a relationship to be a complete human being, but that he wouldn't find a good relationship until he felt complete. Rather than hunt for the right relationship, I advised him to step back from the process long enough to focus on and appreciate what he had to offer another person.

After I worked with Nick for several months, he began making the first tentative steps back into dating. He's currently seeing three women, all of whom have happily gone out for repeat dates with him. "Who knows," he says, grinning. "Someday I might even have to cancel my lifetime membership in that church singles' group."

What? Ask *Him* Out?

Not too many years ago, a woman who asked a man out on a date was described with such unflattering terms as "easy" or "pushy." Common wisdom held that a woman was supposed to bat her pretty little eyes and wait for the man to approach her. To our credit as a culture, this "common wisdom" has been relegated to the stature of past folly. Smart women don't wait for anyone nowadays, in their romantic lives or their professional lives. When we see something we want, we are fully capable of—and allowed to—go after it. This includes asking a man out.

Even so, you want to do it with finesse. After all, there's a slight chance that he might still be a bit uncomfortable with the idea of a woman initiating the date (although all my surveys show men are delighted when a woman shows interest in them). Usually, if you want to ask a man out but are unsure of whether taking the initiative will make him uncomfortable, you can handle it in two or three steps:

1. *Let him know, through verbal and/or nonverbal cues, that you are interested in him.* We've already discussed some general principles of this step earlier in this chapter. Here are a few additional suggestions for a woman approaching a man. First, don't forget to smile at him. Smiling at a man goes a long way toward letting him know you think he is a winner. Second, if it's appropriate, ask him for his opinion about something you know he knows about. Most men love to be asked for their thoughts on a subject. Finally, "anchor" the conversation by touching him in some nonsexual way periodically during your interchange; most men like and really respond to this.

2. *Let him know you would like to go to a certain event, restaurant, or whatever he suggests.* This step is really quite simple, and leads right into Step 3 (if Step 3 is needed). If you're discussing movies, for example, and you discover there is one you would both like to see, take the subtle approach and say something like, "Oh, I'd love to see that," and wait for him to ask you.

3. *If he doesn't respond to Steps 1 and 2, you can just come right out and ask him.* If you feel particularly confident, or if he doesn't respond immediately (and isn't throwing out cues that he really isn't interested), come right out and say, "I think we'd both enjoy (seeing that movie/trying that restaurant). Do you want to go?"

By allowing the actual "asking out" to arise naturally within the course of the conversation, you are using a safety-net tactic, which men have been using for centuries. It's

For HER Eyes Only

Most men are delighted when a woman takes the initiative and shows him she's interested. The trick is to express your interest and then back off enough to let him do at least some of the pursuing. That way, he won't feel "cornered," which, of course, is especially important if he's not really interested. If he *is* interested, he'll appreciate the opportunity to engage in the pursuit.

Heart Brakes

Most men I've surveyed seem to like when a woman touches them in a nonsexual manner during conversation. Interestingly enough, though, the reverse is usually not true; if a man gets "touchy" with a woman he's just met, she is likely to interpret the gesture as predatory.

important to remember that your self-worth isn't tied to the man's response. If you can remember that, you will be infinitely more attractive to him, and he will feel much less burdened with the responsibility for your well-being. Your seductiveness quotient will soar.

If you find, after asking him out, that a man is completely threatened or put off by your invitation, you need to remind yourself that he has probably been trained all his life to react that way, and may need more time to grow accustomed to being around an assertive woman. At that point, you need to ask yourself, honestly, if the man has enough good traits to justify your continued efforts, or if he will ultimately prove to be a source of frustration and pain. You aren't going to "fix" him. You must decide if he is worth the effort.

That might sound pretty cold-hearted, but you need to think, first and foremost, of your own emotional well-being. If you allow your own peace of mind to be diminished, your seductiveness and allure for others will be diminished, as well.

If the man simply declines, don't waste your time beating yourself up about it. Perhaps he really is committed to another activity at that time. And if he's just not interested, be glad you were able to find out early on, rather than investing a lot of time and emotional energy into someone who wasn't a good match for you.

For HIS Eyes Only

Men, you need to keep in mind that when a woman asks you out, she is asking you to share a given experience with her, not to partake of the deepest levels of intimacy with her. An invitation to dinner, or a movie, or a concert is not, in and of itself, an invitation to her bed or to the altar.

Platonic Pothole or Road to Romance? You Decide

Tony has scads of women friends who adore him, but when it comes time to get romantic, they invariably let him know that they "just don't think of him that way." Lynnette has a circle of attractive and adoring men friends who feel they can confide in her about anything, but they never seem to feel that she's date material. Renee complains, "Everyone says you're supposed to be friends before you become lovers. But what happens to me is that I always make friends with a guy, and by the time I want to become lovers, he has me ensconced in a position of being 'just a friend'—and he can't think of me in any other way."

Call it the buddy syndrome, call it pal purgatory, call it the chronic platonic problem— but whatever you call it, it's making many men and women unhappy. It's not a problem for everyone, so if this situation doesn't apply to you, feel free to skip down to the next section. However, judging from the number of questions I'm asked on call-in radio shows, the buddy syndrome is one of today's most common dating problems.

There are many variations of this syndrome, but the good news is that you can overcome it. Again, it's all about taking a proactive approach to your relationships. First you need to understand why you keep getting into these platonic ruts.

There Are Friends...and Then There Are Platonic Friends

One of the biggest reasons for the buddy syndrome is that people get confused about the dynamics of friendship with someone of the opposite sex. You see, there are friends, and then there are *platonic* friends. What's the difference? Well, let's look at some definitions. The Webster's dictionary definition of a friend is "a person who is attached to another person by a feeling of affection or personal regard." According to the same dictionary, platonic means "free from sensual desire."

Think about your opposite-sex friends. If they are truly platonic friends, you think of each other as surrogate brothers or sisters, or, as some people express it, as part of each other's family of choice (as opposed to family of origin). But let's face it: Not every friendship with the opposite sex is, in fact, free of sensual desire. Sometimes you meet someone and there's an instantaneous feeling of attraction. Or perhaps the attraction comes later on.

In any case, the buddy syndrome rears its ugly head when one or the other person focuses so intently on being a friend that he or she doesn't give off any romance signals. While that person may have intended this friendship to be a prelude to "lovership," there is a certain point at which it becomes, instead, just another platonic friendship. And it's all because the person has chosen to act in certain ways that would seem to preclude passion in the relationship.

Obviously, it's best to address the buddy problem at the very beginning of a relationship. Yes, you want to be friends before lovers, but you also want to make sure you actually reach the lovers stage if that's where you want to go.

Wordplay

A **platonic** friendship is an affection that does not involve sexual love or sensual desire. The word is derived from the Greek philosopher Plato (c. 427–347 B.C.E.), who was known for his disdain of sensory experience.

Heading Off the Buddy Syndrome at the Outset

When you meet someone whom you think may have possibilities as a lover, start setting boundaries from the very beginning. Don't act toward this person as you would act toward a platonic friend. Here's what *not* to do:

➤ Avoid lending a sympathetic ear to sad stories about his or her last lover, and don't relate your "lost love" tales either. Later, when you know each other better and have established a romantic link, you can tell each other about your past relationships. For now, though, try to stay away from these subjects. Of course,

123

For HER Eyes Only

A man is more likely to see you as a prospective romantic partner if you establish certain boundaries and give off signals that distinguish you from one of his beer buds. Elise, for example, says, "If he says, 'Hey, look at the legs on that one,' I'll just raise one eyebrow, smile at him, and reply—good-naturedly, of course—'Hey, save it for the locker room.' If I'm attracted to a guy, of course, I want to be a friend to him—but I never let him forget I'm a woman first."

For HIS Eyes Only

A woman is more likely to see you as a prospective lover than as a male best friend or surrogate brother if you set boundaries from the beginning. As one friend of mine puts it, "The problem with some guys is that when they're beginning a friendship with a woman, they act the part of the big brother, and then they're disappointed when that's how she sees them." Let her know that you see her as a woman as well as a friend. Don't look at, or comment on, other women in her presence. Focus on her, and don't forget to give her sincere compliments.

this doesn't imply that you have to come across as being heartless. If the person mentions a recent heartbreak, you can murmur sympathetically, but then change the subject as quickly and smoothly as possible. Ask the person a question about something else that's going on in his or her life now—for example, a question about work—or ask the individual's opinion on a current issue. This shows you are interested, but doesn't take away the idea that there may be some sensual desire between you.

➤ Try not to discuss the people you're both dating now. At this early stage, it's perfectly all right for both of you to be dating more than one person. However, if you listen to the friendly object of your desire tell you about his or her other dates, or if you talk about yours, the person is going to automatically place you in the category of platonic buddy. Don't do it.

➤ Don't ogle other people or flirt with someone else in his or her presence. If you're a woman and you're trying to dazzle the attractive gentleman sitting across the table from you, it's obviously not cool to drool over the hunk at the bar. If you're a guy and you're trying to impress that gorgeous woman you've just met, she's not going to be too wowed by you if you whistle at the babe who just walked in the front door. Save that kind of behavior for your buddies. If you're openly flirting or ogling someone else, the person you're with will assume you're not interested. You'll immediately be put in the platonic slot.

➤ Don't put up with open ogling or flirting. If the other person is the one doing the drooling and whistling, or making the lascivious comments about others, deflect them as politely and charmingly as you can. If the person doesn't get the hint, and/or is being obnoxious or crude, take it as a warning, and find someone who's more responsive to your charm.

➤ Don't take a prospective seducee out with "the gang." It's great to have platonic friends of the opposite sex. Being a buddy and shoulder to cry on is a warm and satisfying role, to be sure, but it's not a sensual one. So don't bring your would-be lover along when you go out with the pack. Otherwise, this person is likely to start looking at you in the same light your platonic buds do. It's best to keep these friendships separate until you've established a romantic link with your intended.

Remember that once you're in the platonic slot, it's difficult to escape. A client of mine has likened it to being in a deep freeze and trying to thaw yourself out. If you find yourself in this deep freeze with someone, know that more than likely it isn't because you haven't acted as a friend toward this person, but rather because you've acted as a platonic friend. (And if I don't do anything thing else in this book but clarify the difference for you, it's worth the purchase price!)

Pay attention to the tips I've given you, and you shouldn't have any trouble avoiding the buddy syndrome. The cardinal rule is this: Until you're certain that this person is not romantic material, refuse to act in a platonic way. It really is a simple principle, and yet people mess up on this over and over. Remember, how you act around the person to whom you're attracted is your choice. Start paying attention to your actions, and you'll be much more pleased with the results.

Popping the Question (No, Not *That* One, Silly! Asking Someone for a Date)

The hows, the whens, and the wherefores of asking someone out are as varied as the situations in which you will find yourself when you get around to asking (or being asked). To attempt to detail the circumstances and their appropriate dialogs would fill a library. For that reason, I'm not going to go too far into the details.

What I will do is remind you that your intent, and your state of emotional attachment to the outcome of the encounter, are the most important factors in determining your success.

➤ *Your intent:* If you know that your intent toward the other person is good, and that you aren't trying to take something he or she might not be willing to give, you will feel much more at ease asking for a date, because you won't be trying to hide anything. You will be seen as an equal, who wants only to share a pleasant experience with another person. You will come across as a delicious seducer, who promises to enrich the other person's life, even if only for an evening. If, on the other hand, your intent is less than benevolent, the other person is sure to perceive you as a malicious seducer—one who makes others feel like prey facing a predator—and will run like heck.

➤ *Your emotional state:* Again, the key lies in being interested, not desperate or needy. If you are a joyful person to be with, and your main motive for asking someone out is simply to share some of your joy—even if only for one evening— you will be naturally alluring.

On the other hand, if you ask someone out with the feeling that your well-being hinges on his or her response, you'll be hiding all of your other, good qualities behind a cloud of neediness. The result of such an approach is rejection, along with the reinforcement of the self-doubt that you already feel and project. Seduction will then be only a wished-for dream.

As you can see, the most important factor in approaching a member of the opposite sex is your own state of mind. Rather than polishing up the words you plan to say, concentrate on appreciating the value of who you are and what you have to offer. Get a clear understanding and acceptance of what you can and should expect from another person in a relationship, and do your best to communicate that understanding.

Nothing is more seductive than a person who has much to offer, is willing and able to share it, and doesn't put a high price on the sharing. Achieve this level of self-confidence, and you'll never need a book or a coach to help you find happiness in relationships again.

The Least You Need to Know

➤ Don't waste your time trying to come up with a clever pickup line; instead, focus on what's unique about the person you're trying to attract, and tailor your approach accordingly.

➤ There's a difference between communicating desire and communicating neediness; the latter is definitely not seductive.

➤ It's perfectly okay for a woman to ask a man out, but she needs to handle the situation with tact and diplomacy.

➤ You can avoid the buddy syndrome, or the platonic trap, by sending out the right signals in the very beginning of the relationship.

➤ If your intent is benevolent, and your entire well-being doesn't hinge on the outcome of one evening, you shouldn't have any trouble getting someone to go out on a date with you.

Chapter 11

Romantic Signals: How to Read Them and How to Give Them

In This Chapter

➤ Reading what his or her body language is really saying

➤ Eye contact as a tool or a weapon

➤ How to make your own body language communicate effectively

➤ The magic of touching

Without even opening your mouth, you speak volumes to the people around you. The way you stand and sit, your facial expressions, and even the way you position your arms and legs serves to communicate your mood or attitude. And of course, the people all around you are busily conveying their own nonverbal messages to you and anyone else who's paying attention.

Although most of us normally use such nonverbal forms of communication quite unconsciously, we can learn to modify the silent signals we send out. This is useful whether you're attempting to seduce that gorgeous man or woman you just met, or you're trying to close a business deal. I'm not suggesting you try to "lie" with your body language, just that you learn to observe what you're communicating. That way you can address—and, if necessary, modify—your attitudes. Similarly, you can learn to read the nonverbal messages of others around you.

This chapter will help you become more observant of body language in other people and in yourself. It will also help you ensure that what your body is saying is consistent with what you really feel. Realize, of course, that this is general information, and some of the nuances we discuss may vary from person to person, and culture to culture. Since this is not the forum for a detailed discussion of international body language, however, we'll stick to basic principles that apply to most contemporary Western cultures.

Developing Your "Body Literacy"

I can understand how intimidating the study of body language can seem when you first consider it. There have been quite a few scholarly—and a few less-than-scholarly—works that describe in detail what every posture signifies, and what every gesture really means.

While I have no desire to discount the value of all the work that's been done on the subject, I will say that you already know the most important information, even if you aren't consciously aware of it. It's really very easy to "hear" what another person's body language is saying to you, once you make a conscious effort to notice it.

Imagine, for example, that you are talking to someone, and you notice that she's keeping her arms folded tightly across her chest. Think about how you feel when *you* assume that same posture. One reason you might do it is that you are cold; folding your arms is an attempt to keep in your body heat and keep the chills at bay. But you also might assume this position if someone is making you uncomfortable, perhaps by being overbearing. Logically, then, if someone adopts this stance while talking to you, he or she is unconsciously trying to remain insulated from a source of discomfort. When you're confronted with such a situation, ask yourself what you might be doing, or saying, to make the person uncomfortable. Another possibility is that the person is shy or self-conscious, and he or she stands like that as a matter of habit. (Then again, maybe it's just chilly in the room!)

Ask the Love Coach

Try the following exercise at the next party you attend—it will help you develop your body language literacy. Observe someone who is talking with a group of people (don't try to horn in on a private conversation between two people), just out of your range of hearing. Look closely at the person whom you've chosen to observe. Look at the person as if he or she was on television with the sound turned down. In your mind, make up a brief story about this individual, describing his or her part in the current scene. Then approach the group and find out how close you were. You might be surprised at how accurately you can assess someone with such an exercise.

When you're talking to somebody who's standing or sitting across from you, learn to really notice the person's position. Without studying the position of each hand, foot, arm, or leg, you can determine, very easily, whether an individual's overall attitude is one of openness or whether he or she is "circling the wagons."

Is the person leaning toward you as you talk, or away from you? Are this individual's hands open, as if he or she were accepting a gift, or clasped, as if clutching a purse, protecting it from thieves? These descriptions may be exaggerations, but you get the point. There's no rocket science involved in interpreting body language, just common sense.

It's really quite easy to become literate in body language. For more examples of body talk, see the Body Talk table later in this chapter.

Ask the Love Coach

There are powerful truths to be found by reading body language; most people have a lot more control over what they say with words than what they communicate nonverbally. Recently I was sitting in a restaurant and happened to notice Clarissa and Richard sitting across the room. They looked to be on their first date together. Clarissa was playing with her hair, giggling, and leaning forward as Richard was speaking. She anchored her own remarks a couple of times by reaching across the table and touching Richard's arm. Meanwhile, I saw Richard sitting up very straight, with his shoulders back; but when Clarissa spoke, he leaned forward and listened intently without interrupting.

The next day both Clarissa and Richard called me separately, each saying they had noticed me in the restaurant and wanted my opinion on what I had observed. Clarissa was uncertain about how Richard really felt about her, but I told her, "That man really likes you." Richard was equally uncertain about how Clarissa felt. "Call her and ask her out again," I advised.

If you know body language, you can tell what's going on between two people without hearing a word they're saying. Needless to say, Richard and Clarissa went out with each other again—and I'm happy to report they're still dating.

Eye Contact: Magic or Menace?

We humans have long held that a person's eyes are the "windows to the soul," and we tend to place great substance in how a person maintains—or avoids—eye contact during conversation. It is here that the "reading" can get a little tricky. Some people simply aren't inclined to make heavy eye contact, and tend to look away frequently. This doesn't necessarily support conventional wisdom, which says that such people are usually deceitful. The person may simply be shy.

By the same token, just because someone looks unceasingly into your eyes when he or she speaks doesn't mean this person is necessarily a paragon of integrity. On the contrary, deceivers may actually be consciously forcing themselves to maintain eye contact to convince you that they are truthful and/or interested. Or they may even be trying in some way to manipulate you, or to intimidate you with their steady, unwavering gaze. Look closely into the eyes that stare into yours, and try to read what is behind them.

Other factors that can influence your interpretation may be the result of the individual's genetics, rather than his intent. For example, it's said that someone with close-set eyes is somewhat shifty, or someone has "beady little eyes" if her eyes are small. While I am certain that each of us can recall someone who fits these descriptions (physically and in personality), to be fair, we need to at least consider our prejudices when we make our interpretation.

By using common sense and your instincts, you can get a pretty accurate idea about the person, regardless of how long he or she looks into your eyes. Remember: The foremost factor in seductiveness is intent, and the best way to read that intent is on an intuitive level.

Body Talk: Saying It Without Words

If it's important to know how to read body language, it's equally as important to know how to "speak" with your own body. You probably know what you want to say. Now we're going to look at a few ways to say it, clearly, without uttering a word. Keep in mind that this isn't about deception, and it's not about engaging in the sort of forced posturing that's as obvious as a rhino in a phone booth. Instead, what we are trying to do is make you aware of what your body language is saying, so you can be certain that it mirrors what you really feel.

Just as you choose your words when you are describing a situation to another person, you can also choose your body language. This isn't being deceptive. It is simply exercising your communication skills to describe your thoughts as accurately (or sometimes as diplomatically) as possible.

Once you have really focused on the individual you're with, and decided what you want to communicate to that person, go over the checklist in the following table, comparing your posture and positioning to the items listed. Is your body saying "I'm interested" or "Get me outta here"?

Ask The Love Coach

Don't let your body language sabotage you. My client Nancy had a disagreement with a coworker one afternoon, and it remained unresolved at the end of the day. She had a reception to attend immediately after work, and, almost immediately upon her arrival, met a very interesting man whom she definitely wanted to get to know better. He seemed interested in her as well—at first, anyway. As they talked, she noticed his interest seemed to be wavering, and she was puzzled.

"Then I happened to catch a glimpse of myself in a mirror," she says. "Here I was, standing next to this perfectly gorgeous guy, and my arms were folded across my chest, there was a shadow of a frown on my face, and I looked like somebody who'd just sat on a pine cone." Fortunately, Nancy remembered what she and I had previously discussed about nonverbal communication. She was able to stop and ask herself, *Is this the image I want to show this guy? Am I really focusing on him, or is my coworker standing here between us?* She immediately switched her focus to her new friend, centering her attention on his attractive smile. Before long, her face and her body language reflected her change in attitude, and she was able to recapture his interest.

As Nancy discovered, we can sometimes let things that have absolutely nothing to do with the other person (or our feelings about them) affect the way we act. This can distort what we are trying to communicate, and can short-circuit the seduction. Try to really focus on the person across from you, thinking about the things you find attractive about him or her. You'll find that as your focus shifts from the difficult situation you're worried about to the pleasant situation you're in now, your body language will reflect the shift, and you will look much more approachable.

Body Talk

Come Hither!	Go Thither!
Lean forward	Lean away
Smile	Frown, scowl, or look bored
Make eye contact	Look everywhere else
Hands relaxed and empty	Clenched fists or clutched item
Palms out	Knuckles out

continues

continued

Come Hither!	Go Thither!
Feet flat on floor	Ankles crossed and locked
Legs look relaxed	Knees pressed tightly together
Animated responses	Impassive responses (or none)
Fiddling sensually with a prop	Put prop aside brusquely
Subtle touching	No physical contact

Now let's look at some specific examples from our list, and see how they apply to your own body talk.

Leaning with Meaning

Have you ever been talking to someone and noticed the individual leaning forward in his or her chair as if ready to pounce? Didn't you feel as if the person was really excited about what you had to say? Though you don't want your partner to feel like wounded prey faced with a hungry predator, you do want to physically convey your interest. Leaning toward someone says, quite simply, that you want to be closer, while leaning away lets that person know that you'd rather be somewhere else.

Positions the Kama Sutra Never Mentions

The way you position your body, especially your arms, hands, legs, and feet, can give someone a fairly clear indication of how you feel in his or her presence. While you can't (and shouldn't) try to lie with your body—any more than you should lie with your words—you can choose to be conscious of how accurately your position communicates your feelings. Think about whether you do any of these things:

➤ Do you assume a position that looks defensive, even though you're sitting with a person you like? Is this because you're shy or self-conscious, or because you have something on your mind that is adding to the stress of meeting someone new?

➤ Notice your hands. Are they open, as if waiting to accept a gift, or clenched tight, as if you were holding your last dollar in a room full of pickpockets?

➤ If you're a woman, are your legs so rigidly slammed together that they're screaming "You're never getting in here!" or are they more relaxed, saying "I have no need to protect myself from you."

➤ If you're a man, are you hovering over the woman you're interested in as though you're about to pounce on her—and is she subtly but progressively drawing back and looking around as if she's plotting her escape?

While I have presented some extreme examples here, you should ask yourself where your body talk falls on this spectrum. When I owned my own dating service, I made videotapes of clients as part of their membership package. As a coach, I have also videotaped clients in order to help them improve their presentation techniques or interaction skills. Upon viewing the tapes, many people are astonished at how frightened—or overly eager—their positions make them look.

Smile Without Guile

Smiling is one of the most dynamic forms of body talk. When you smile at someone sincerely, you're telling the person that you are enjoying the time you are spending together.

➤ *When a woman smiles….* It is especially true for women that a smile goes a long way toward seducing a man. He wants to please you, and may even have a lot of his own self-image tied up in his ability to please. Therefore, when you smile at him, you're telling him that you're enjoying his company and that he's doing all right with you.

➤ *When a man smiles….* A man's smile can communicate the same acceptance as a woman's, but his *intent* has a bigger effect on how the smile is interpreted. No woman likes to feel as if she's an hors d'oeuvre on a plate, waiting to be consumed. She wants to feel wanted, even lusted after, but she wants to be desired as a whole person, not just as a repository for a man's lust. So ask yourself, guys, whether your smile is expressing your appreciation for the person in front of you or for the person you hope will be writhing around naked later on. It really makes a big difference.

Eye Gotta Be Me

Since we've already determined that the eyes are the windows to the soul, it makes sense to be conscious of what your eyes are saying to the other person. The phrases "bedroom eyes" and "undressing her with his eyes" are good descriptions of some of the things your eyes can communicate to your partner. They speak so clearly of your intent—and your spirit—that they can deafen your partner to what you might actually be saying.

If you look at the person you're with and find yourself thinking that he or she is absolutely delightful, that delight will shine like a neon sign in your eyes. If you're looking at the person, however, and thinking this individual is the answer to all your emotional needs, that person will inevitably see you as some kind of emotional vampire, waiting for the opportunity to drain all of his or her energy.

Beyond the intent behind your eyes, how you physically focus on someone has an effect upon how you are perceived. You want to look into the other person's eyes while you are with him, but not with an unbroken stare. Look away from time to time, and allow the person some emotional space. You might even look at the person's hands sometimes while she's talking to you, as the hands provide animation to the dialog.

Animated Annie, or Wooden Wanda?

Consider also whether your responses to your partner's conversation are animated and alive, or stagnant and dead. If you look as if you're bored with someone, that person will give up on you in a hurry.

One caveat: Don't get all carried away with this animated-response principle, or you'll look like a puppy greeting its master at the door after a day-long separation. That can be scary to anybody. Find a middle ground—one that expresses your interest but doesn't make you look like a blithering nincompoop, or someone who hasn't had a date since Nixon resigned. Act toward that person as you would toward anybody you find interesting. Keep your eyes on him or her during the conversation, smile often, nod when appropriate—in short, make it apparent that you are really listening to what this person is saying, and you genuinely enjoy being in his or her presence.

Heart Brakes

There are those people who see rejection as a challenge to over-come. For people like this, you can forget about subtle hints to let them know you're not interested. You might just want to invest in a good fly swatter, though!

Ask the Love Coach

There is a process called mirroring, which, as it happens, is practiced not only by humans but also by our closest relatives in the animal kingdom, the apes. You simply mirror the verbal techniques or gestures of the person you are trying to attract. You can mirror his tone of voice, for instance. Or if she puts her chin in her hands, you do the same thing. Be sure to do it in a flirtatious manner, so it doesn't look as if you're mocking the person. Done with finesse, this is definitely a case where imitation is a sincere form of flattery.

The Proper Use of Props

Yet another way that you can seductively communicate without saying a word is through the use of props. Now, I know this sounds really staged, but it's something we all do unconsciously. All I'm suggesting is that you make yourself conscious of your movements and use them to your advantage.

Men, imagine you're sitting across from a very lovely woman, and both of you seem to be enjoying each other's company. You notice that her fingers are moving ever so delicately, up and down the stem of her wine glass. What comes immediately to mind? With this subtle movement, she has increased the level of your interest, and you find yourself fantasizing about her. (Women, are you paying attention to this?)

I have also heard that some women have an equivalent response to a man who lightly (and apparently absent-mindedly) runs his fingertip around the rim of his glass, occasionally even touching his finger to his lips to moisten it. There are any number of ways that you can inspire your partner to fantasize about you, without being crude or even obvious. Use your imagination.

Once you do, you'll find any number of props you can use to seductive ends. Again, subtlety is the key. Use what's on hand; don't go out of your way to find a suggestive object. After all, you want your actions to be smooth and natural. The wine glass suggestion I mentioned earlier is a good example of a sensual prop, and there are many other objects you can use: a pen, a straw, a scarf, or a lipstick, for example. A woman playing with her hair can convey a seductive message to the man sitting across from her. A man gently running his fingers over his silk tie can send a sensual message to his partner. Be playful, and, by all means, have fun with props. Don't fiddle with them nervously, however—that's definitely not sensual.

Heart Brakes

It is unnecessary—even inadvisable—to describe what your movements represent when you touch someone. The sensuality of your touch will speak for itself. No need to spell it out ("When I caress your long, beautiful fingers, it makes me think of your long, lovely legs.") The message will come across loud and clear, and will actually be diminished by the telling.

For HER Eyes Only

I have learned, through personal experience and through talking to hundreds of men, that a light, seemingly unconscious touch on a man's knee or thigh has the effect of immediately causing him to fantasize about the woman he's with. If you really want to put some passion in his thoughts, try a gentle touch while you're talking with him, and watch his eyes light up.

Seduction: It's More than Mental—It's Also a Contact Sport

Despite what some people may think, foreplay begins long before any clothes start coming off, and even before any decisions are made about having sex. In that time of

For HIS Eyes Only

A woman loves gestures that aren't necessarily sexual but that create an ambience of safe intimacy. Gestures such as guiding her gently by the arm as you're walking, or putting your jacket over her shoulders if she seems cold, can have a cumulative effect that she'll find very seductive. If she's already attracted to you, these gentle gestures will enhance her feelings. If she's not certain of her feelings for you, your overtures won't seem predatory or threatening. Just remember, you don't have to formally ask permission before you make each move—but do pay attention to her reactions.

For HIS Eyes Only

How can you tell if a woman is...well...interested? Once you've learned to read the signs, it's easy to tell, even from across the room. Some of the most common flirtatious signals: She smiles at you and glances at you repeatedly, tosses her head, and/or flips her hair. Close up, behaviors such as leaning in to you and whispering to you can be signs of flirtatious behavior.

exquisite tension when neither person knows where a relationship might go, even the slightest contact can be a source of sparks or revulsion. Intent and finesse are what separate the two.

Since the brain is the primary erogenous zone (see Chapter 4), your initial acts of seduction must be more mental than physical. The whole idea is to get your partner thinking about you in a sexual light, and to enjoy those thoughts. As I've said so many times before, your intent will be communicated very clearly to your partner. If all you're interested in is a sexual encounter, all your words and deeds will carry at least a subtle undertone that your partner will hear and see. If, however, you see your new partner as an emotional, intellectual, and even spiritual delight, as well as a potential romantic and sexual partner, that balance of intent will also come across.

So how do we turn up the heat without getting burned? Certainly a spontaneous grope for your partner's more personal parts would be counterproductive. It is here that your finesse plays such a crucial role. You want your partner's passion to build slowly to a fever pitch. You want this person to be excited about exploring new experiences with you. But you want this person to feel as if the seduction is his or her idea. So you plant little seeds. If the situation is right—and the chemistry is there—these seeds will blossom.

Some of the most effective seeds you can plant take the form of sensuous touches. They seem to be completely spontaneous, done almost absent-mindedly. Yet they are very effective in sparking thoughts in your partner's mind.

It is impossible to overstress the importance of intent and finesse where the art of sensuous touching is concerned. Perhaps more than any other aspect of a seduction, there is a very fine line between what is welcome and alluring and what is unwelcome and even offensive.

You need to be very conscious of your partner's boundaries, and respectful of his or her concept of personal space. Some people think nothing of giving a peck on the cheek, embracing, or being embraced by a new acquaintance, while others reserve any physical contact whatsoever for people with whom they already feel intimate. Go slowly with your attempts at physical contact, and read your partner's reactions every step of the way. If you do it right, your sensuous touching can lead you both into a truly delicious seduction.

You have at your disposal many different tools that you can use to communicate with your partner. You may impress someone with your words, dazzle him with your smile, and mesmerize her with your eyes. With the right little touches, you will complete your delicious seduction. Always remember, however, that a seduction that doesn't make both of you feel good is not worth pursuing.

For HER Eyes Only

Some guys are bold and obvious when expressing their interest in you. Others are more subtle. Some of those across-the-room signals that mean he's interested include: preening behavior, stroking his tie, or an eyebrow flash upon catching your eye. Closer up, be on the lookout for subtle gestures, such as touching your arm or putting his hand on the small of your back to guide you while you're walking together. All of these can be signs that he finds you enticing.

The Least You Need to Know

➤ It's really quite easy to read basic body language, just by using your powers of observation.

➤ Eye contact is very important, but it is a two-edged sword; it can intimidate people as well as attract them.

➤ Whether you want to attract someone or repel them, it's important that your body language reflect your intent.

➤ Touch can be very powerful, and touching someone can be seductive even if the touch isn't overtly sexual.

Chapter 12

Flirting: Tickle, Tease, or Torture

In This Chapter

➤ What is flirting, anyway?

➤ The good, the bad, and the ugly

➤ How to get over your fear of flirting

➤ Harmless flirting: testing your equipment

➤ Destructive flirting: Scarlett fever

➤ Purposeful, seductive flirting: when you know what you want

---

At one time or another, nearly everybody has flirted with someone they find attractive. For many people, flirting is nothing more than a fun and harmless way of interacting. But flirting isn't always harmless, and it can sometimes be quite destructive. On the other hand, it can also be a powerful prologue to that delicious seduction we all long for. It depends upon several factors: your intent, the other person's expectations, and the actual results. In this chapter, we'll explore the different types of flirtation, and I'll share some pointers on how to flirt seductively.

The Flavors of Flirting

Webster's dictionary defines *flirting* as "acting amorously or seductively without serious intent." But just as the word "seduction" has changed in meaning over the years, "flirting" has undergone a similar transformation. It no longer necessarily means acting without serious intent, although it certainly *can* mean that. Let's begin by defining our terms.

There are three kinds of flirting:

1. *Harmless flirting.* I like to think of this as equipment-check flirting. It's just a way of testing one's attractiveness to the opposite sex, with no serious intent, but with no harmful results either.

2. *Destructive flirting.* Maybe it's a woman who comes on to every married man at the party, while the wives stand around seething. Perhaps it's a married man who flirts constantly and outrageously with other women, even (or especially) in the presence of his wife. Or maybe it's your blind date, who's too obviously *not* blind whenever another attractive woman walks by your table. If flirtatious behavior causes discomfort, anger, or unhappiness, it is destructive. The destructive flirt may not necessarily be flirting with harmful intent, but he or she is flirting without regard for the results.

3. *Seductive flirting.* This is meaningful flirting. It's flirting with a serious purpose, and that purpose is pleasure (without pain). We'll go into the particulars later on in this chapter (also see Chapter 11 for more advice).

Wordplay

Webster's dictionary defines **flirting** as "acting amorously without serious intention." But that's really more descriptive of the old-style flirting. Remember, the single element that truly separates delicious seduction from malicious seduction is intent, and the same goes for flirtation. Keep your intent clear and kind, and your flirting will be sweet, your seduction a delightful experience for both of you.

Before we discuss the different types of flirting, I want to say a few words to those of you who have cold feet about the whole thing. I know you're out there, so come on in, sit by the fire and let's get you warmed up.

Hope for the Flirt-O-Phobe

Many people have anxieties about flirting, and as a result they don't do it well, or they don't do it at all. If so, they may be missing out on a lot of fun. For, despite my many caveats about destructive flirting, the truth is that harmless flirting *can* be fun, and seductive flirting can greatly enrich your seduction experience.

Most people with flirting anxiety are simply afraid of rejection. The good news is that much of this fear can be overcome by shifting your mind from the idea of flirting to the idea of simply *connecting with another person.* When you connect with someone, you make a link or a bond with that person, and not necessarily with romantic or seductive intent. You can make a connection with the gas station attendant, the person in line behind you at the supermarket, or the woman who's checking you out at the bookstore (by this, I mean she's ringing up your purchase, not "checking you out" in *that* way). In fact, connecting with people in these neutral situations is a great way to begin getting over your anxiety about flirting. After all, what is flirting but just another way of connecting with other people?

I'm going to share some secrets for connecting. Master these, and flirting will come naturally. (Also see Chapter 5 for some extra help.)

➤ *Your state of mind is the most important determinant of your happiness.* Your happiness doesn't depend on your state of matrimony or relationship; it depends on your state of mind. Seducing someone that you're wild about may ultimately be your goal; but remember, getting there is half the fun. And you do want to have fun, don't you? Otherwise, what's the point? Whether you want to be a great seductress or seducer, or you just want to form a connection with that woman who works at the bookstore, cultivate a joyful state of mind, and the rest really will come easily.

➤ *Don't be too attached to the outcome of your connection attempts.* I've said this so many times that you might call it the Love Coach mantra, but it's so important that I'm going to keep saying it. When you're connecting with someone, or even flirting with that person, you're not going to hit the mark every time. It's like striking a rock 99 times, and it doesn't crack until the 100th swing of the pick axe. You need a little practice, particularly if you haven't been out there flirting in a long time (or ever). Remember, you're going to start simply by connecting, making conversation, and talking to people. Learn not to be disappointed if the outcome isn't exactly the way you would have liked.

➤ *Remember that everyone wants to connect with a happy, confident person.* Do whatever it takes to reinforce your confidence and your self-esteem. Remind yourself that you're a unique and worthwhile person. If you need some inspiration, go back to some of the exercises in Chapters 3 and 4.

➤ *Smile, for Pete's sake!* Okay, I admit it, this is another one of my mantras, and if you've read some of the earlier chapters, you'll know it. It sounds so simple, but if you learn the art of the genuine smile and practice it as often as you can, people will be drawn to you. Try smiling at people whom others rarely smile at—that grouchy librarian nobody ever talks to, the post office attendant stuck behind the service counter at lunch hour, or that check-out clerk in your supermarket who looks like she's never smiled a day in her life. See if you can't light up that person's eyes. When you smile, you give away a gift of joy.

➤ *Practice eye contact.* But practice it in moderation; you want to look interested, not predatory. Look away occasionally when you're talking to someone, but do return your glance frequently, and be sure to smile.

➤ *Genuinely care and have empathy for the people with whom you're connecting.* If you make a genuine attempt to see the world through the other person's eyes, the empathy and caring will come naturally. See Chapter 5 for more about this.

➤ *Don't forget that laughter and humor are fun—and sexy!* Laughing with somebody is one of the most delightful experiences you can share.

➤ *Find things that you have in common with people and talk about that.* Don't forget that most folks are comfortable around people with whom they have something in common.

➤ *Find something that you really like about someone and share it with that person.* Remember, if you like someone, that individual will almost always like you back. If not, you don't need to be hanging around with that person, right?

➤ *Be approachable.* It's fine to maintain a level of mystery, but no matter how beautiful or how handsome you are, people will not approach you if you don't look happy, friendly, and receptive. In fact, stunningly good-looking people often have more trouble than average-looking people in this area, because others automatically assume that beauty renders a person unreachable.

Heart Brakes

Don't be a self-rejecting flirt. Let's say you're thinking of asking that attractive person you've just met to dance, but you don't do it because you're afraid of rejection. Bad choice! It can't hurt to go ahead and ask the person to dance. The worst that can happen is that the answer will be no. Even if it is, it might be for a reason completely unrelated to you. Maybe this person has two left feet, or maybe he or she is already involved and doesn't want to be tempted. In any case, don't reject yourself without even consulting the object of your attention. And remember, the people who lose out are not the ones whose flirtations are rejected; the only losers are the ones who never get in the game.

The first step, then, is to get out there and practice simply connecting with people. The next step is to overcome your resistance to actual flirting. While flirting may seem to come naturally to some people, it is a skill that anyone can learn. So go ahead and try it. And yes, you have to practice. Just like playing tennis, riding a bike, or anything else, your flirting will improve with practice. The important thing is that you get out there and do it!

Now that you're feeling better about flirting, let's explore the different varieties of flirtation.

Testing, Testing: One, Two...Wow!

Harmless flirting can be fun and ego boosting. Jill just ended a long-term relationship and went through an intense grieving period of several weeks. Jill did little but sit around the house trying to decide if life still had any meaning. She finally came to the conclusion that it did, and knew it was time to dust herself off and get back out there in the action.

However, she wisely decided she really wasn't ready to date yet, so instead she elected to go out with a couple of girlfriends for a night of harmless flirting, or "equipment testing." They decided to go to a new club across town.

Ask the Love Coach

There's nothing wrong with engaging in harmless flirtation to test your attractiveness, if you are clear about your intentions and don't lead anybody on. Set boundaries for yourself, and don't cross them. Remember, it's very easy for people to misconstrue signals, particularly if their judgment is impaired by alcohol. Don't let an innocuous "equipment test" turn into a cruel tease.

Jill was still a bit shaky after having been out of action for so long, but she prepared herself by taking a leisurely bath and playing some music that really got her in the mood. As she applied her make-up, she studied herself in the mirror, focusing on her best features: her large blue eyes, her long, blond hair, and her fantastic, easy smile. People have told her she looks a lot like a younger version of Goldie Hawn.

By the time Jill walked into that club, she had psyched herself up. She was thinking, "I'm a dead ringer for Goldie Hawn. In fact, I'm even more adorable." So she strode right in and put on her biggest smile. First she looked all around the room—not at the people, but at the colors and the decor of the club. She soaked it all in: the music, the rhythm, the laughter and noise. She really felt good about herself, and more alive than she had in weeks. She laughed and joked with her friends, and ordered a nonalcoholic drink.

Ask the Love Coach

We flirt for many reasons. For some people, flirting is a means of convincing themselves that they are worthy and desirable. For others, it's merely a tool to be used to satisfy sexual urgings. And for a pitiful few, it's a weapon to manipulate and dominate other people. For the practitioners of delicious seduction, however, flirtation is but one of the ways to communicate that we, ourselves, are seduced by the wondrous flavors of life.

Before too long, a man walked up and asked Jill to dance. He wasn't really her type, but that wasn't what she was after. She went to the dance floor with him, danced several dances, flirted a little with him, and had a delightful time. After awhile he took her back to the table, and said, "Would you like to go somewhere quieter, where we can talk and get to know each other better?"

Jill replied, "No, thanks. I'm really here just to have a good time dancing. But hey, you sure are a great dancer, and I've had a wonderful time."

He shrugged good-naturedly and said, "Well, okay, maybe I'll see you on the dance floor later! If you'd like, maybe you'll give me a call someday if you'd like to go out dancing again." He gave her his card and left with a good attitude, because she hadn't led him on, and she hadn't made him feel rejected. Before too long, Jill noticed another man looking at her from across the bar. She looked at him briefly, then she looked down, and then she looked up again, making eye contact and smiling briefly. She looked down again and started to twirl a strand of her hair. This was definite preening posture—in other words, unmistakable flirting!

The guy came over and said, "May I buy you ladies a drink?" They said, "Sure," and began to talk to him, but he zeroed in on Jill. Finally Jill said, "Let's dance." He was a great dancer, and she really liked the way dancing with him made her feel sensuous and sexy again. He seemed to be quite turned on to her, but she stuck to her vow not to get involved with anyone. So, just as she did with the first man, she let her new dance partner know that she was there that night just to have a good time dancing. He seemed disappointed, but didn't push it.

For HER Eyes Only

When you're flirting, you can really wow him with eye contact if you do it right. Look at him briefly, then look down, and then look up again—making the actual eye contact, and smiling briefly. This is very important; eye contact without a pleasant smile is just staring, and that's not very sexy.

As the evening progressed, Jill's self-esteem and self confidence steadily rose, but not at the price of anyone's feelings. She flirted in a way that didn't lead anyone on, or damage self-esteem.

Later on in the evening, she noticed another man making eyes at her. But she also noticed he was there with his girlfriend, and this was definitely a violation of the ethical boundaries she'd set for herself. So she looked down, not giving him a second glance, and struck up a conversation with someone else.

By the end of the night, Jill had danced and had fun, laughed, and told stories with her friends. As people said good night to her, she felt wonderful. She went home and had a restful night's sleep, knowing that, yes, her equipment still worked—and when she gets ready to use it again, it will work just fine the next time, too.

As God Is My Witness, I Shall Never Flirt Destructively Again!

You can be pretty sure that those are words Scarlett O'Hara never said. We all remember the image of Scarlett seated so demurely at the center of a circle of fawning would-be suitors. With deft movements and subtle words, she held out to each of them the promise of her attentions, even her affections, if only they played their cards right. In one scene of *Gone With The Wind*, she was flirting madly, leading the men on, enraging their women, and generally causing mayhem. Her intent was meaningless, beyond her desire to feel good about herself—everyone else's feelings be damned. The character of Scarlett was, in her fickleness, the epitome of the old-fashioned flirt—the destructive flirt, if you will.

What we so often forget is that Scarlett, as adept as she was at flirting and seduction, ended up alone and unhappy. Her very fickleness caused her to lose the one man she truly loved—and who truly loved her.

The old style of flirting generally had one very clear and very short-term objective: attract someone's amorous attention. There was little or no thought given to the "next step," much less the final outcome of the actions. All that mattered was to get another person to notice and want you.

That's not to say that such an objective is inherently bad, of course. We all want to be noticed and desired. To some extent, we all wish to be seductive. It's in our wiring to want, even need, to attract the attentions and affections of another human being. And, as we just saw in Jill's example above, flirting can be a fun and harmless means to gain this attention. Unfortunately, however, there are still many Scarletts (and their male counterparts) running around out there, flirting with disaster.

It happens all the time. A client of mine named Hannah told me about two couples she observed at

For HER Eyes Only

Nearly every woman will admit to having led a man on at one time or another, for the sole purpose of boosting her ego. Unfortunately, to establish a pattern of this type of behavior is to perpetuate all the negative elements we've been trying to get away from. Flirting for vanity's sake may give you some temporary emotional reinforcement, but in the end will make you feel ugly inside. If you are going to practice equipment-check flirtation, be sure to do it in such a way that it is not harmful to the man you're flirting with, or to you.

Heart Brakes

Don't ever practice harmful flirting. If someone who is obviously with someone else begins flirting with you, don't flirt back. And, of course, if you are with a date, do not under any circumstances flirt with anyone else other than your companion. It's just plain rude. Set your boundaries and don't let anyone violate them.

a dinner party recently. It was an intimate gathering at a home in a ritzy part of town. One of the men, Fred, had brought his date, Melissa. Melissa was pretty and person-able, and Fred found her quite attractive. They had been going out together for nearly a month. But then Fred noticed his business associate Phil's date, a pretty blonde named Connie. So, Fred began to do what Fred does best: flirt. He would make comments—some subtle, some not so subtle—about how pretty Connie was. He'd make eye contact with her, wink at her, and laugh a little too loudly at her jokes.

Connie, who had no particular attachment to Phil (beyond the fact that he'd brought her to the party), began to respond to Fred's overtures. As a matter of fact, she found him quite attractive, and she figured, from the way he was behaving, that he didn't have any particular attachment to Melissa. Fred, however, didn't have any serious intentions toward Connie, other than a desire to grab her attention. Once she began responding flirtatiously to Fred, he quickly grew bored, and turned his amorous attention to my client Hannah, who had the good sense to ignore him.

Meanwhile, Phil was furious, as was Fred's date Melissa, and Connie was just feeling humiliated. What Fred had accomplished, in the space of a single evening, was to make three people very upset. This was definitely a case of harmful flirting.

Ask the Love Coach

If the person you're trying to attract seems to be practicing old-style, destructive flirtation, should you dismiss this individual as a potential partner, or should you offer the benefit of the doubt? It depends. He or she may well be a wonderful person who simply doesn't realize that things are done differently now. Pay attention to your gut feelings, beyond whatever physical attraction you may have. If you think this person really might have promise, try getting to know him or her a little better; reserve your judgment until you feel you have some more "facts." Maybe this old-style flirt is a diamond in the rough. If this person's behavior is truly offensive, however, don't stick around for the abuse. It's not your job to "fix" anybody.

How do you avoid harmful flirting? It's really just a matter of common sense and decency. If your intent is honorable, and you project those good intentions to those around you, you shouldn't run into any problems. And, since it is impossible to know for certain what a new acquaintance is thinking or, therefore, what his or her inten-tions are, you can only make sure your own motives are pure. Here are some pointers:

➤ *Ask yourself exactly what your flirtation is supposed to be saying to the other person.* Are you promising just a bit of harmless and nonsexual fun, a night of steamy passion, a sizzling affair that lasts until you both get bored, or a possible lifetime together? Be careful what you're communicating.

➤ *Ask yourself if you are being truthful to the other person.* Are you giving subtle hints that you might be willing to offer something you really aren't willing to give? You certainly don't want to find yourself in the uncomfortable position of having your actions "write checks that can't be cashed."

Perhaps you have the idea that the only way you'll make any headway is by offering the object of your desire what you think he or she wants. This may be as miniscule as a telephone call, as intimate as a sexual liaison, or as all-encompassing as an eventual trip to the altar. Keep in mind, though, that there's just no way you can determine the needs of someone you've just met. You can, however, be sure of what you are willing to give, and limit even your most subtle "promises" accordingly. You don't want to emit those confusing mixed signals we've all had to figure out at one time or another.

➤ *Don't flirt with somebody who is obviously with someone else.* Sometimes this is hard to discern. We've all seen the married flirt who doesn't wear a ring and makes the rounds at parties, hitting on every attractive person in the room. But usually you can tell who's with whom. If you have any doubt whatsoever, ask. If you're intimidated by such a direct approach, just play it safe and don't flirt with someone whose status you don't know.

➤ *If you're with somebody, don't flirt with anyone else.* 'Nuff said.

For HIS Eyes Only

How many of you men out there have worked hard to put on your best show for a woman, just so you could get her to have sex with you—only to avoid her after you'd achieved your goal? How did you feel when all was said and done? Did you feel like a better person, or like a louse? The guys I've talked to about this said their most common lingering feeling was that they'd "gotten something over" on the woman. And a few have admitted the often unstated, though obvious extension of this: They feared that who they really were wasn't good enough to get and keep her attention and affection. When you feel this way, you'll more than likely tend to continue a pattern of deceit, which ends in unsatisfactory relationships.

Flirting As a Prelude to Passion

You've spotted someone whom you find particularly attractive, someone you want to get to know better. You aren't necessarily looking for a soul mate, but you wouldn't head for the hills if one appeared, either. What you do want is the opportunity to get to know this person, spend some time together, and determine whether he or she is as attractive to you as you think. It's time to turn on the charm.

This is where your literacy in nonverbal communication really comes into play (see Chapter 11). Many of the preliminary signals you send out during seductive flirting are the same as those used during harmless, equipment-check flirting (and, unfortunately, during destructive flirting too). The difference, of course, lies in your intent, and, if things go the way you've planned, in the results as well.

Heart Brakes

Giving out false signals can be very damaging, to both the sender and the recipient. For example, people who give hints that they are interested in a long-term relationship when they truly aren't cause immeasurable damage to their partner's ability to trust (and, ultimately, to themselves). On the other hand, people who proclaim they aren't interested in a committed relationship, but are devastated when such a relationship doesn't develop, are setting themselves up for inevitable hurt. You are perfectly entitled to your own set of priorities and limits in your relationships, but it is your responsibility to yourself and to your partner to communicate those priorities and limits.

The Anatomy of Seductive Flirting

Truly seductive flirting is a synthesis of virtually everything we have talked about so far. It involves the approach techniques, the principles of connecting, and all the various forms of nonverbal communication we've discussed. Seductive flirting is your unique expression of the sultry seductress or sexy seducer you have become. This is where you really begin to test those elements of seductiveness you've been developing. When you're flirting seductively, you are flirting on several levels:

➤ *Your physical self*, through your general appearance, your body language, and your facial expressions.

➤ *Your intellectual self*, through your conversation.

➤ *Your emotional self*, through expressing empathy with the person you're trying to attract, and through your attempts to get beyond this person's surface.

➤ Your *essence*, or *spirit*, which, as defined earlier, is at once a blend of the other ingredients, and an element in and of itself. Your essence is reflected in your self-confidence, your sense of self-worth, and your intent.

Okay, maybe that's all sounding a little abstract, so let's get to some concrete stuff. Just how *do* you flirt seductively?

The Sweetest Sale You May Ever Make

If you've ever had any sales training, you probably learned various formulas for making a sale. The formula for seductive flirting is roughly the same, except, of course, the product you're selling is yourself, and the medium of exchange is pleasure rather than money (well, I'm assuming). Here is a simple formula that you can use as a guideline for your own seductive sale (see Chapters 10 and 11 for more information).

➤ *Attention:* You can grab that attractive person's attention even from across the room, if you just know the right signals. Smiling and judicious use of eye contact are great beginnings. Lip licking, playing with various props (your wine glass, your tie) can also be quite intriguing.

➤ *Interest:* The process began when someone first noticed you, but it really hits its stride when you approach that person, or that person approaches you. Now you can use some of the up-close signals, such as whispering, leaning in, or tender touching. Presumably the verbal communication has begun, too—another powerful way of building interest.

➤ *Desire:* Here's where you're beginning to make this person really want you. Turn up the heat a notch with a thigh touch or other mildly erotic gesture. Continue with the verbal communication too, creating a sense of empathy with the person, and making the object of your desire feel emotionally safe with you. (Make sure you feel emotionally safe too, of course.)

➤ *Conviction:* At some point, this person is going to become convinced he or she *must* find out more about you. Congratulations; you're almost there.

➤ *Action:* Now you've really come to the point where something's gotta give. This is where you "close the deal"—you ask for a date and the person accepts (or you are asked for a date and you accept).

Ask the Love Coach

The most successful flirts are those who feel that the world—and life itself—flirts with them. Take the time to be tantalized by something as simple as the scent of a newly mowed lawn or the taste of a fresh strawberry. Look for the beauty in the world around you, and you will mirror that beauty back for all the world to see.

When you come right down to it, seductive flirting is really as simple as finding your prospect and selling your seductiveness to that individual. As for commissions and bonuses, well, that's entirely up to you and your partner!

Flirting, as we have seen, can be grievously misused. However, if you maintain your conscious commitment to the integrity of your own behavior, you will find that flirting can be a deliciously sensuous activity—a source of pleasure for both you and the person with whom you're flirting. Done properly, it can provide a real boost to both your egos, and get a new relationship off to a wonderful start. So stamp that word "integrity" on the inside of your eyelids where you'll be constantly reminded, and get out there and have—ahem—a *ball!*

The Least You Need to Know

➤ Flirting can be many things: a harmless ego boost, a destructive game, or a powerful prelude to seduction.

➤ If you have a fear of flirting, you can get over it if you think in terms of simply connecting with people, not flirting with them.

➤ When you are flirting, know what you want (and are prepared to give) and keep the signals you send clear.

➤ To be successful at seductive flirting, you need to be literate in nonverbal communication, as well as the principles of connecting.

Ring!

Chapter 13

A Seductive Guide to "the Big D": The Date

In This Chapter

➤ "The Three Phases of Evening": Anatomy of a date

➤ Using the date as groundwork for seduction

➤ Keeping the interest—and fun—alive

➤ Ending the date seductively

➤ Rating your date

Now that you've put so much time, thought, and energy into honing your own style of personal allure, and have successfully attracted someone, it's time to hit the playing field and go out on a date. While you've made a great first impression, you now are faced with "fleshing out" the image you've projected so far.

Equally important, it is also time to actually begin the process of deciding whether or not you want to seduce this person. Assuming the answer is yes, you will be using the date to pick up clues that will help you set the stage for a successful seduction. (And assuming the answer is no, you'll still want to end the evening as graciously as possible, with no hurt feelings.)

If this sounds like a lot of work, relax; it's not. The first point to remember is that even if your ultimate goal is a steamy seduction, your aim on the first date should mainly be to have fun. In this chapter, I'll share some secrets on how you can not only have fun, but can use that first date to learn more about this person, in order to begin planning a delicious seduction.

Ask the Love Coach

It's not unusual to experience the jitters before (or during) a first date. The biggest reason people feel anxiety on a date is that they are afraid they will fail to be desirable to the other person, and may ultimately be rejected. Try to concentrate on not becoming attached to any particular outcome, and look at the date as an opportunity to just connect with another person. Practice this technique, and a lot of pressure will be relieved. You'll be much more able to just relax and enjoy yourself, which will go a long way towards making you more seductive.

The Beginning: Getting Off to a Great Start

Before you even arrive at your date's door (or he or she arrives at yours), do a little mental preparation. Remember that you aren't looking at this date as your make-it-or-break-it chance for a long-term relationship, so you're ready to enjoy whatever experiences the two of you share. To keep this perspective real, just remind yourself that you are here primarily to get to know someone new.

The key point to remember is that you want to concentrate on connecting with this person. Remember the connecting principles we talked about in previous chapters? I've recommended practicing these principles with everybody you meet. Well, here's a secret: Practicing them with your date can make your seductiveness quotient go through the roof.

Focus on Your Date Instead of Yourself

To truly connect with another person, you have to focus on that person. Focusing on your date rather than yourself has several seductive benefits:

➤ *It makes you more appealing.* Your date will be flattered by your attention, and will feel he or she is really special to you.

➤ *It makes you more observant.* By focusing on your date, you will be able to pick up clues about this person that will point the way towards successfully seducing him or her.

➤ *It takes your mind off yourself.* Being more concerned with the other person than with the impression you're making has a way of taking the edge off those dating jitters.

So, as you make your "final approach" to actually meeting your date, remind yourself to observe him or her more closely than you are observing yourself. As you greet your date, hold on to the knowledge that you are already succeeding, or you wouldn't be going out in the first place. And, as you look into your date's eyes, notice how pretty they are, instead of fretting about what those eyes might be seeing. You'll be starting out on the right foot for a wonderful evening.

Show Up on Time

Sometimes we let our excitement about a date blur our judgment, and we show up early. Other times, we may allow some distraction to make us lose track of time and we show up late. Neither of these is very seductive.

By showing up on time—not too late and not too early—or being ready when your date arrives, you are saying that you respect this person enough not to waste his or her time. You can start the date off right by making such a simple, clear statement.

Don't Try Too Hard to Impress

Once the date has gotten underway, don't quit focusing on your partner. Beyond simply maintaining the (hopefully favorable) first impression you've made, your date—and you—now have an opportunity to discover the wonderful qualities you each possess, just beneath the surface. But the only way either of you can hope to make these discoveries is to simply relax and be yourselves.

Heart Brakes

One of the biggest allure-killers is the fear that you're not "measuring up" to your date's desires and expectations. By getting so wrapped up in concerns about the impression you're making, you end up coming across as fearful and insecure. Remember that confidence is very seductive, whereas a lack of confidence is a real turn-off.

Heart Brakes

Just as arriving late is a sign of disrespect, so is arriving too early. It is likely that, by showing up early, you will catch your date before he or she is ready to see you—not a great way to start off a first date.

In the first hour or so of a first date, both people tend to feel pressure to get their message across as quickly as possible. There often seems to be the feeling that unless you impress your date as much as possible right off the bat, the encounter will fail. That feeling has probably ruined more dates than any other single factor. Your date will be far more pleased by the knowledge that you are having a good time than by a recounting of all that is wonderful about you. And remember what we've said about people who talk about themselves too much? That's not at all seductive. Altogether too many potentially great relationships have been stopped dead in their tracks by people who were so anxious to impress that they came across as being incredibly self-centered and insecure.

Ask the Love Coach

Always remember that a date is not so much a test of your desirability as it is an opportunity for both of you to decide whether or not you enjoy each other's company. Ask yourself the really important question: Are you enjoying your time together? Or are you just wondering how you're doing? If the answer to the first question is yes, the date—and the relationship—will have a much better chance of being a happy one.

I'm not suggesting that you be coy or reticent. I'm only suggesting that you remember to place your focus on your partner, and maintain a degree of mystery about yourself. A little mystery can be extraordinarily seductive.

Flattery Will Get You Anywhere—or Nowhere at All

All of the great lovers throughout history have known the seductive power of sincere compliments. A few honest compliments can get your date off to a wonderful start. Everybody likes to know they are appreciated and attractive, and complimenting your date is a direct way of letting that person feel appreciated. If she's wearing a really pretty outfit, tell her that you think it looks good on her. If he just got a new haircut, tell him how sharp it looks. Just remember:

➤ *Give honest compliments.* Zero in on the qualities of your date that you really like, and let him or her know you are impressed. If your date has a quick wit, for example, say so. If your date is a snappy dresser, compliment his or her taste. Be generous with your compliments, but keep them realistic. The corollary to this is....

➤ *Don't make up a compliment just to flatter your date.* Your deception will be embarrassingly obvious, and you will appear phony in your date's eyes. Besides, if you have to invent something to flatter your date, why are you even going out with that person in the first place? Find something you really like about your date, and comment on it.

To Be Interesting, Be Interested

I think we've just stumbled across another Love Coach mantra. Being truly interested in your date is just about the most seductive thing you can do. You know how good it makes you feel when somebody is truly interested in what you have to say or what you are about. Your date is no different in this respect. If your date is talking about something and it becomes apparent that he or she has strong feelings on this topic, listen attentively and offer your own reflections. You don't need to agree with everything he or she says, but it is very important that you honor your date's opinions and feelings by accepting the importance he or she ascribes to those ideas.

While many people are good about showing initial interest in the person they're trying to seduce, too many seem to forget to continue to show interest once they're out on a date. They start things off by talking too much about themselves or simply neglecting to ask the other person questions. That's not seductive.

If you remember to concentrate on whatever you find interesting about your date, rather than what you think your date will find interesting about you, that *is* seductive. So relax, focus outward instead of inward, and you and your date will both have a terrific time. The evening will fly by.

During the Date: Keeping It Fun (and Seductive!)

Well, you've been together for a couple of hours now, and you've both been enjoying the newness of each other. Almost without knowing it, you find yourself shifting into a more intimate atmosphere. And no, I don't mean the clothes are starting to come off—at least, I hope not. (More on that in a while.) What is happening is that you both find yourselves sharing little "secrets" about yourselves, little clues that give one another a better indication of what you're each really all about.

It is at this point that you need to be careful. Though you want the other person to know more about you, and you, in turn, want to know more about your date, you also want to keep it light. There are two reasons for this: First, so you can both concentrate on enjoying yourselves, and second, so you can maintain that all-important air of mystery. Here are some do's and don'ts:

1. *Do share stories about some of your favorite experiences, but make sure the stories add to your mystique rather than detract from it.* Seductive people share stories about themselves, but they know there's an art to it. For the reasons given above, you want to keep your story on the light side. And although you don't want to appear boastful, you do want to tell stories that cast you in a favorable light. Perhaps you can strike a middle ground with a humorous tale of a time when you were less than perfect, and the funny things that happened as a result of your own mistakes. You will be communicating that you are secure enough to admit to being human and that you don't have issues with everything that didn't go your way.

2. *Don't unload your entire emotional or romantic history, especially the traumatic parts.* Seductive people know that nothing is less alluring on a first date than hearing a blow-by-blow recounting of someone's love life, especially the parts that are unpleasant. Don't dwell on the past; focus on having a good time right now, with the person who's sitting across the table from you.

Ask the Love Coach

There's a lot of seductive wisdom in the old colloquialism, "Dance with the one who brought ya'." Focus on the person you are with right now, because you aren't out with an old ex; you're out with someone new. Leave the exes—and your issues with them—at home. Or better yet, toss them out entirely. The only "baggage" you should bring with you is the wisdom you've gleaned from your past relationships. Other than that, the only way to focus on the new is to get rid of the old. That way, you'll truly be able to give your new friend a chance.

Always keep in mind that the objective is to make the date fun, while keeping the flames of interest burning. It's really not all that difficult. All that's required is the use of some common sense and honesty.

Are We Having Fun Yet?

Seductive people know there's an old saying pertaining to the issue of fun: You're not bored; you're *boring*. If you are really enjoying yourself on a date, your date is going to feel at least partly responsible, and he or she will feel good about that. Now think about it: Who would you rather be with—a person who seems indifferent to the experience of being out with you, or one who seems to be genuinely enjoying the time you spend with each other? Would you prefer to hang with a person who seems all wrapped up in his or her issues, or someone who can overlook minor inconveniences and have a good time? You know who you'd rather be with. Trust me, your date feels the same way.

If you pay attention, you will inevitably get clues from your date about his or her definition of fun. You may discover you both love the adrenaline rush you get from amusement-park rides, or you both get all warm and fuzzy when you see one of the delightfully sophisticated new children's movies.

Heart Brakes

Nothing turns a date sour as effectively as a person who gets upset over minor annoyances. If a waiter spills water on your good suit, make a joke of it. Ask him if he knows a good dry cleaner and leave a good tip, anyway! Remember two key points: 1) Don't sweat the small stuff 2) It's all pretty much small stuff.

There's Fun, and Then There's Fun

Having fun is, of course, the main point of the first date. If you're observant, however, you can also use these moments of innocent first-date fun to gather clues that will help you plan your delicious seduction of this person. No, you're not going to have sex on the first date, but it's never too early to begin discovering ways to push your date's "hot" buttons.

For example, do you remember the principles of Neuro-Linguistic Programming (NLP), discussed in an earlier chapter? Throughout the afternoon or evening, observe your date and see if you can tell if he or she is visual, auditory, or kinesthetic. Not only can you use these observations when it comes time to actually set the scene for seduction, you can put them to immediate use on the very first date.

If he was blown away by the jazzy soundtrack in the movie you just saw together, take note; you're with a man who is moved by music. Certainly you can envision a seduction scene with similar music playing softly in the background. For now, however, ask him to describe how the jazzy music made him feel, and what it reminded him of. Really listen as he talks, and experience it with him.

If she exclaims in delight at the feel of the soft breeze on her skin as you're sitting in the park, pay attention; you probably have a sensualist on your hands. Think of warm baths and loving massages—someday. Right now, touch her gently from time to time as you're talking; brush her hair away from her face, or run your finger over her arm, as lightly and sweetly as a breeze.

Ask the Love Coach

What if you and your date are attracted to each other, but discover you have virtually no common ground where interests or passions are concerned? Is the date a failure, the seduction doomed? Not necessarily. If you can't seem to find any areas in which you share any enthusiasm, consider doing something neither of you has ever tried before. Perhaps neither of you has ever been to an opera, or a big-band concert, or a tractor pull. Just by doing something new together, you will establish a degree of kinship, based on the sharing of a new adventure. The unknown, while a trifle scary, is also very exciting and can be absolutely seductive. This is a chance to stretch your respective comfort zones and have a wonderful—yes, even seductive—time in the process.

Encourage and participate in your date's expressions of delight, so that from the very beginning, he or she associates you with enchanting experiences. This is a subtle but powerful way to lay the groundwork for a delicious seduction.

Again, it's all about focusing more on your date than on yourself. Not only does this make you more alluring in your date's eyes, it will ultimately make you a better seductress or seducer.

The End? Going Gentle Into That Good Night...

Okay, so you've spent the evening (or afternoon) with this new person, and you've learned more about his or her personality, dislikes, and history. You've completed whichever activity you decided upon, whether it be dinner, the theater, a picnic, tractor pull, or mud wrestling tournament. Now come the big questions. What do you do next? Assuming you want a repeat performance, how can you leave your date with a lingering image that will make him or her want to see you again? How can you end the date on just the right seductive note?

Ask the Love Coach

The end of the first date can be an awkward time, but it doesn't have to be. If you're comfortable with the boundaries you've set regarding intimacy, you shouldn't have any trouble saying good night graciously. A hug or a simple good night kiss, and an acknowledgement that you had a wonderful time, should leave your date with a warm feeling—and you'll both still respect yourselves in the morning.

S-E-X: Don't Jump the Gun, or You Might Shoot Yourself in the Foot

The first rule to remember, both for safety's sake and for the sake of seductiveness, is not to rush into intimacy.

Of course, there's nothing wrong with kissing on the first date. A simple goodnight kiss can be very seductive, especially if it leaves your partner longing for more. Whether it's a kiss on the cheek, a warm brush of your lips against those of your partner, or a lingering mouth-to-mouth exploration, a kiss can be a very warm and pleasant way to end an evening. Simply do what feels comfortable for you both.

But please don't let the action get much sexier than a lingering kiss (which, of course, can be very sexy indeed). I always advise against having sex too early in a relationship, especially on the first date. Besides the obvious danger of sexually transmitted diseases, consider this:

➤ Having sex with someone whom you haven't really gotten to know is a sure-fire way to short-circuit even a potentially steamy relationship. It is only natural that you allow yourself to be quite vulnerable when you have sex with someone. If you don't really know each other very well, however, sharing that vulnerability will usually give rise to some strong doubts—about yourself, the other person, and the new relationship itself. And your partner will probably be having the same doubts. You both may end up so embarrassed about it that you'd just rather forget it ever happened. On the other hand...

➤ By stopping short of a sexual relationship, you effectively heighten the delicious tension that is such a significant part of seductiveness. We're going to go into the art of tension-building in juicy detail in the next section, but for now, suffice it to say this: By keeping the other person wondering what it would be like to have sex with you, you are making the whole process of seduction much more enjoyable for both of you. And there's another beneficial side effect; you are also encouraging his or her interest in you as a person. Even though the sexual desire may be a primary force in causing the person to want to see more of you (no pun intended!), it has the effect of putting the focus on the other aspects of your persona as well. This helps the object of your desire to get to know you even better, and find more about you to like—and, of course, to be seduced by.

Heart Brakes

Beyond the inevitable emotional gamble of having sex early in a relationship, there is the very real danger of contracting a sexually transmitted disease. Even if a person seems nice, or not the "type" to carry such a disease, that certainly is not an accurate measure of his or her physical health. Too many nice people have had their lives forever changed or even ended because they had sex with someone whose disease simply wasn't evident. I ask you to be intelligent and responsible when making choices that can dramatically affect your own life and that of your partner.

Repeat Performance?

If you have found your companion to be charming, attractive, interesting, and all those other delightful qualities that make you feel really excited about being alive (and excited about the prospect of eventually seducing him or her), don't just stand there; let your date know what a great time you've had. You don't necessarily have to come out and say that you would like to see this person again, because you can get the point across quite well in other ways.

For HIS Eyes Only

Men, here's a hot tip for end-of-the-date behavior: Don't make any attempt to kiss her! This is especially effective if (1) you have a reputation as a ladies' man or (2) you feel she's a bit out of your league. It's also important for you to have given her clues during the evening that you actually find her very attractive. While I don't usually advocate playing games with each other, the disparity between your other actions and words, and your failure to even attempt to kiss her good night will leave a woman wondering. Don't just leave her hanging, though; either use the suggestions I gave earlier (that is, trace her lips with your fingertips), or go ahead and ask her out again. The end result will actually be an increase in her interest in you. It's all part of the delicious art of sexual tension, only it goes even deeper than that.

Heart Brakes

NEVER PURSUE SOMEONE WHO IS OBVIOUSLY NOT INTERESTED IN YOU.

➤ *For you women*, a big smile at the end of the date can speak volumes. A light touch on his hand, his cheek, or even his lips can set the idea in his mind that you enjoy his company. It doesn't take any grand gesture to make him feel like a winner, just a few subtle clues. And if he leaves feeling like a winner, he will almost certainly be back.

➤ *For you men*, the same thing goes about the big smile. Let her know what you enjoyed about the time you spent together, and that you think you'd like to see her again, but don't push for a set time or date just yet. A woman who feels truly beautiful at the end of the date with you will probably be more than enthusiastic about seeing you again. As for kissing her, don't push it; do what comes naturally for both of you. In fact, there are some alternatives to kissing that can be very seductive to a woman (also see sidebar). Trace her lips with your fingertips, caress her cheek, and, perhaps, say, "You'll be hearing from me." (And keep that promise.)

Of course, these gestures of delight could very well result in someone bringing up the subject of a second date, and that person may as well be you, right? After all, if there's going to be a seduction, you've got to go out again. So why not go ahead and ask for a second date then and there? The worst your partner can do is say no. And remember, if you avoid asking the person because you're afraid of being rejected, then you are doing your own rejecting. At least, by making an attempt, you stand a chance of getting a yes. You're also displaying confidence, which is very seductive.

If your date doesn't quite say yes, but doesn't give you an unequivocal no, either, maybe he or she is simply undecided. Your partner may well need time to "rate the date." Don't give up. Go home, do your own date rating, and go about your life. If you haven't heard from this person within a week or so, pick up the phone yourself. If he or she still seems to be hedging, it's probably time to start looking for someone else. It makes no sense to waste your time on somebody who just isn't interested in you.

If, however, both of you are interested enough in each other to go out a second time, there is only one more fundamental rule you need to follow: *Have fun!* Remember, the whole purpose of all this effort, of the seduction, and, indeed, of being together in the first place, is to enjoy yourselves. If you keep it honest, and continue to be fully present with each other, the enjoyment will come naturally, and it will be well worth all the effort and uncertainty you have both faced in the process.

Or...Polite Exit?

If you know by the end of the date that you don't want to go out with the person again, be courteous, but clear. I don't care if your date was an insufferable bore, and you spent the entire time wishing you would be abducted by terrorists, just to get away. You owe it to your date—and to yourself—to be as kind as you are honest when you decline the offer for another interaction. Tell the person that you appreciate his or her interest, but you don't feel that the two of you are a match. Don't try to lay blame, and don't feel that you have to put the other person down. It simply didn't work out; you're just different people. Wish the person the best, and go your separate ways.

For HER Eyes Only

Worried because he hasn't called you back after the first date? There are any number of reasons a man doesn't call back, even if he is genuinely interested. Even if both of you had a great time on your date, sometimes a man just has to think about it for a few days. He might even be worried that he'll seem too eager if he calls you back right away. Give him at least a week, and if you haven't heard from him, go ahead and give him a call. Keep it light, and don't put any pressure on him, but let him know that you are still interested. If he simply thought *you* weren't interested, this will show him that you are.

No matter how disastrously incompatible you feel the two of you are, make every effort to end the date on a congenial note. Allow the other person the dignity of leaving with his or her self-esteem intact. (That's what you'd hope someone would do for you, right?)

Ask the Love Coach

The Golden Rule is a wonderful guide to follow, during the date and afterward. Do unto others as you would have them do unto you.

Rate Your Date

Now that you're home, and alone at last, it's time to evaluate your experience. Whether or not you've made a commitment to go out with this person again, I strongly suggest you take at least a few minutes to contemplate your time together. Nobody is asking you to decide right now if this person is your soul mate—but you don't want to seduce, or be seduced by, someone who is completely wrong for you. What you need to do now is pay attention to your gut feelings, beyond whatever feelings of lust this person may have stirred in you.

To put things in perspective, it helps to ask yourself some questions.

So...Just What Are Your Gut Feelings?

I realize it's probably late, and you may be tired, so you don't have to grill yourself tonight. For now, just ask yourself a couple of fundamental questions:

➤ How do I feel after having spent time with this person? Do I feel excited? Happy? Disappointed? Or do I feel uneasy, as if I'd been protecting myself the whole time? Or do I have mixed feelings (or no feelings)?

➤ Do I feel a deep hunger for this person, or did he or she take my appetite away? Do I want to jump this person's bones at the earliest opportunity, or take a long shower to wash his or her presence away?

More than likely, what you feel will be somewhere between any extremes I've listed here. What is important is that you look at how you feel *right now*, right after you've parted company. These immediate feelings will be your most astute guides in proceeding with—or terminating—your new relationship.

Now you can go to bed and get some sleep (but pay attention to your dreams). And then, the next morning, perhaps while you're enjoying your first cup of coffee, review the date in your mind again.

Okay, Now Ask Yourself These Questions

Remember in Part I, when we went into some detail to explore the various elements of seductiveness? You can use these elements as reference points to help you judge the seductiveness potential of your new relationship. Consider your general impressions of how you clicked with your date on these levels:

➤ *Physical chemistry*. Was it sizzle or fizzle? Are you really attracted to this person, or do you just think he or she would be an attractive accessory, making you the envy of all your friends? Does this person really seem to be attracted to you?

➤ *Intellectual compatibility*. Was there mental electricity between the two of you, or just so much static? Do you have compatible interests, at least to the point that you could converse intelligently with each other? Do you feel you're intellectual equals, or do you sense that one of you seriously outranks the other in brain power?

➤ *Emotional attunement.* Did his or her presence feel like a warm, sweet breeze, or just so much hot air? Did you feel good about yourself in this person's presence, or uneasy for some reason? Did you like each other?

➤ *Harmony of spirit.* This may be harder to determine after just one date, unless you read auras, but do pay attention to any feelings you may have—positive or negative—about this person's vibes. Did he or she seem like an ethical and honest person, or did you get the sense that this person was trying to hide something? Again, you don't want to ignore those gut feelings.

Now take a break, and then come back and think about the date some more. (I promise we're almost through with the cross-examination.) Ask yourself these questions:

1. Did we have fun together?
2. Was there powerful physical chemistry between us?
3. Did we treat each other respectfully?
4. Did we touch each other in a tender, caring way?
5. Did we genuinely seem to like each other?
6. Did I feel good about myself while I was with this person (and did that person seem to feel good about him- or herself too)?
7. Does this person seem to be free of obvious critical flaws, such as addictions or a violent temper?
8. Would I like to go out with this person again as soon as possible?

But Enough About You—What About Your Date?

If you have decided you want to continue the relationship and progress toward seduction, it's time now to return your focus to your date. A truly seductive person will take the time to reflect not just on his or her own feelings, but on what he or she learned about the other person. Review the evening, and ponder on the clues you picked up about your date. Ask yourself:

➤ What have I learned about this person? What are his or her likes and dislikes? What is his or her idea of fun? How can I make our dates more fun for this person, so he or she will associate me with good times?

➤ What kind of cues does he or she seem to respond to most favorably: visual, auditory, or kinesthetic? How can I best appeal to this person's senses, in order to create seductive experiences that will make him or her long for more?

You can't possibly hope to learn everything there is to learn about a person after one date, but if you've kept your eyes and ears open, you'll have picked up some very useful clues that will help you refine your approach, and make the seduction all the more delicious. Keep on looking for more clues as you get to know the person better; the more you learn, the better a seducer or seductress you will be.

Whether or not a long-term relationship is your goal, you do need to take some time to do some thinking during the interval between the first date and...well, whatever comes next. If your date passed the tests in this chapter, and if you have paid attention to what you've learned about your date, the two of you may well be on your way to a deliciously seductive experience. So pour yourself another cup of coffee, and allow yourself the delight of fantasizing about whatever (or whomever) comes next!

The Least You Need to Know

➤ Even if your ultimate goal is a steamy seduction, your aim on the first date should mainly be to have fun.

➤ The best cure for date anxiety is to focus on the other person, instead of on the impression you're making.

➤ Use your first date to begin picking up clues about what turns your partner on; these observations will help you set the stage for a delicious seduction.

➤ Kissing on the first date is okay, if both of you are comfortable with it, but try to avoid getting physically intimate too early in the relationship.

➤ If you're interested in going out with someone again, you should let the person know, but if he or she is definitely not interested in a repeat performance, don't waste time in pursuit.

➤ If you're not interested in going out with someone again, be honest but be kind. Remember the Golden Rule.

➤ No one expects you to decide if a person is your soul mate after only one date, but you should ask yourself some fundamental questions to determine whether or not you want to continue the relationship to the seduction stage. You don't want to seduce, or be seduced by, someone who is completely wrong for you.

Part 3
A Night to Remember

You have become the alluring seductress or seducer you've always wanted to be, you've attracted the person whom you think you want to seduce, and now it's coming down to the wire. We'll begin this part with a chapter on determining whether or not this person really is a good sex partner for you. (Don't get into bed with your partner before answering the questions in this chapter.)

Next we'll explore how to make the most of that delicious period of tension leading up to lovemaking. Seduction, after all, is not just an act; it is a process—and I'll share some tips and techniques to help you savor every moment. Then we'll discuss the anxieties and fears you may have as the time of that first lovemaking approaches. And then at last, in the chapters you've been waiting for, we'll talk in delicious detail about using seduction to bring you to that long-awaited explosive lovemaking.

If you've chosen your partner wisely and well, and you open yourself up to learning all you can from your new lover, it's very possible that the explosive chemistry between you will continue long past that "night to remember."

Chapter 14

Should We or Shouldn't We?

In This Chapter

➤ Engaging your brain for thinking as well as fantasizing

➤ Safe sex as part of that sweet seduction

➤ More good reasons not to have sex too soon

➤ Tough questions to ask while you still have your clothes on

➤ Peeking into the future

Since this is a book about seduction, the underlying assumption is that, sooner or later, you're going to end up in bed with that attractive person you've had your eyes on. If you've stuck it out with me to this point, I can assume that you are acting with integrity, with the goal of creating a seduction experience that will be pleasurable and enriching for both you and your partner.

This is precisely why you need to do some intense soul-searching before the fact. At the same time you are plotting your delicious seduction, you also need to be asking yourself, and your partner, some probing questions (no pun intended). Even if you're not planning on spending the rest of your life with this person, give careful thought to what you intend to do. After all, you are about to embark on the most physically intimate act possible between two human beings. Not only does this involve potential physical risks, but there are significant emotional concerns as well. Despite what you've seen in the movies, in real life you can't just fall into bed with someone and assume that the details will take care of themselves.

Consider this, then, the reality-check chapter. I promise we'll get to the juicy stuff, beginning in the next chapter, but please don't skip this one.

Sex in the '90s and Beyond: A Cautionary Note

It's a sad fact of life that when we think about sex these days, we have to consider the growing danger of sexually transmitted diseases, or STDs. A few decades ago, before STD became the acronym of choice, the biggest sex-related hazard besides getting "PG" was catching VD. Syphilis and gonorrhea were the most common of these venereal diseases, and were curable if caught in time. The freewheeling '70s brought another affliction (that is, besides disco and leisure suits): genital herpes. Herpes, unfortunately, is incurable, although symptoms can be brought under control, and the condition isn't fatal.

But then the '80s hit, and with them came ominous reports of a new disease. This one has no cure either, and it is deadly. While recent research has led to life-prolonging drug protocols, an actual cure for AIDS is probably still years away. And I don't mean to sound pessimistic, but if some of the doomsaying experts are correct, we can look forward in the future to the rise of more STDs, as yet unnamed.

All the more reason, then, to exercise both caution and candor with your potential partner. If things are really beginning to heat up between the two of you, now is the time to stop, look, and consider the following:

➤ *Have you discussed AIDS and other STDs to your mutual satisfaction?* Given all of the hazards we've just discussed, I'm astonished that so many couples *don't* talk to each other about STDs. You might think this problem is restricted to younger people, who traditionally behave as if they don't take their own mortality seriously. But many older couples are reluctant to face this issue, as well. Some are simply embarrassed, in which case I tell them, "If you're embarrassed to talk about safe sex with someone, why do you feel at ease having sex with that person?" Some people say they're afraid of offending the other person by even implying the person might be diseased. Since there has been such intense publicity about these diseases, I'd venture to

Heart Brakes

Most discussions of sexually transmitted diseases, or STDs, emphasize AIDS because it is fatal. But this doesn't mean you can afford to ignore the possibility—or consequences—of other STDs. For example, Hepatitis B is easily spread through sexual contact, and it is on the rise. This disease can lead to cirrhosis of the liver or liver cancer. (Hepatitis C is even more insidious; many carriers don't even have symptoms.) And even though herpes, chlamydia, and genital warts may not pose a death sentence, they can have very serious consequences and adversely affect the rest of your life (not to mention put a real damper on sex). In the United States, about 40 million people currently have some sort of sexually transmitted disease, and each year there are about 12 million new cases. Anyone who is considering having sex needs to be aware of STDs. Consult your health-care practitioner for information on testing.

guess that your partner is as concerned about this issue as you, and will actually be grateful you brought it up. And for those who *are* offended by this subject, I offer the reminder that even the so-called "nicest" people can and do get AIDS and other STDs. Still other people have told me that they don't get into safe-sex discussions because, they rationalize, their partner isn't the promiscuous type. To these people, I say, "Okay, maybe your partner hasn't been promiscuous. Maybe he or she has only had one sexual partner before you. But what if the first partner *was* promiscuous, or was an intravenous drug user?" The bottom line is, you can't let embarrassment, fear of awkwardness, or mistaken assumptions prevent you from looking out for your health. Don't enter into a sexual relationship with someone until you feel safe about this issue.

➤ *Have you each been tested for STDs, particularly for HIV?* HIV, or Human Immuno-deficiency Virus, is the virus that causes AIDS. There are a number of facilities that provide tests for HIV. The cost varies, depending upon whether it is a private clinic or a publicly funded facility. Call your local health department for more information. If you're particularly worried about confidentiality, there is an over-the-counter home HIV test available now for about $50.00.

Even so, most experts recommend that HIV testing be supplemented by counseling, particularly if the test results are *positive*. Remember, though, even a *negative* test doesn't necessarily mean that you're home free. Almost all people develop HIV antibodies within three months of infection, but with some people, it can take up to six months. If you engaged in behavior that can transmit the virus during the six months just before your test, you may be infected but still test negative because your body may not yet have produced antibodies. To be sure, you must be retested at least six months after you last engaged in behavior that can transmit HIV.

➤ *Have you decided on the logistics of safe sex between the two of you?* Condoms are often lauded as the best defense against STDs, but they are not foolproof. It's true that latex condoms do offer a measure of protection. Even so, condoms can break. Furthermore, some people are allergic to latex or the spermicides that come with certain types of condoms. I can't specifically recommend any one method; I can only advise you to discuss all safe-sex issues with each other and, if

Heart Brakes

A *positive* HIV test result does not necessarily mean you have AIDS at that point, but it does mean you will most likely develop AIDS.

A *negative* result simply means that no HIV antibodies were found in your blood, which usually means you are not infected. Even so, this does not mean you are immune to HIV; nobody is. You still need to practice safe sex.

Heart Brakes

Condoms are not necessarily the sexual answer to a suit of armor. They can slip off, break, or even lose their effectiveness if they are past the expiration date on the package (*always* check this). In addition, studies have shown that the AIDS virus can penetrate condoms made of lambskin.

For HER Eyes Only

We often think of men as being the ones who balk at safe-sex precautions, such as condom use. But let's be fair, ladies. I've talked to hundreds of men and women about this issue, and I've found that, in many instances, the woman doesn't even bring the matter up in the first place. That's because she automatically assumes, without even asking, that her partner is going to be displeased; or she finds such talk unromantic or unpleasant; or she may even assume it's the man's job to deal with it. Remember, it's your body, and there is nothing even remotely romantic or pleasurable about a sexually transmitted disease or an unwanted pregnancy. If he is resistant, or doesn't want to talk about it, *you don't belong in bed with him*. Find someone who cares as much about your welfare as he does his own pleasure.

necessary, with a health-care professional. That way, you can come up with a mutually agreeable protection plan.

Besides having a frank dialogue with your partner, I recommend that you stay as informed as you possibly can about these matters. Keep yourself current on the latest health reports in the media. (The Internet is a wonderful information source for up-to-date health matters.) There's plenty of information on safe sex out there, so educate yourself, and discuss it with your partner *before* you get caught up in the heat of passion.

Remember, if you don't feel comfortable discussing these topics with your partner, you might want to question why you *do* feel comfortable having sex with this person. And if you're worried that all this planning will somehow diminish the experience, it won't. On the contrary, the realization that the two of you are looking out for each other's welfare will make the seduction all that much sweeter.

When More Than Your Imagination Is Fertile

Have you discussed the possibility of pregnancy and birth control? For some older couples, or couples in which one partner has undergone sterilization, this won't be necessary. But for everybody else, the same rules that apply to STDs apply here: Use caution and candor.

Men, you can't assume she's on the Pill or taking care of contraception in some other way. Ask her. And women, don't wait for him to ask; you bring up the subject. With the wide variety of contraception options available, and the wealth of information that is equally available, there's simply no excuse for ignoring this important matter.

Laura thought she had it all under control. A successful investment banker in her late 30s, she had been off the Pill and celibate for a couple of years when she began dating Steve, a lawyer who was a few years younger. She didn't want to go back on the Pill, but felt confident that she knew her own body well enough to know when her "safe" times were. Since Steve had an aversion to condoms, Laura used contraceptive foams or suppositories.

One afternoon, however, she and Steve had a little too much champagne after celebrating his triumph in a tough case, and they ended up making love on a couch in his office. They used no contraception, and it really wasn't a safe time for Laura; however, she shrugged it off, rationalizing that her fertility was probably on the decline anyway. A few weeks and one missed period later, Laura was gasping at the positive result on her home pregnancy test. A visit to her doctor confirmed what the home test had indicated, and now she and Steve were faced with a choice.

Laura was glad to have choices, but was still very distressed over the situation. Neither abortion nor adoption were options she felt she could live with, so she decided to have the baby and raise it herself. Steve wasn't ready for marriage, and besides, he really wasn't "the one" for her. Steve did, however, agree to pay child support and to be part of his child's life as much as possible.

Granted, the consequences could have been much worse if Laura had been very young, or hadn't had any money, or Steve hadn't been willing to participate financially and emotionally. Nevertheless, there were consequences—for Laura, for Steve, and for their child. These could easily have been avoided if Laura and Steve had not been careless about birth control.

When Lust Hits, Go Slow

Even after you've addressed the questions of STDs and birth control, there are still several other matters to consider when deciding that all-important question, "Should we or shouldn't we?"

Again, you need to take your time in making this decision.

In a previous chapter, we mentioned that one good reason for taking your time is that it gives you both an opportunity to build the tension. Of course, there are many other reasons to wait. To begin with, when you let yourself get confused by passion or blinded by lust, there's a danger that you will either enter into a sexual relationship with the wrong person, or with the right person at the wrong time. Either one of these possibilities can have serious consequences for your happiness.

The Wrong Person...

Sexual desire can be very deceptive; when you're overcome with it, you can easily be blinded to a person's imperfections and even a person's critical flaws. Unfortunately, once you've established a sexual bond with someone, you've created a link that could be permanent. Remember in Chapter 1 where we said that seduction has lasting effects? Sex, for better or worse, utterly changes the dynamics of a relationship. It has been said that sex is the glue that keeps relationships together. Unfortunately, it can also be the epoxy that keeps you bonded to someone long after you've decided you want the relationship to end.

...Or the Right Person at the Wrong Time?

Having sex with someone before you are really ready can spoil the relationship, even if the two of you might have been truly compatible. I've counseled many people who have made this mistake. Their story is always a variation on the same theme: What began as a passionate interlude ended in awkwardness, self-consciousness, remorse, and doubt. Both sexes suffer, each in his or her own way:

➤ Women may find themselves unable to have an orgasm. This leads some women to fake it in order to keep their partners from feeling they're less-than-adequate lovers.

➤ Men may have difficulty getting an erection, even though they're very attracted to the woman they're with. This leads to feelings of inadequacy, and often causes the woman to have doubts about her attractiveness (which is usually such a sensitive issue for women anyway).

Heart Brakes

Sex can keep a good relationship going through the tough times, but it can also keep a bad relationship from ending, long after it has stopped being good. Keep in mind that, for better or for worse, having sex with a person will create a bond between the two of you. Choose your partner(s) carefully.

Unfortunately, people who scarcely know each other are not inclined to drop back a yard or two and honestly discuss what's on their minds. Instead of afterglow, couples in the throes of the sex-too-soon syndrome are left with a list of unspoken fears: What does he/she really think of me? Did I perform up to his/her expectations? If he/she doesn't want to see me again, does that mean that I didn't perform well, or that I'm just not desirable enough?

It's unlikely that these two people will want to discuss these fears with the person who seems to be the very source of their discomfort, so they withdraw from each other. Each person's withdrawal feeds into the other person's fears, making that person withdraw even more—until that seedling of a relationship has shriveled up and died. That's why I recommend waiting until you really know someone before jumping into bed.

Heart Brakes

By having sex with someone before you're really ready, you can not only destroy the opportunity to build a wonderful relationship, you can end up cheating yourself (and your partner) out of some really remarkable sex.

So...How Can I Tell If This Is the Right Person?

I have devised a few questions to give you a better idea of whether or not the person you want to seduce is someone you *should* be having sex with. Some of the questions will look familiar, because they appeared in the "Rate Your Date" section in Chapter 13. But now that you are moving ever closer to having sex with this person, you need to ask them of yourself again. Review all the questions below, and answer them honestly. By doing so, you will develop a clearer picture of what your prospective lover is like, and you'll also get a better idea of your own needs.

If even one of your answers is "no," then you seriously need to reconsider your plans to seduce this person. On the other hand, if you just don't know the answers at this point, you simply need to take more time to get to know the person. In any case, the time to review this list is *now*. Some questions simply are not best answered with one's feet in the air!

➤ *Is this a person who you want to become more like?* When you have sex with someone, you are exchanging more than body fluids. You also exchange *energy*. No, I'm not going off on a metaphysical tangent here. The truth is, as you become more intimate with another person, you become more alike. You pick up aspects of each other's personalities, some of each other's pet phrases or cherished opinions, even some of each others' habits (good or bad). Maybe this is why people often comment that couples who have been together for a long time even begin to look alike. At any rate, in ways both subtle and obvious, you will become more like the other person, and vice versa. If you don't like the idea of becoming more like this person, you might pause to consider this.

➤ *Do you feel this person would be a suitable partner for your sister, brother, or best friend?* This one has been a real litmus test for several clients and friends of mine. It's definitely a question that compels you to look at your partner from a different perspective than you may be used to. And, should your answer be "no," ask yourself: "If this person isn't good enough for someone I really care about, why is he or she good enough for me?"

➤ *Is there genuine physical chemistry between the two of you, or does one of you look upon the other as just another trophy?* I assume that you wouldn't be spending your time and energy becoming a delicious seducer or seductress just for the sake of making your friends gasp with envy when they see that *Baywatch*-babe lookalike or that handsome hunk on your arm. Similarly, I would hope that your partner isn't using you for such a shallow purpose. Don't misunderstand me; there's nothing wrong with feeling a little surge of pride in the fact that your partner is so obviously attractive to others; but this pride should be a pleasant byproduct of a relationship that is based on genuine—and mutual—passion.

Ask the Love Coach

While most of us condemn the idea of using another person as an accessory to define ourselves, the truth is that we all do it to some extent. We may not do it consciously or with manipulative intentions, but we all find ourselves attracted to people who make us appear closer to our ideal image, just by being around them. The most blatant examples are the striking blonde that many men want to have on their arms, or the "bad boy" that so many women seem to pursue. There's nothing wrong with feeling a little proud of your partner, as long as you're not using the person solely to bolster your self-image.

➤ *Do you feel attraction on other levels besides the physical?* Are you intellectually attracted to this person? Do you truly like him or her? Do you also feel emotionally secure when you're around this individual? For example, do you get the feeling that any confidentiality will be respected, and that it's safe to display your vulnerability to this person? Do you feel protective toward this individual and want to touch him or her in a tender and caring way as well as a passionate one? Does he or she feel the same way toward you? These questions are very important, because even if you're not looking for your life mate at this point, you don't want to seduce someone you don't like and respect, or for whom you feel no tenderness.

➤ *Is this a person whose company you could enjoy without having sex?* In fact, would you have this person as a friend if you knew you would *never* have a sexual relationship? Of course, if you're in one of those Harry-met-Sally situations and have been friends for a long time before becoming lovers, you already know the answer to this question. But even if this person has been a romantic prospect from the time you first met, you want your relationship to have a solid basis of friendship as well as passion.

➤ *Does this person appear to be free of critical flaws?* Sometimes it seems there's a fine line between a charming quirk and a genuine flaw. The difference is that while a quirk may become a mere annoyance once familiarity sets in, a critical flaw can be a serious threat to your happiness (or even to your life). That's why it's important to avoid becoming sexually involved with someone who has a critical flaw. Some of the more obvious critical flaws are addiction to alcohol or other drugs; rage or violent tendencies; or criminal behavior. Other flaws, perhaps less dramatic but equally serious, include immaturity, irresponsibility, or unavailability—either emotionally or legally (the person is married). Do yourself a favor and stay away from anybody who has critical flaws, or who in any way doesn't seem right for you. Remember, you can't change this person—you can't cure the addict's addiction, you can't persuade the drug dealer to turn away from a life of crime, and you can't make your married lover leave his or her spouse if your lover doesn't want to. A relationship with a person who has a critical flaw is a dead end.

Heart Brakes

Trust is a very important part of seduction. If you don't feel you have a solid basis of friendship with the object of your desire, you'll really miss out on some of the best seduction there is.

Ask the Love Coach

When Tricia found out her boyfriend Kyle was married, she was devastated. Sure, there had been signs along the way that he was hiding something, but she had brushed them aside because he was so attractive. By the time she knew the truth, she had fallen in love with him. Nevertheless, Tricia knew that breaking up with him was the right thing to do. The problem was that she was always stymied in her efforts by Kyle's emotional or sexual manipulation. For nearly a year she was sustained by his earnest and tearful promises that he would leave his wife as soon as he possibly could.

Finally, with coaching, Tricia found the strength to leave Kyle for good. The last she heard, he was involved in yet another passionate affair, and still hadn't left his wife. "I squandered a year of my life on this man," Tricia said. "But I guess I got off easy, because some women I know go on for years with their married lovers, living on false hopes, and wasting their lives away."

Don't get sexually involved with a person who is unavailable for *any* reason, or who has any other critical flaws.

Enjoy the Moment, But Don't Forget to Look Ahead

Let's say your partner (and you) have passed all of the tests. Do the clothes start flying off now? Well, not so fast; I've still got a few questions for you. Whether or not a permanent commitment is in the cards, you need to look beyond that glorious night of passion you are planning. After the seduction, what's next? How will the two of you feel about each other and about yourselves? Will your morning-after experience be champagne brunch or coyote love? What do you and your partner hope to gain from the relationship, besides a good romp? Might this relationship actually have a future?

Nobody can predict the future with 100 percent accuracy, but you can certainly come up with a working version, based on what you know about yourself and your prospective lover. We're going to discuss "the future" in more detail later on in this book, but it's never too early to begin thinking about it. Ask yourself (and your partner) the following questions, and pay attention to your gut feelings. Questions 1 and 2 are particularly important, because if the two of you have radically differing expectations, that can spell big trouble. You might feel somewhat uncomfortable with questions 3 through 6, but don't let that stop you. A little honesty at this point can mean the difference between afterglow and after burn.

1. What am I expecting from this relationship (beyond a good time in bed)?

2. What is my partner expecting from this relationship (beyond a good time in bed)?

3. Will he/she still like me afterwards?

4. Will I still like him/her afterwards?

5. Will I still like myself?

6. Will my partner still like himself/herself?

The Bottom Line: Choose with Care

Things may have been simpler in the old days, when the only officially sanctioned sex took place within marriage. Nowadays, going to bed with somebody no longer necessarily means a lifetime commitment. Even so, I believe sex is far too important to be entered into frivolously, and choosing a sexual partner is not to be taken lightly. If you want your seduction experience to be truly delicious and sweet, you must take time to consider the wisdom of your choice—before you abandon yourself to passion. As artist and writer Kent Nerburn wrote, "Choose carefully and tenderly. Touch has a memory of its own." It does indeed, and if you are mindful of your choices, that memory will be one of perpetual delight.

The Least You Need to Know

➤ Even if you're not expecting a lifelong commitment, there are many reasons to think carefully before having sex with someone.

➤ Don't have sex with anyone until the two of you have discussed AIDS and other sexually transmitted diseases, and have come up with a mutually agreeable protection plan.

➤ Don't have sex without addressing the issue of contraception, if applicable.

➤ Being blinded by lust can cause you to have sex with someone who's wrong for you, or it can ruin a relationship with someone who would have been good for you.

➤ Don't go to bed with someone unless you feel something more than physical lust for that person. You may not be in love, but you should feel intellectually attracted to and emotionally safe with this individual.

➤ Whether or not you are seeking a long-term relationship, you do need to think beyond the seduction, so you'll have an idea of where the relationship is going.

Chapter 15

Setting the Stage for Seduction

In This Chapter

➤ Building the tension with seductive fantasy

➤ Tantalize, don't terrorize

➤ A vacation for which you don't need a travel agent

➤ Hints for her

➤ Hints for him

You may be the most seductive, alluring human ever to walk the earth, but if you don't get your partner thinking of you in seductive terms, you might well end up in that "platonic purgatory" we spoke of earlier. Remember, the brain is the most powerful erogenous zone we have. It only follows that touching this zone with just the right balance of suggestiveness and restraint will elevate the delicious tension that is building between the two of you.

In this chapter, we'll look at some simple things you can do to inspire your partner to see you in a sensuous light as you move closer to your first sexual encounter with each other. We will look at the art of using little tricks—without trickery—to let your partner see how attractive and desirable you really are, and to ensure that you have a firm place in his or her fantasies.

I Had This Dream About You...

James and Donna are sitting across the table from each other in a quiet little restaurant. The appetizer of steamed artichoke and drawn lemon butter has just arrived.

James plucks the first petal, dipping it thoughtfully into the delightfully pungent liquid, and draws it across his teeth, savoring its taste and texture. Swallowing, he smiles as he begins to speak.

"I had the most delightful dream last night…yes, you were in it. As a matter of fact, you were at its very center. And no, it wasn't that kind of dream! Would you like me to tell you about it?"

He takes another petal from the artichoke, the silence hanging heavily as he absorbs its flavor. Finally, he speaks. "We were in a place I'd never seen, but it looked like a villa somewhere on the Mediterranean. There were these beautiful Renaissance paintings on all the walls, which were covered with this very intricate gilded wallpaper. Statues were everywhere.

"We entered what I assumed to be our suite, and it was absolutely breathtaking. A basket, filled with succulent-looking fruit, sat on the table in the foyer. The windows were opened wide, and a soft breeze was making the gauze curtains billow gently. We looked at each other and just smiled. It seemed like we were completely immersed in this place that was so unfamiliar, yet, at the same time, very comfortable.

"Then, it seemed like we fast-forwarded, until we were in the most exquisite bathroom, actually a suite of its own, and you were sitting naked in a huge marble tub. You were almost entirely covered with bubbles. I took a pitcher from the little stand by the tub, and poured warm water over your head. You closed your eyes as the water flowed over you, and I sat mesmerized, as the bubbles ran down your body.

"I picked up a pitcher filled with a shampoo that smelled like sweet coconut. Not the artificial smelling stuff you can get at the drugstore. This smelled like fresh coconut. I was almost tempted to taste it, it smelled so delicious. Anyway, I worked it between my hands, and began to massage it into your hair. You sighed as I worked the foam into your scalp, and it was uncanny, I could actually feel the smooth texture of your wet hair. I rarely have dreams that are so vivid and detailed, but in this one, I could see, feel, hear, and smell everything. Anyway, I spent this delightfully long time shampoo-ing your hair, and I really loved watching you, because you seemed to be enjoying it so thoroughly.

"When I picked up the pitcher again and rinsed the lather from your hair, the last of the bubbles were washed from your body. I just sat there, drinking in the vision, until I looked into your eyes again. It seemed like your smile was coming, not just from your lips, but from your eyes, from every part of you. We looked into each other's eyes for what seemed like hours, speaking, but not speaking, if you know what I mean. Then I woke up, and you were nowhere to be seen. I have to admit, that was a letdown. I guess I just assumed that, as real as the dream had been, you would be there, lying next to me. It was over an hour before I could get back to sleep."

The above scenario was based on a real dream, as told to one of my clients by a real (and very poetic) man. Naturally, this is not a script for you to recite to your date. Remember that the core of delicious seduction is absolute integrity. But the way in which this dream was presented can serve as a guide that you can use to turn your own dreams and fantasies into elements that plant and nurture the seeds of desire. Let's take a look at these elements, and review some guidelines for sharing your own delicious dreams or fantasies.

➤ *Knock before entering.* First, and foremost, you need to make certain your partner feels completely safe with you, or he or she will not be able to let go enough to be entranced by the images you describe. You will notice that early on in the preceding dialogue, the dreamer asked whether the listener was interested in hearing about the dream, followed by assurances that it wasn't "that kind" of dream. Of course, it *was* "that kind" of dream, but it was presented in a non-threatening manner.

➤ *Fantasy, like spice, should enhance and inspire, not overwhelm.* As the description of the dream progressed, there were subtle hints at sexual interest, yet no outright mention of it. The dreamer acknowledged that the other person was naked, and described how the bubbles were being rinsed away, leaving the person completely exposed. There was no overt talk of the details, yet the listener was guided to think of what it would be like to be so completely exposed. The image is "fleshed out" (pardon the pun) only enough to inspire the listener to begin his or her own fantasy. This is a much more powerful aphrodisiac than a detailed description, because you have enlisted your partner's mind in your seduction.

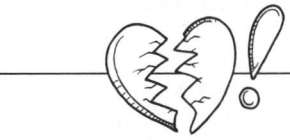

Heart Brakes

Remember: A dream (or fantasy) in which you do not feel safe *is* a nightmare. Keep it light!

➤ *The most powerful statements fall between the lines.* The dream goes on to speculate about the desires and feelings that may be growing in both partners, yet does so with absolute subtlety. The point that the dreamer made about looking with relish upon his partner's naked body is clear, yet flows seamlessly into the statements made by his protracted eye contact. It is a whisper, speaking much more clearly than a scream.

➤ *Let your date see the desire that is building in you.* As the dream concludes, the dreamer lets the other person know how pleasant the shared experience was, and how much its passing was mourned. This tells the other person that the dreamer wants more, yet provides the safety net of "it was only a dream," should the intimacy prove threatening or more intense than he or she is comfortable with.

Ask the Love Coach

Let your partner fill in the blanks of your fantasy or dream. Too much detail, and it will be like watching a movie instead of participating in a relationship. You want your partner involved.

The dream scenario that opens this chapter is a good example of how to involve a partner, perhaps to the point of getting him or her to fantasize about you, too. The man began by enlisting his date's permission to relate his dream to her. Once she gave the go-ahead, he provided just enough descriptive detail to make the dream seem real, pique her interest and get her imagination fired up.

Did it work? In spades. "What he left unsaid was just as powerful as the things he said," declared Donna, my client whose date had shared this dream. "He really made me feel that I was in the scene he described, and afterwards, I couldn't stop fantasizing about him. Let's say it added a delicious dimension to our seduction."

By setting the stage in the description of your dream, you are inviting your partner to become a participant in his or her own fantasies. By approaching a potentially erotic encounter, yet leaving it hanging, you have allowed your partner to complete the scene in his or her own imagination. You will have created a fantasy that is perfectly tailored to your partner's deepest desires, and is therefore incredibly powerful. You will also have allowed your partner to have some space, so that he or she doesn't feel crowded or intruded upon. This is the perfect setting for a seduction, achieving that delicate balance between danger and comfort that spells eroticism.

Welcome to Fantasy Island

Most of us, no matter how reserved or conservative we are, have fantasies that linger in the back of our minds, taunting us when we allow our thoughts to wander. We typically keep these fantasies hidden from all but our most intimate companions. But as we've just seen with the dream scenario above, the sharing of such private thoughts—or the suggestion that you may be a part of the other person's fantasy—can be a powerful means for connecting with the person you want to seduce.

The most powerful tool at your disposal here is subtlety. You don't want to give your partner a point-by-point description of a fantasy involving the two of you. It is better to plant a seed of an idea, and allow your partner to fill in the blanks according to his or her own desires.

Say the two of you are out on a particularly beautiful evening, and the chemistry seems to be there between you, but is, as yet, undefined. You look up at the night sky and state, almost absent-mindedly, how wonderful it would be to have a sailboat and a month's vacation time. Your partner's first question would likely be to ask you where you would go. You could simply smile and answer, "Everywhere. Want to come along?" Your partner would naturally be intrigued. As you describe the details of your fantasy, you go just far enough to get the other person involved.

"I can see the sky, bluer than I've ever seen, with only a wisp of clouds. We sail into a deserted bay, drop anchor, and swim to shore. Once we get to the beach, we fall down on the warm sand to catch our breath. The sun seems to be shining only for us, and this wide expanse of beach feels like a whole other world, where we are the only inhabitants. Then I would lean over and kiss the nape of your neck, and taste the saltiness of the water on you." Before you know it, you have your partner fantasizing about spending time in some tropical paradise with you, alone, nearly naked, and being tenderly kissed. Once again, you have made your partner an active participant in his or her own delicious seduction, with the primary erogenous zone—the brain—providing guideposts to the alluring images that nobody outside his or her mind can equal.

Bringing your partner along on such a "fantasy journey" requires you to do only three things:

1. Pay attention to the clues you are given as to his or her own desires.

2. Use a little creativity in painting the mental picture.

3. Always be subtle in your descriptions.

Done properly, this can pave the way for even greater fantasies being brought to reality in your relationship.

Secrets for the Seductress

There is a widespread notion that seduction is much easier for a woman than for a man. Billy Crystal once said that the difference between men and women on a date is that men spend the evening wondering if they're going to "get lucky," while women already know. While this may, on

Heart Brakes

When you share a hidden fantasy with your partner, be sure that you're not giving out information that he or she isn't ready to accept. If the fantasy is a sexual one, don't go into explicit details. If it is a romantic fantasy, give enough information to let the person know you're interested, but not so much that he or she feels you're looking for a premature commitment.

For HER Eyes Only

A feather can have more impact than a baseball bat. You can let him know you're thinking about him, but don't always tell him *what* you're thinking.

the surface, seem to ring true, neither men's nor women's attitudes toward sex are quite this simplistic, as you probably know from reading the previous chapters in this book. The very act of seduction carries as many risks for women as it does for men.

The delicious seduction of the new millennium, however, isn't about shallow, meaningless encounters. It's about two people sharing more than bodily fluids. It's about actually touching each other on multiple levels.

Toward this lofty goal, there are many things you women can do to inspire a man to think of you in a seductive way, yet still maintain his interest in you as a person. The first rule is: Always be subtle. To subtlety, add a bit of spontaneity, visual appeal, and presentation, and you've got a seductive mix that will have his mouth watering for you.

Subtlety: Letting Him Fill in the Blanks

Just as I described in the dream at the beginning of the chapter, you can let your partner know that you see him in a sexual way, without beating him over the head with details. You can relate your own dream, or perhaps give him a very brief description of a fantasy you have, leaving the delicious details to his imagination. Done with the appropriately light touch, this can be a more powerful aphrodisiac to the man than the most blatant X-rated narrative.

Here's an example. Say the two of you are watching a movie, and there is a scene that tickles your fancy. In the movie *Sirens,* there is a scene where a very proper young woman is tied to a tree by three of her playful friends, and must wait for a supposedly blind hired hand to untie her. To some women—and men—the fantasy of a woman being gently but firmly restrained (with no malicious intent, of course) is very exciting. Imagine what your date's reaction would be if, while watching such a scene, you elicited a soft, yet obviously excited, sigh.

His mind would immediately begin racing, with thoughts of you in such a predicament and with himself as the hired hand (who is, of course, not really blind). Most men are so visually oriented that they could play this scene out to its conclusion, with the two of you making passionate love in the shade of the tree. With a simple sigh, you have elicited his tendencies toward fantasy.

By using such a subtle approach, you have gotten his motor running, while still maintaining your own safe boundaries. If he doesn't seem amused by your little outburst, you can simply say that the situation seemed really frightening, and you're off the hook. On the other hand, if he takes your cue, you will get your point across in a subtle manner, without having to go into a long description of the eroticism you saw in the scene.

There are many other ways that you can enlist the man's help in creating your own aura of seductiveness. With the right words (and the right touch) from you, he will be a very willing participant in his own sweet seduction.

Ask the Love Coach

Don't forget that a sensuous touch can be very effective in getting a man's mind moving in the direction you want. Even the slightest touch on his arm will make him keenly aware of your physical presence. If you casually touch his thigh while the two of you are talking, it will almost certainly cause him to think about how your fingertips would feel on other sensitive spots. Yet you will have left alive the element of mystery, and he'll be wondering if you are aware of the thoughts you are inspiring, or just casually making an innocent gesture.

Spontaneity: Being a One-Woman Surprise Party

Another way you can bring a man to desire you is by simply being spontaneous, even in a completely nonsexual way. To be ready to jump into a new experience, excited by what it has to offer you, tells a man that you are hungry for life, and that you won't be a wet blanket who needs convincing before attempting something new. Most people crave spontaneity in their lives. With this in mind, you can direct some of that craving toward yourself, just by being open to new things.

Of course, you have a right to set boundaries, and to avoid doing something that makes you feel unsafe or that otherwise makes you feel uncomfortable. Ask yourself, honestly, if the situation is really risky, or if it's just new to you. Find the perfect balance between your good judgment and your desire for fun, and you'll have a wonderful time.

Not surprisingly, this spontaneity principle also extends to sex (more on that in Chapter 17), and to expressions of affection. Say, for example, that the two of you are walking down the street on your way to the restaurant. Your conversation is light and lively, even nonsensical at times. The two of you are just laughing and enjoying the evening— and each other. At one point, as you lean close to hear him whisper something funny about a person nearby, you punctuate your laughter by kissing him briefly, almost absent-mindedly, then continue your conversation as if nothing had happened.

Heart Brakes

A man loves spontaneity, and if you typically respond to his spontaneous actions or ideas with reservations, excuses as to why the suggestions are impractical, or with obvious "issues" about what those actions mean, you'll be telling him, just as clearly, that you aren't the one he should look to if he wants to do something fun.

He'll be pleased by your spontaneous act, and left wondering whether the kiss was significant, or merely a response to a whim. His interest will definitely be piqued, and he will perceive you as someone who is full of delightful surprises. You just may start him wondering what other wonderful surprises are in store for him.

If He Likes What He Sees, He'll Want to See More

Since men are, for the most part, very visually driven creatures, a significant part of your seductiveness lies in your physical appearance. Each woman has her own particular beauty, and her own unique look (see also Chapters 3 and 7). It is your uniqueness that attracted him to you in the first place, so you will want to emphasize and project those individual qualities that he obviously finds so delightful.

Over and over again in surveys, men have told me that what they want is a woman who is comfortable in her own skin, and who isn't overly self-conscious. They want a woman to be as attractive as she can be, yet who isn't afraid to be seen with tousled hair and make-up that hasn't been retouched in a while. They're turned on by a woman who is stylish in her own way, and conscious enough to want to look good for him, yet not so self-conscious that she can't enjoy herself.

Here are a couple of other points to remember:

➤ *One of the sexiest things you can wear is an honest smile.* By showing you're happy while you're with a man, you raise your attractiveness quotient significantly. That smile is not just a matter of positioning your face a certain way. It comes through in the form of a happy, pleasant voice and the way your eyes twinkle when you're having a good time. A smile is really a combination of all your expressions, telling your partner that you are glad to be around him. You will make him look all the more forward to that moment when you're wearing nothing *but* that beautiful smile.

➤ *Femininity is incredibly sexy.* As we discussed in an earlier chapter, true femininity is the quality that makes a man feel masculine around you. It makes him feel like he has something precious to offer you—not as your "knight in shining armor," and not as the hero who can save poor, helpless, little you from danger, but as someone who feels strong, capable, confident, and sexy in your presence.

You've come this far, and you feel like you're ready to take things to the next level. By paying just a little attention and making sure that what you're communicating is what you really feel, you can set the stage for a wonderful experience to unfold. Be aware of what a man wants—spontaneity, confidence, an open mind—and let him see that you may hold the answers to his desires. You will, for all practical purposes, have seduced him already.

Secrets for the Seducer

It may come as a surprise to you men, but many of the same things that you look for in a woman, she is also looking for in you. You each want to feel that your partner is really interested. What makes the two sexes so different (well, besides the obvious things) are the ways in which we express our interest, and the little signs we look for to show us our date is really interested in *us*.

There are some things that are easy for a woman to overlook, yet are very important to a man. By the same token, women seem to place great importance on some matters that may seem insignificant, even alien, to men.

Atmosphere Is Everything

Remember the little seduction scenario I described in Chapter 1, where the man prepared a sensuous bath for his lover? The seductive power of this scene lies first of all in the man's intent—his desire to please his woman. But the gesture is made all the more alluring by the man's attention to even the tiniest details: the rose petals marking the path to the bathroom, the champagne chilling within easy reach, the candles softly illuminating the room, and the sweet fragrance of the bath oil he had added to the water. Not even the temperature of the water, warm and inviting, was overlooked in his attempt to create a sensuous environment.

Such little details may seem unimportant to a man, yet to a woman, they add up to a total experience that completely wraps her in the knowledge that her man appreciates and cherishes her. A woman cannot help appreciating a man who would put forth such an effort for her enjoyment, especially when she realizes that this attention to detail just isn't in his everyday nature.

My advice to you men is to make even the most mundane of activities a sensual delight for your partner. While you might not be at a point in a relationship where a sensuous bath would be

Heart Brakes

Don't let your attention to the details become an obsession. If one of the little things you've done in preparation for a seduction scene doesn't quite work, or if it doesn't please her as much as you'd hoped, just let it go and move on to the next thing. Once you've made your preparations, shift your focus to what really matters: the complete enjoyment of the experience. Remember, even the most finely orchestrated seduction scene needs some breathing room for spontaneity—and humor!

For HIS Eyes Only

Don't forget the flowers! While a dozen red roses may be making a statement you aren't certain you want to make, it's always a nice touch to add flowers to an occasion you spend with your partner. Even a single rose, placed on the car seat where she will find it when she gets in, will delight her. Or you can present her with a bouquet of wildflowers that you picked on the way over to her house. Either way, you won't be implying anything more than your appreciation of her.

appropriate, you can, just by paying attention to the little details, make your partner feel deliciously seduced.

For example, if the two of you are going on a picnic, you could choose a place that is out of the ordinary, such as a botanical garden or the landscaped grounds of an art museum. In your picnic basket, hide a bud vase with a flower. Forget the paper plates and cups, and use actual plates and stemware. And when you get to your destination, dazzle her with a table befitting a four-star restaurant, right down to the cloth napkins and tablecloth. I promise you, her response will be more positive than if you had taken her to the four-star restaurant, because she'll know how much thought you put into making the scene just right.

Even if all you serve is fruit and cheese, you will have created a sensuous experience she'll never forget. She won't be thinking of the money you spent, but rather of how much of yourself you put into the day, and she'll appreciate your "investment" more than you can imagine.

Heart Brakes

There are no "little things" where atmosphere is concerned. When you are setting the stage for a delicious seduction, keep in mind how important those supposedly minor details are to a woman. The seductive mood of the picnic described in this chapter, for example, would be diminished if you used some flimsy paper plates and cups. You might think this is silly, but just by overlooking this simple detail, you have failed to show your date that you are really focused on pleasing her, on delighting all of her senses. Instead of it being a perfect experience in every way, it will come across as a clumsy attempt at seductiveness.

Tell Me More About My Eyes

It's nearly impossible to overstate the importance, at this stage, of letting your partner know you think she is physically beautiful. Particularly as you move closer toward making love, she'll be eager for signs that you find her attractive. Since our culture places so much emphasis on women's physical beauty, her sexual responses are very much influenced by how she thinks you perceive her. The truth is that many, if not most, women harbor anxiety about their sexual attractiveness (we'll talk about this more in the next chapter).

You can allay her anxiety by telling her she is beautiful. You can tell her with your eyes, of course, by gazing appreciatively at her (without leering, of course). But we women like to hear what you're thinking, too, so give her frequent (but not excessive) compliments, and be sure they're sincere. And don't focus on just one aspect of her beauty, such as her gorgeous legs or her creamy skin. Vary your compliments so she'll know you find "the total package" ravishing.

If you truly make her feel that your eyes are a mirror for her beauty, she will be more than willing to reveal *all* of that beauty to you when the time comes.

Patience, Patience, Patience

As you move closer to your first sexual encounter with your partner, it's easy to become impatient. But it's important, men, to remember that women are very sensitive to feeling pressured. What you want to do is create for her a sense that you have all the time in the world, and that you are prepared to wait as long as she needs you to—because you know that she will be more than worth the wait.

In Chapter 17, we'll discuss why the timing of that "first time" should be up to the woman. But for now, I'll just advise you to rein in your desire, and learn to bask in the moment. If you do, both of you will savor the process of seduction to the fullest. And when you finally do end up in bed, it will be all the sweeter for the wait.

Your own imagination, appealing to your partner's, is a powerfully seductive force. If you really listen to what your partner is saying, even between the lines, he or she will tell you how to completely enthrall and delight, and make the task of seduction much simpler.

For HIS Eyes Only

Women love to hear sincere compliments about their beauty from a man to whom they're attracted. This works out well, because most men, in the early pursuit stages of a relationship, find that complimenting their partners comes quite naturally. But don't just reserve the compliments for the early stages; a woman likes continual reminders of her attractiveness. She'll never tire of knowing you appreciate her beauty, and that you don't take it—or her—for granted.

The Least You Need to Know

➤ Dreams and fantasy can be powerful tools to heighten sexual tension.

➤ A woman can increase her seductiveness to a man by being subtle and spontaneous, and by concentrating on her own unique visual appeal.

➤ A man can increase his seductive appeal to a woman by paying attention to atmosphere, appreciating her physical beauty, and creating a sense that he wants to savor each moment rather than simply rush into sex.

➤ A delicious seduction is an entire experience, not just a single act.

Chapter 16

Pre-Game Jitters

> **In This Chapter**
>
> ➤ Why getting there isn't *all* fun
>
> ➤ Men's sexual anxieties
>
> ➤ Women's sexual anxieties
>
> ➤ Shared sexual anxieties
>
> ➤ "Perfect sex" happens only in the movies
>
> ➤ Taking the pressure off of the first time

So you've made the decision to seduce your partner, and "Will we or won't we?" is no longer a question of "if," but just a matter of "when." If you're like most people, you're experiencing some mixed emotions now. For most of us, the interval leading up to that first lovemaking is characterized not only by an exquisite feeling of excitement, but also by anxiety and even fear. No matter how self-confident or experienced you are, no matter how well you know your partner, no matter how sure you are that you are doing the right thing, that "time before the first time" can be as scary as it is exhilarating.

If it's any comfort, your partner will most likely be experiencing those pre-game jitters too.

All of this, of course, is perfectly normal. Whether you're a man or a woman, it's only human to feel nervous before becoming intimate with someone. Many fears are coming into play, including that most basic one: fear of the unknown. So although it may be true that "getting there is half the fun," it's also true that the process of getting there isn't *entirely* fun.

In this chapter, we'll talk about some of the most prevalent fears of men and women. They're really not all that different from each other; they're just manifested in different ways. We'll also discuss some of the fears shared by both sexes. Facing up to your fears allows you to put them in perspective, thus preventing them from putting a damper on your excitement and anticipation. And once you've moved past these fears, you are well on your way to a delicious seduction.

His Fears

Traditionally, men have been expected not only to initiate relationships in the first place, but to take the active role in lovemaking as well. Our society has long called on men to perform on many levels, including sexually. These requirements are responsible for much of the anxiety men feel about sex.

That "Size" Thing

There's a pervasive notion in our society that bigger is better. The bigger your car or house or bank account, the more important you are. It's bad enough that we often judge people by such superficial criteria—but what's even worse is that many men seem to believe the bigger-is-better concept applies to their genitals as well. And many guys fear they're not big enough. Despite all of the reassurance we women give them, despite those clever sayings such as, "It's not the quantity, it's the quality," lots of men still equate penis size with sexual prowess.

Heart Brakes

So, you don't believe that men are worried about size? Just take a look at some of the ads in the back of men's magazines for penis enlargement products. The amount of advertisements speaks volumes about the demand, and thus, the anxiety over this issue.

The truth is, guys, you men are far more concerned with penis size than we women are. Study after study has shown that fewer than 50 percent of women care at all. If you ask me, many of these women are more influenced by some misguided notion of what they're supposed to like, than they are by personal experience. Most women say they prefer an average-sized penis to a super-sized version. Furthermore, many women actually experience pain or discomfort during intercourse with a man who is unusually large.

The people who are experts in these matters say that the average erect penis is about seven inches. Ultimately, however, what's important is not how many inches you have, but what you do with them (and, I might add, with the rest of your appendages as well). So forget those "Long Dong Silver" flicks, and concentrate on pleasing your partner. She'll love you for it.

Performance Anxiety

For too long in our society, the onus has been on men to perform—in sports, at work, in the battle-field, and in the bedroom—especially in the bedroom. If you believe the old stereotype, men are supposed to be like Energizer batteries: always ready, willing, and able to keep going and going and going…. No wonder so many men approach the sex act with anxiety or even dread.

Well, first of all, the truth is that men *aren't* always ready. Women are finally finding this out, now that more of us are taking the initiative with sex these days. Secondly, every man has, at one time or another, experienced performance anxiety. The fears are mostly unspoken: *What if I can't get it up? What if I go off too quickly, before she's satisfied? What if she's expecting me to go all night? What if she doesn't like my technique?* Let's look at these concerns one by one.

➤ *"Getting it up"* is, of course, a paramount concern for men. Until recently, guys didn't talk very much about erection difficulties. There was too great a stigma. These days, the issue is more out in the open; but as a society, we still don't deal with it in a very mature way. Look at those silly sitcoms that treat impotence as the joke of the week. For that matter, look at the very word "impotence," with its implica-tion of loss of power and virility. The clinical term is "erectile dysfunction," but whatever you choose to call it, it can happen to any man, at any time—even young men. Some of the causes include stress, fatigue, too much alcohol, lack of exercise, smoking, poor diet, heart disease, or various prescription drugs. If it happens to you, it's not the end of the world, or even of your sex life. It helps to have an understanding partner (show her this book). And if erectile dysfunction is a chronic prob-lem, see your doctor. There are plenty of treatments available today, including the much-touted virility pill, Viagra.

Wordplay

Impotence is a misleading word that generally refers to the inability to have an erection. The proper term is *erectile dysfunction*. Erectile dys-function, or ED, can be a one-time or occasional occurrence, or a chronic condition. It affects millions of men of all ages and circum-stances. At one time, ED was thought to be chiefly a psychological problem, but now medical experts say that in up to 80 percent of cases, the cause is at least partly physical.

For HIS Eyes Only

By now virtually everyone knows about Viagra, the so-called virility pill. Men of all ages who have experienced erectile difficulties have found this drug makes a remarkable difference. In fact, some doctors are even recommending Viagra to help alleviate problems that may merely be a result of those pre-game jitters. Viagra works not by producing sexual desire, but by amplifying signals at the nerve endings, easing the pathways for normal sexual stimula-tion. Ask your doctor for more information.

For HER Eyes Only

If he has difficulties having an erection, don't blame yourself or him. In fact, rid yourself (and him) of the notion of blame altogether. The latter may be easier said than done, because many men do tend to reproach themselves. Just be gentle and loving, without being overly solicitous, and let him know that he's more than an erect penis to you. If he still seems to be in the mood for sex play, have him satisfy you orally or manually, or, if you feel at ease about this, let him watch you masturbate. It's very likely the erection will take care of itself when he witnesses your climax. Otherwise, make light of the situation. If necessary, just forget about sex for awhile, go and have fun, and come back and try again later.

For HER Eyes Only

A man's primary sexual need is to feel that he's the best lover you have ever had. Simply by enjoying yourself with him, and letting him know you enjoy him, you allay his fears and go a long way toward meeting his primary need.

➤ *"Going off" too quickly* is a concern for some men, particularly younger ones. But keep in mind that "too quickly" is a relative term. As long as both of you end up satisfied, it really doesn't matter who climaxes when. If you do feel you have a problem with premature ejaculation, there are definitely some very pleasurable ways around the problem. First of all, if you're really concerned about climaxing right away, either because you haven't had sex in awhile, or because you just find her so intensely exciting—or both—tell her! I bet she'll understand, and then the two of you can take it from there. Perhaps you'll want to satisfy each other orally first, and then have leisurely inter-course later. You work it out. On the other hand, if you have a chronic problem with climaxing too soon (and not being able to have another erection later), there are many exercises and techniques you can use to prolong the pleasure. See some of the tips in the next two chapters, and pay a visit to your bookstore or library for books that cover the matter in more detail. Also, see the list of resources at the end of this book.

➤ *Going all night* sounds like a great fantasy if you're very young or you actually believe some of those XXX-rated movies, but in reality, very few women are turned on by the prospect of nonstop "pumping." The idea of a man who's a perpetual piston, driving his woman to ecstasy dozens or hundreds of times, just doesn't have much bearing in reality. In fact, even though women are more readily multiorgasmic than men, there are many women who are satisfied with one orgasm. For these women, anything more is overkill. Even women who like to climax over and over again in one session like a little variety. On the other hand, the idea of making love around the clock can be pretty appealing—as long as there are a few extended rest periods, with maybe a meal or two from room service thrown in. Even tigers, who sometimes mate for nearly two days running, rest in between matings!

➤ *Sexual technique* is more than what you do; it is who you *are*. Technique can be learned, of course (see the next chapter for a few tips and tricks), but the most important thing to remember is that *each new lover is a new learning experience*. What drives one woman into throes of ecstasy may leave another one cold. If you focus on pleasing your partner rather than on impressing her with your performance, and if you open yourself to learning what she likes, technique will never be a problem for you.

Her Fears

Even if the birth control issue is all taken care of, women can have many anxieties about sex. Most women have some degree of insecurity about their physical attractiveness—which isn't hard to understand, given our culture's obsession with female beauty. Many women also worry about their sexual response. Will they be able to have an orgasm? What if they take too long to have one? Let's look more closely at some of these female fears.

Showing Him Her Physical Flaws for the First Time

If men have felt the burden of performance all these years, women have borne the burden of being beautiful. It's not enough that men are naturally visual creatures; we women also have all of those cultural images to deal with. While surveys have revealed that more men than you might think are dissatisfied with their looks, let's face it: Beauty has always been a bigger issue for women. With women, the beauty question often goes beyond mild dissatisfaction with their looks, and can become a real fear complex. Sure, we can tell ourselves a dozen times that we have gorgeous lips, or legs to die for, and that even Cindy Crawford doesn't really look like Cindy Crawford. Even so, the prospect of appearing nude before a new lover for the first time can strike terror into even the most gorgeous woman.

The plain truth is, though, that most men—no matter how crazy they are for the centerfolds and the *Sports Illustrated* swimsuit issue, and no matter how much they ogle women in public—have a

For HER Eyes Only

Be sure you show your appreciation for *his* body. After all, many men have insecurities about their bodies, too.

For HIS Eyes Only

Make your woman feel beautiful. Anything you say or do to compromise this feeling can diminish her ability to enjoy having sex with you. If you make her feel beautiful by complimenting her and lavishing all of your loving attention on her body, you will alleviate her fears about her attractiveness, and you'll be meeting a primary emotional need.

tendency to suspend their judgment once they're in a one-on-one situation. They simply don't bring the ratings signs into the bedroom. Once your clothes fall off and your new lover beholds your nakedness for the first time, he's not going to hold up a sign with your rating in big red letters. He's going to be overcome with excitement, because a real woman, no matter how "imperfect," is infinitely more thrilling than a two-dimensional image ever could be. More than likely, his reaction is going to be, "Wow."

It's normal to be nervous about being naked for the first time with a new lover. But if you've practiced the techniques in this book, and have learned to care for and love your own body, your nervousness will quickly pass, and you will be able to abandon that beautiful body to the pleasure it deserves.

The Big "O"—You've Come a Long Way, Baby

Once upon a time in polite society, women weren't expected to enjoy sex. Where intercourse was concerned, they were taught to assume an attitude of indulgence, if not thinly disguised revulsion. It was, in other words, perfectly okay for a woman to lie back and think of the laundry or her mother's pound cake recipe. She could remain still and silent until the deed was over, and the man would think nothing of it. In fact, if she moved or made a noise, he was likely to become alarmed, fearing she'd suddenly turned into some sort of brazen hussy.

Well, thank goodness those days are gone. But, unfortunately, we've arrived at the opposite extreme now, and women are expected to have an orgasm every time they have sex—not just once, but again and again and again. Not only does this put more pressure on a man to perform, but it puts pressure on a woman to have multiple orgasms, and very obvious ones at that. In fact, you could say that the "big O" is the female equivalent of male performance anxiety.

As a result, many women feel pressured to "prove their womanhood" (and assure him of his manhood) by faking orgasms. Almost every woman has faked an orgasm at one time or another, and almost every man insists he can tell the difference between a false climax and the real thing. Whether or not this is so can make for some lively dialogue between men and women. Can anyone forget the diner scene in the delightful movie *When Harry Met Sally*?

Some women really do go all out and make a spectacle of their feigned passion, just as Sally did in the movie.

For HIS Eyes Only

Men, just because you've heard that a woman is theoretically capable of hundreds of orgasms, this doesn't mean that your partner is one of those women who has to climax five dozen times before she's satisfied. If you're not sure what her preferences are, ask her. Some women have varying preferences, so at times your woman may be multiorgasmic, and at times she may be satisfied with one (or even none). Every woman has her own level of pleasure, and her own cycles. Don't make her feel she's under any obligation to measure up to some arbitrary standard you may have read about in "Penthouse Forum." Otherwise, she may end up faking orgasms.

Years ago, Workman published a humor book called *The Dieter's Guide to Weight Loss During Sex*. According to the book's facetious calorie counter, the calories burned during orgasm could be broken down as follows: Real—27 calories burned. Fake—160 calories burned. That's probably not too far off the mark.

All joking aside, however, I don't recommend ever faking an orgasm. No matter how kindly your intentions, faking an orgasm is an act of deception. When you've done it once, it's too easy to do it again. And what you end up doing is cheating yourself and your partner out of a beautiful—and genuine—experience.

It's far better to be honest with your partner from the beginning about your pleasure level. Of course, it's entirely possible that your patterns can change as your relationship grows. But this should be a natural progression, not a contrived one. Here are some pointers to remember.

➤ *Learn to appreciate your own sexuality, and don't try to measure up to some arbitrary standard.* If you're satisfied with just one orgasm per session, or if you need a half an hour or so between orgasms, so what? There's no rule that says you have to be multiorgasmic every time, or at all. There's also no rule that says you have to have an orgasm through intercourse. As a matter of fact, many women either can't have an orgasm with vaginal intercourse alone, or it's very difficult for them to have one that way. But who cares? It's been said that any orgasm is a good orgasm, and I have to agree. Remember, everyone is different; let your body be your guide to what pleases you.

➤ *Tell him honestly what pleases you.* Let him know in an attractive way, however, so he won't feel as if he's being corrected. And if you're satisfied after one good orgasm—whether manual, oral, or vaginal—certainly let him know that, too, and reassure him that he's under no obligation to keep going and going until he "gives" you a dozen climaxes. Of course, you don't want to just roll over and fall asleep if *he's* not finished yet, but neither do you want to fake orgasms just to keep things going.

➤ *Be willing to learn and grow.* You may not be multiorgasmic now, but that could change with time. Or maybe, like so many women, you've never had an orgasm through intercourse—but that could change, too. Be open to these changes, and willing to experiment with your lover. Particularly if you're young, you may still be learning to define your sexuality, and your peak may be years ahead.

➤ *If you just can't have orgasms at all, be honest with him (and see your doctor).* There are many reasons women don't have orgasms.

For HER Eyes Only

Experts now disagree on whether or not there's even such a thing as a woman's sexual peak, but many women report that it takes years of experience for them to really come into their own sexually.

Sometimes the problem is a lack of sexual desire, and sometimes it is an inability to get sufficiently stimulated. Many factors can be responsible: stress, fatigue, anger, embarrassment, various medications or surgeries, or a combination of causes. Be honest with your partner so he won't feel that he is the cause of your lack of response. And see your health-care practitioner; most cases of female sexual dysfunction (the term "frigidity" is passé) are treatable.

Shared Fears

Since sex is such an intimate act, it brings up many emotional issues that aren't necessarily relegated to one gender or the other. Some fears are common to both men and women.

Rejection

If everything doesn't go just right during lovemaking, if one partner seems even moderately displeased about something, the other partner can interpret that displeasure as sexual rejection. And, at some level, both men and women may feel the fear of being "seduced and abandoned." For both sexes, the fear of rejection or abandonment can create a fragile emotional state. On the other hand, the rejection issue may not be a problem at all. If it is, the best antidote is to talk about your fears with each other. Even if the sex doesn't work out, and you ultimately end up parting ways, you'll both leave with your self-esteem intact.

Who Else Is in Here with Us?

Once upon a time, men were experienced and women weren't (or at least they weren't supposed to be). Nowadays, women are as likely as men to have multiple lovers in their past. As a result, both sexes may be faced with that silent question, "How do I measure up to his/her past lovers?"

It's normal to be curious about your lover's past. (Of course, I hope you've long since covered all the safe-sex issues, so that curiosity is your only motivation for wanting to know more about your partner's past loves.) As you get to know each other better, you'll almost certainly share more stories from your respective pasts. Just remember these rules:

➤ Don't be obsessed with the notion that your lover is comparing you to past partners. Assume that your new love is with you because he or she truly wants to be. Certainly, don't ask your lover questions such as, "Was I better than...?" Of course, don't compare him or her with *your* past partners, either.

➤ Everybody has a past, but remember that in bed, it's more important than ever to realize that you're with *this* person—right here, right now. Act accordingly.

➤ If you are still haunted by ghosts from your past, or if one or the other of you has some unfinished business, you need to deal with it before you become sexually involved with each other.

Your past will always be a part of you, but it doesn't have to haunt you. Sex just works best when both parties put the past in its proper place, and practice the art of "being in the moment" with each other.

Primal Fears

Some sexual anxieties go deeper than the influences of culture and gender stereotypes. The physical act of sexual intercourse gives rise to primal fears that may not even register consciously, but are there to a greater or lesser degree. I'm not going to go into a discourse about the psychosexual implications of coitus; I'll leave that to the scholars. Let's just acknowledge that each sex can experience different fears related to the sex act itself.

Heart Brakes

Don't have pictures of your past love(s) on display, particularly in the room where you make love. That's a sure way to put a damper on your new affair.

➤ *A man,* by the act of entering a woman, is entrusting the most vulnerable part of his body to her. In a very real sense, this is a type of surrender for him. And he might, at some level, experience an irrational fear of being "consumed" or "smothered." This fear may be one reason why men sometimes experience mixed feelings toward their lovers, particularly *after* sex (for other reasons, see Chapter 19). A woman needs to be aware of this fear, and she needs to be careful about seeming possessive or smothering.

➤ *A woman,* during the physical act of intercourse, must literally open herself and allow a man to enter her. Even in the context of the most tender and loving relationship, this is still an "invasion" in a physical sense. In order for it to be a delightful experience, a woman must let go and be comfortable with making herself truly vulnerable to her partner. It's only natural that this might create feelings of anxiety, however subtle they might be. A man must realize this fear exists in her at some level, and he must gently encourage her to open up, but at her own pace.

Ask the Love Coach

In a magazine interview a few years ago, the actress Rebecca de Mornay beautifully expressed the primal physical bases of men's and women's sexual fears. She said that the dynamic of men and women can often be illuminated directly in the act of intercourse. Since the man becomes hard and pushes inward, and the woman becomes soft and closes around him, the man fears suffocation, while the woman fears aggression and, ultimately, abandonment.

De Mornay was expressing an idea that has engrossed psychologists for decades (and many other thinkers for centuries). Many people today would scoff at the notion that sex can create fear on such a primitive level, but it's a point worth considering. No matter how sophisticated we become, our primitive impulses are still there below the surface, and they are almost certainly responsible for some of our ambivalent feelings about sex.

Reality Bites Back

It's not enough that sex with a new person brings up that fear of the unknown for most of us, plus all those other anxieties, cultural and primal, that we've just discussed. We also have popular culture standing at the bedroom door, feeding us notions of how we "should" look, feel, and behave. In the movies (well, at least the mainstream flicks), the act of lovemaking is always perfect, devoid of any awkwardness. The lighting is just right, and there's usually lovely music playing in the background to add that erotic ambiance. Safe sex is never an issue, and nobody ever seems to suffer from nervousness, shaky self-confidence, or a negative body image. You don't see men contemplating their penises and wondering if they're big enough, nor do you see women fretting over the cellulite on their thighs. That just wouldn't sell at the box office.

In our minds, we know those perfect little lovemaking scenes in the movies aren't real. We realize they're the product of hours of rehearsing, who-knows-how-many takes, and careful editing. And we may even accept with good grace the fact that most of us don't look like Julia Roberts or Brad Pitt (who still wouldn't look as good as they do if not for the skill of the makeup artists and lighting technicians). Yet at some level, most of us are influenced by the cinema's false representations, as well as the thousands of other images presented by TV and the print media. We can tell ourselves these images are merely the product of our youth-oriented, performance-obsessed culture, that they're the creations of shrewd marketers and have little bearing on the everyday lives of real people. But that doesn't stop many of us from feeling an undercurrent of anxiety about not measuring up.

I hope this chapter, and many of the previous chapters in this book, have helped put some of these issues in perspective for you. The truth is that we all have fears and anxieties about sex. I'd be willing to bet that virtually all of those actors and actresses and models we idolize have these fears too, off-camera.

As for measuring up, this is a concept that has no place in a delicious seduction scenario. It won't even be a concern if you place your focus on your partner instead of on some standard that has no bearing in reality. The formula is really quite simple: If you pay attention to details, you will learn what turns your partner on. Knowing that, you can easily set a seduction scene geared to please him or her—soft lighting, sensual surroundings, his or her favorite jazz musician on the CD player (we'll have more tips on setting the scene in later chapters). In short, a lot of focus, a little imagination, and a desire to please will make you a hit with your partner, and you won't even need a crew of technicians and make-up artists.

The First Three Times Don't Count

Before we leave the subject of pre-game jitters and get back to the good stuff, I want to leave you with one final tip. No matter how compatible you are with your partner, and how at ease you are with each other, your first shot at lovemaking may not be all fireworks. In fact, the opposite might be true. If so, don't be dismayed. Remember, you're two real people in a real situation; only in movies and romance novels does the first time proceed without a hitch.

To help relieve the pressure, I'm going to give you one of the Love Coach's rules for lovemaking: The first three "games" don't count. Think of the first few times as pre-season games before football season begins. More than likely, you'll fumble a bit. This is understandable when you realize:

➤ Both of you will have a certain level of anxiety—yes, even after reading this chapter. Nervousness just comes (no pun intended) with the territory.

➤ People are complex, and everyone is different. It's going to take time for you to get to know each other's lovemaking style and preferences. The more you learn about each other, the better lovers you will be for each other—and you can't possibly learn all there is to know in one session.

For HER Eyes Only

To ease his performance anxiety, let him know that "the first three times don't count." Don't tell him the moment you're in bed together, of course. It may sound to him as if you're really not expecting much from him (or that he shouldn't expect much from you). Find a way to work it into the conversation beforehand. Bring up the subject by telling him you're a little nervous as well as excited, but you've calmed your nerves by remembering the Love Coach's rules about the first three times. (If he's a football fan, he'll like the preseason game analogy.) He'll appreciate your frankness about your anxieties, and, even if he doesn't admit it, he'll feel relief from pressure. Just be sure to keep the conversation on the light side.

This is not to imply that everything is going to be perfect by the fourth time or so, but by then, you'll be on your way to knowing each other better. It is my hope that your lovemaking will just keep getting better and better as you go along.

Take That Fear and...Transform It!

The basic animal act of sex comes more or less easily and naturally to our species, as it does to most species. That's part of nature's plan. The fine art of lovemaking, however, is more complicated. Even if you're not obsessed with arbitrary standards of sexual performance or physical beauty, it's quite natural to have some anxiety about being a good lover. And it's perfectly normal to be nervous before making love with someone for the first time. If you have a good honest relationship with your partner, the two of you can dilute some of your fears simply by talking about them with each other.

Practicing positive self-talk is also helpful. Self-talk, as you may recall from Chapter 4, is the little voice in your head that constantly makes judgments about you and the world around you. Self-talk is really nothing more than a series of thoughts, and, since thoughts create feelings, you can change your feelings by changing your thoughts. With conscious effort, you can redirect any negative thoughts into positive ones. If you consciously and constantly tell yourself that what you're feeling is excitement about the upcoming seduction, and not fear, you just may end up convincing yourself.

After all, your body really doesn't know the difference between anxiety and excitement. Both emotions cause many of the same physiological reactions, such as increased heart rate and more rapid breathing. It's up to your mind to make the interpretations, and you have the power to direct your mind. In fact, with a little practice, you might be surprised at how easy it really is to turn your anxiety back into excitement.

The Least You Need to Know

➤ It's natural to feel anxiety and fear as well as excitement before making love with someone the first time.

➤ Men and women have many of the same fears about sex, but they're manifested in different ways.

➤ Don't be influenced by media depictions of sex; perfect sex only happens in movies and romance novels.

➤ If you think of the first three times you have sex as being like warm-up games before the season begins, you won't feel so much pressure to make the first time flawless.

Chapter 17

Tonight's the Night: Lovemaking 101

In This Chapter

➤ Knowing when it's "time" (and who gets to decide)

➤ Making the first move

➤ Handling last-minute jitters

➤ Lovemaking—from delicious build-up to afterglow

Even though you have used your delicious creativity to make the experience of "getting there" exquisitely sweet for both of you, you've always known that sooner or later you would want to actually *get there*. And now here you are at last, on the verge of making love with your partner for the very first time.

Making love is what this chapter, and the next one, are all about. I'm going to share with you some tips to help you make the most of the explosive chemistry that has brought you to this point. In years of working with clients I conducted several detailed surveys about men's and women's most powerful sexual turnons and turnoffs. (The top-ten lists are in my book *Cracking the Love Code.*) The information in this chapter and the next, was gleaned from those surveys, and from ongoing feedback from clients of all ages and levels of experience.

Ask the Love Coach

So, you think tonight is going to be *the* night, (or today's going to be the day, as the case may be) and you're having another bout with those pre-game jitters that we talked about in Chapter 16? Nervousness just before the fact is certainly normal, but there are many ways you can psych yourself up for that first time. The initial step is to relax. Whether you meditate, take a long bubble bath, or just sit in a darkened room and listen to music, make some quiet time for yourself. As you become more relaxed, begin thinking sexy thoughts. Call on your most steamy fantasies, or go back to the exercise in Chapter 7. If you're a woman, do the exercise, and if you're a man, envision your partner doing this exercise, standing naked before her mirror and getting herself prepared for you. Also remember that your partner probably has the jitters too, and the two of you can help each other over the hump (in a manner of speaking!).

Getting Started: When...and How?

Many of my clients have asked me, "When is the best time in a relationship to begin having sex?" Surveys I have taken with my clients revealed that the average couple has their first sexual encounter on the third date. I believe that for most people, this is way too soon to have sex. So when *should* the first time be? There is no absolute "best" time for everyone; each couple is different. It may sound simplistic to say, "When it feels right, do it," but if you have taken care of the necessary details we talked about in earlier chapters, and all systems are "go," the two of you really are the best judges of the right time.

The Woman Says "When"

When it comes right down to it, the woman should be the one who actually chooses the time of the first encounter. This is simply because during the sex act, the woman has to open up and receive a man, physically as well as emotionally. In a sense, she is in a more submissive role (even if she's on top). Therefore, feeling safe is more of an issue for women than it is for men. If a woman doesn't feel safe with a man, she may end up having sex with him, but her responses will be stunted, and it will not be a very pleasurable experience for her.

Making the First Move

A client of mine named Christy shares a delightful story of spontaneous sex and perfect timing. She and her boyfriend Paul had been dating for several weeks and decided to take a trip together. Even though they knew each other quite well, and had discussed safe-sex issues to their mutual satisfaction, they hadn't had sex yet. They had a tacit understanding that the relationship was headed in that direction, but Christy wasn't sure she was quite ready. They agreed, therefore, that they would have separate rooms on their trip so there would be no pressure. The first night, they shared some intense kissing and fondling, but Christy got cold feet, so they ended up staying in their separate rooms. The next day they decided to go on a picnic. Christy put on a sundress, and underneath it, she wore nothing but a skimpy little pair of panties.

As they got into their Jeep, they began kissing passionately. Paul slid his hand up Christy's dress, feeling the little lace panties but not going any further. Christy was beginning to get very turned on again, but was still somewhat hesitant. So they headed out to the little country store near their motel to buy their picnic provisions, fondling each other along the way. Once inside the store, Christy slipped into the restroom, and it was then that she made up her mind to take control of the seduction. She pulled off her panties and put them in her purse, knowing full well this seductive gesture would send a clear message to Paul that it was time. Then she rejoined Paul, they finished their shopping, and off they went in the Jeep.

They drove for a half-hour or so, until they reached a wooded area by a creek, a perfect little spot to have a picnic. Paul parked the Jeep and was starting to gather up the food when Christy said, "Stop. I have something I want to talk to you about." All at once, she got up and straddled him right there in the Jeep, and began kissing him intensely. He slid his hand up under her dress and found that those little lace panties were gone. They took each other right there, and it was one of the most passionate lovemaking experiences either one of them had ever had. After that, there were no more separate rooms.

Women, if you feel safe and you feel ready—and particularly if you know *he's* ready—there's no reason not to make that first move. Christy is very glad she did, and so, as you might imagine, is Paul.

If you've read this far in the book, you probably know that these days, it really doesn't matter who makes the first move, as long as someone makes it.

Heart Brakes

Guys, most women are really turned off by an ambiguous approach. Not only does it give them the feeling that the man really doesn't know what he wants, but it makes them doubt their attractiveness to him. An assertive approach—not to be confused with an aggressive one!—spells competence to a woman. And women, if you're indecisive in making your move, you'll confuse him, or he might interpret your actions as coyness or teasing, which he'll probably resent. Be assertive (without being pushy), and even if he's not quite ready, he'll be flattered by your obvious desire for him.

Just remember that "it takes two," so pay close attention to the other person's reactions, and act accordingly.

➤ *For women:* If you and your partner have taken care of all of the rational details, such as safe sex and birth control, and if you truly feel emotionally safe with this man *and* sexually attracted to him—then go for it! Make that bold first move. More than likely, he'll be thrilled. Remember, though, that he has as much of a right to say, "No, not yet," as you do. Pay attention to his cues, and if he's not ready, back off for now.

➤ *For men:* If you're going to make the first move, be assertive, but pay close attention to your partner's response. If she's not ready, *don't push her.* Remember that it should be up to the woman to ultimately say when. Emotional safety is a big issue for women, and if you pressure her into having sex before she is truly ready, the experience will be diminished for both of you.

Relax! It's Not a Competition

Before we go any further, let's stop for this reminder: Sex should be fun. And it will be a lot more fun for both of you if you keep these points in mind:

➤ *You don't have to and shouldn't even try to do "everything" the first time out.* Don't strive to use every position or oral-sex technique you've ever read about. Concentrate on pleasing and being pleased, instead of impressing your lover with your repertoire of sexual tricks.

For HIS Eyes Only

Laughter is not only an aphrodisiac, it can also be an expression of pure delight. This is particularly true for some women during sex. For these women, laughter is simply a spontaneous expression of their joy. Unfortunately, some men misinterpret this, and think they're being laughed at. Not to worry, guys; if she gets the giggles in bed, consider it a sincere compliment!

➤ *You don't have to like everything you try, and neither does your partner.* If, for example, you've heard that women are supposed to go wild over a certain technique, but *your* woman doesn't like it at all, that doesn't mean there's anything wrong with her, or even necessarily that you are doing it wrong. People are individuals, and they don't come with standardized instructions.

➤ *Don't be afraid to ask your lover to be your teacher.* Perhaps there's some aspect of sex play in which you feel uncertain about your abilities, either because of inexperience, or because you're out of practice. Don't worry; just ask your partner to be your guide. Inexperience is nothing to be ashamed of, and more than likely your lover will be pleased by your eagerness to learn.

➤ *Don't forget that humor has a place in a healthy sexual relationship.* In other words, lighten up! You already know that the first three times don't count. But no matter how many times you've made love, leave room in your sex life for the unexpected. That way, if the dog comes bounding into the room and jumps on the bed while you're engaged in a steamy caress, you can laugh about it and just go on with what you were doing (well, after you send the dog out of the bedroom and shut the door).

Ask the Love Coach

The teacher-student role can be seductive in and of itself. Don't be afraid to let your lover be your teacher, both in and out of the bedroom. Asking your partner to teach you about something he or she knows about (and that you would sincerely like to learn more about), will raise that person's self-esteem and will make you even more seductive.

➤ *Remember that it's not a race, but a journey—and getting there is half the fun.* Many people, particularly men, tend to approach situations with specific goals in mind. While setting goals is essential in business ventures, temper that inclination in the bedroom. As we've said before, your only goal should be a mutually pleasurable lovemaking experience.

Ask the Love Coach

A truly delicious seduction engages all of the senses. Whether you're a man or a woman, if you're setting up the seduction scene, pay attention to details. Consider scented candles and fresh-cut flowers; soft and pleasant lighting; sheets of silk or high-thread-count cotton; romantic music; and, to appeal to your taste buds, an extravagant treat such as a very expensive wine or perhaps a box of champagne truffles. Create an unforgettable sensory experience for you and your partner.

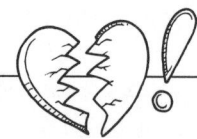

Heart Brakes

Alcohol can be an icebreaker for some people; in low doses it is a stimulant, and it can reduce inhibitions. But for many would-be lovers, it's too easy to cross the line from slightly stimulated to numb, because alcohol becomes a depressant after you've had a few drinks. And *if* it reduces your inhibitions, it can also wreak havoc on your judgment. Remember that there is going to be a morning after, and *don't do anything sexually while you're drinking that you wouldn't do sober.*

For HIS Eyes Only

While you may think that Seth's actions to soothe the anxiety of his virgin wife Sara might take some of the sizzle away for him, just the opposite was true. Putting his climax on the back burner just caused his sexual tension to mount, ultimately creating a magnificent orgasm. Deliberately building sexual tension is a very seductive technique, both for the seducer and the person being seduced.

Easing into the Situation

So you've made your first move, and your partner has indicated that your overtures are welcome. What if you're still feeling a bit awkward, or you're nervous about making the next move? There are several ways to loosen up and ease into greater intimacy.

I want to share with you the story of Seth and Sara, a couple of octogenarians who got married back in the days when most women were still virgins on their wedding night. That first night, Seth took his bride into the bedroom and sat her on his lap. He began kissing and caressing her through her clothes, and continued to caress her until she had an orgasm. Then they talked and danced to the music on the Victrola, and had a little champagne, followed by more kissing and caressing. Eventually he began touching her under her clothes, and finally he began to slowly undress her. But they did not have penetration until much later that night.

What Seth did was to create a safe environment for Sara, and a feeling that the two of them had all the time in the world. There was no rushing toward a goal, no "wham-bam-thank-you-ma'am." Seth made Sara know that her pleasure was very important to him. So Sara's introduction to sex was slow and gentle and exquisitely sweet—and, needless to say, even though they've been married for nearly 60 years, that woman still looks adoringly at Seth.

Whether or not this is your first time to have sex, if it is your first time with a new partner, it's going to take both of you some time to open up to each other. This is where seduction can become not only the lead-up to some pretty steamy sex, but a tool to help you both feel at ease. Just take it slowly and gently, and let your only goal be one of mutual delight. Even if you don't have a problem with nervousness, you can use some of the seductive suggestions below to help you get *really* ready:

> ➤ *So…how'd you make out last night?* Why not have a good old-fashioned make-out session, complete with what used to be called "heavy petting," or "second base"? Or why not play around a little with "dry humping," in other words, sex with all

your clothes on? Think back to when you were a teenager and sex was forbidden. Almost-but-not-quite "doing it" will help you get to know each other's bodies better, thereby increasing the level of trust between you.

➤ *There's the rub.* Even if you're not quite ready for a full body massage, giving each other a sensuous shoulder rub or back rub can help both of you relax and loosen up. Or try a foot massage. This is one of the most profoundly sensual experiences you can give each other. After all, your feet are just about the most sensitive parts of your body (they have over 7,000 nerve endings!), and a warm but firm caress by a loving partner, particularly on the soles of the feet, can be very erotic. Try it.

Ask the Love Coach

According to practitioners of various *zone therapies* such as acupuncture, acupressure, and foot reflexology, areas of your foot are connected via pathways called *meridians* to different parts of your body. Massaging the areas above the soles of the feet and under the ankle bone supposedly stimulates the sex organs in both men and women.

➤ *Good clean fun.* A warm, fragrant bath together, in a room lit with nothing but candles, can be one of the most relaxing and intensely erotic experiences you can create for each other. If you're still a little shy, make it a bubble bath with lots of bubbles, and you can let the bubbles fall away (or let your lover brush them away) gradually.

Ask the Love Coach

Remember that seduction is a process. Even if your night to remember doesn't result in sexual intercourse—because one of you decides you're not quite ready, or for any other reason—that doesn't mean the night was a failure. After all, you're seducing an entire person, not a set of genitals. And intercourse, while very desirable, is not the only goal. If the chemistry is right, the sex will happen; sometimes it just happens in stages instead of all at once.

Wordplay

For most people, the word **foreplay** means certain acts that lead to sexual intercourse. Foreplay generally implies a greater level of intimacy than just kissing or holding hands, such as fondling each other's genitals or having oral sex. But foreplay can mean different things to different people; for example, some people aren't comfortable with oral sex, but perhaps a bout of passionate kissing is their prelude to intercourse. If your foreplay doesn't end in intercourse—or if it occurs some time *after* intercourse—what's important is that it is a mutually pleasurable experience.

For HER Eyes Only

We women really have an advantage when it comes to satisfying a man, because the single most important thing we need to do to please him is to really enjoy ourselves. Nothing makes a man feel so good about himself, so manly, as knowing that he is bringing his woman to new heights of pleasure.

It's very likely that once the two of you are relaxed and have begun opening up your senses to each other, the rest will come naturally. Whatever happens, the most important point is that you both enjoy the experience. Despite the popularity of terms such as *foreplay*, please keep in mind that *there is no set script for you to follow*. For example, if you end up satisfying each other manually or orally the first time, and don't even have intercourse, so what? If you begin with intercourse and don't have oral sex until much later, who cares? As long as you're both left with a feeling of delight, then your night to remember has been a success.

Tips for the Sizzling Seductress

Women, here are some secrets that will make him feel as if he's the best lover you've ever had—which, as you may recall from the previous chapter, is his primary need in the bedroom.

If You'll Be Jane, He Will Be Your Tarzan

Men love to be with a woman who really enjoys sex, especially when she lets her man know how much she enjoys sex with *him*. Behind the sexism in the old saying about a man wanting a "whore in the bedroom" lies a great deal of truth. Your passionate cries, as well as your pleas for him to continue doing what he's doing, will leave your man wanting to pound his chest with pride. That's not, by any means, a put-down of the man, but rather an acknowledgment, even a celebration, of the fact that he wants so badly to please you.

Be a Gentle Teacher

Every man would like to think he's doing everything perfectly to bring you to the heights of passion. The truth is that it is impossible for any man to know all your unique desires, or to know your body well enough to be perfect in his technique. It's up to you to let him know what really feels good to you, as well as what doesn't feel so good. When your man does something that doesn't turn you on, realize how important it is for him to feel as if he's pleasing you, and use diplomacy when you let him know what you want.

If you just come right out and say that you don't like what he's doing, he will feel, at least to some extent, that he is failing. This can put a real damper on his motivation, and can even short-circuit the whole experience. Try, instead, to let him know what he does that you do like, whether by actually speaking, or by guiding his hands, mouth, or whatever in the direction you want it to go. This way, you won't be telling him that he's failing, but that he could be succeeding more in another way. And you both win.

An Orgasm by Any Other Name...

It was Freud who perpetrated the notion that the only "mature" orgasm for a woman was a vaginal orgasm, achieved through sexual intercourse. But let's face it, from a physiological standpoint, the vagina alone is just not a very efficient orgasm-producer for most women. In fact, many experts on human sexuality are now saying that vaginal orgasm without any other stimulation is more the exception than the norm. If people thought otherwise for so many years, it was probably because so many women were faking it. And they were faking it because of that arbitrary norm created by the same person who brought us penis envy. Does that make any sense for the new millennium? I don't think so!

Remember, any orgasm is a good orgasm. Let your body be your guide, and let your lover know what you like.

Let There Be Light

As you know by now, your man is, by his nature, very visual. He readily responds to images. If you want to really tantalize him, leave the lights on when you make love. He won't be noticing the extra few pounds you're carrying around, because he'll be too caught up in the sensory delight created by the whole seductive picture of the beautiful woman who lies naked beside him.

For HER Eyes Only

If you're extremely self-conscious about your body and leaving the lights on will hinder your experience, try using soft lighting. Pink lights can be especially flattering.

Adonis Reborn?

All right, so maybe he doesn't have the physique of a Greek god, but you still find him incredibly attractive. Let him know that you love his body. Rub his biceps and comment on his sexy arms. Squeeze his tush and tell him how delightful you think it is. I'm sure you can think of a number of other ways to let him know you love the way he looks (and feels, and tastes, and smells). It's very seductive to let him know that you see him as a sex object now and then.

Right Here in the Parking Lot?!?

Most men crave spontaneity and they long for a woman who can act immediately on her desires, or play along with his. When you get a "wild hair" to do something new, don't be afraid to act on your impulse, so long as your actions aren't likely to do either of you any harm. And when he springs a new idea on you, try to keep an open mind as well as your wits. If your typical reaction to his ideas is positive, he will welcome you as his companion in the fun times.

The Sweet Seducer: Not Just the Same Old In-And-Out

Guys, here are a few tips to keep your woman happy in bed, before *and* after.

Let Her Know She's Beautiful

As I said in the last chapter, a woman needs to feel that she is beautiful to the man with whom she is making love. Tell her she is beautiful—with words, but also with your actions, and keep telling her throughout the course of your lovemaking. If she has agreed to keep the lights on, you need to make her feel glad she did! Let her know you savor her. As your eyes, hands, and mouth wander down her body, linger at each new turn, devouring the tastes and aromas that are so uniquely her. Make every touch show her how very appealing you find her. Let her know you find as much pleasure from the feel of your hand resting upon her hip, or from the swell of her breast against your palm, as you do from the feeling of your penis inside her.

By the way, some women are somewhat self-conscious about how they look when they "lose control" and abandon themselves to orgasm. Be sure to let her know she has never looked more beautiful to you.

Ask the Love Coach

Some men try to model their sexual techniques on what they have seen in X-rated movies, or learned from their world-wise friends during their adolescence. You should realize that the vast majority of X-rated films are produced by men, to cater to men's fantasies, and have very little basis in women's sexual needs. The best way to find out what your woman's sexual needs are is to let her show you.

Make Her Know You REALLY Want to Please Her

If there is a goal you need to strive for with a woman, it is to let her know that her enjoyment is of paramount importance to you. Ask her what she likes, and pay attention when she tells you (or shows you). The key is to take your time. A "stop and smell the roses" attitude is important in all aspects of life, but especially with sex. Too many times, I've heard women complain that the minute they started responding to a man's touch, he would immediately shift into what amounted to a sprint toward intercourse and, ultimately, his own orgasm, leaving the woman feeling like she was just an accessory to his own pleasure.

On the other hand, I've talked to a number of women who said that their man made them feel as if they were a temple at which he worshipped. Every woman dreams of being with a man who seems not just motivated, but almost obsessed with ensuring that she experiences all the pleasure she desires.

Always Make Her Feel Safe

Remember that to fully give herself up to an experience, a woman must feel both emotionally and physically safe with you. Even if a woman is the type who craves adventure, she wants to know that you aren't going to put her at risk, either physically or emotionally. Oscar Wilde once wrote that "Some temptations are so great it takes great courage to yield to them." No matter how deliciously seductive and alluring you are, if a woman doesn't feel really safe with you, she will not open up to you completely.

Heart Brakes

Remember that many women cannot have an orgasm through intercourse, or through intercourse alone. However, many women are still reluctant to be completely honest about this with men. If your woman *does* tell you that she has difficulty in this area, be grateful for her honesty—but don't take it as a challenge. Don't feel obligated to be the great lover who finally makes her come via intercourse. Otherwise, you'll be putting pressure (and not the pleasurable kind) on her and on yourself. Just concentrate on giving her pleasure in whichever way she desires.

Afterplay

The image of two people, turning away from each other after sex and lighting a cigarette, has become a clichè of sorts, rating right up there with the man who falls asleep immediately after sex. Unfortunately, the clichè reflects a tendency we have to hide ourselves away once passion subsides, and we realize just how vulnerable we have been with another person. (Of course, there's also a physiological basis for the desire to sleep after sex.) In any case, it's important that you use the moments immediately after making love to set the memory of your sweet seduction.

What you want to do is let your lover know that even though passion is no longer the driving force, you are still very glad to be there with him or her. Don't abandon your partner by immediately turning over and falling asleep, or jumping up and running to take a shower. Instead, hold each other for awhile. Gentle caresses and soft conversation can make this time of afterglow almost as sweet as the seduction itself. And if you do feel a need for a shower, ask your lover to join you. But don't be surprised if this starts a whole new cycle of play!

In the next chapter, we'll continue our exploration of the art of making love. I will share a wealth of seductive secrets that can truly make any night with your lover—whether it's the first night or not—"a night to remember."

The Least You Need to Know

➤ The timing of the first time you have sex should be up to the woman, because emotional safety is a greater issue for women.

➤ It doesn't matter who makes the first move, but if you do, be unequivocal about it. However, pay attention to your partner's responses, and if he or she isn't ready, don't push.

➤ There's really no set script for sex, and one couple's foreplay may be another couple's main event.

➤ The single most important thing a woman needs to do to please a man sexually is to enjoy herself when she's in bed with him—it'll really make him feel that he's a wonderful lover.

➤ It's important that a man let his woman know she's beautiful—not just while he's trying to get her into bed, but during and after lovemaking as well.

➤ A delicious seduction doesn't end when the sex act is over; it's important that you hold each other and enjoy the afterglow.

Chapter 18

A Seductive Potpourri: Tips and Tricks to Make the Night Complete

---

In This Chapter

➤ Getting yourself *really* in the mood

➤ Feathering your love nest

➤ The allure of the unexpected

➤ Clothing and other playful props

➤ Kissing and other oral delights

➤ The entire body as an erogenous zone

Now that we've gone over the basics for your "night to remember," let's rewind the film, slowing down on some parts so we can review and enhance them. While we're reviewing, I'm going to give you a bag of goodies to nibble on—a mouth-watering mix of tips and tricks you can use to help make the seduction complete. We'll be covering a lot of ground here: everything from tips on building the perfect love nest to some tasteful advice on techniques for pleasuring your partner.

As I said in the last chapter, you don't have to try everything your first time out; take what fits your own sweet seductive plans, and leave the rest for the good times yet to come. So, sit back, relax, sift through these tidbits...and enjoy planning your perfect seduction.

Seductive Is As Seductive Thinks

As you know, your brain is the most erogenous part of your body. In Chapter 4 and in various other parts of this book, I've discussed how your thoughts can make you feel and act sexy (or not). Remember in Chapter 15, when our friend James set the stage for his seduction of Donna by telling her his dream about the bath in the Mediterranean villa? Later in the same chapter, I gave an example of seductive sharing of a fantasy vacation. These are wonderful ways to appeal to your partner's mind, and help get him or her thinking of you seductively. But what else can you do to enhance your own preparedness?

In Chapters 16 and 17, I talked about the importance of relaxation, gave you tips to alleviate performance pressure for both you and your partner, and I gave you some ideas for preparing yourself mentally. Just to be sure your bag is full of tricks and treats, here are some more techniques you can use to help get yourself primed and ready.

Two Enthusiastic Thumbs Up!

As you've probably guessed by now, I love the movies, and not just for entertainment purposes. For the seductress or seducer, film can be a rich source of erotic images and ideas.

In preparing for your night to remember, imagine yourself as the actor or actress in a movie you thought was hot, hot, hot. For you women, it might be Kathleen Turner in *Body Heat*, or *Kim Basinger* in *9¹/₂ Weeks* or *The Marrying Man*. For you men, it might be Antonio Banderas in *Desperado* or Leonardo diCaprio in *Titanic*. (If no movie or star comes to mind immediately, check the list a little later in this chapter.)

Try visualizing yourself as that seductive screen god or goddess. Have the confidence—in your body, your kisses, and your touches—that you think this sizzling seductress or seducer would have. Understand that you are not comparing yourself to these icons; you are merely using their images to amplify your own erotic feelings, which will help you project your sexiness to your partner. This technique really works. If you think sexy, you'll be sexy—and you will get rave reviews from your lover.

Ask the Love Coach

Remember, sometimes you've got to fake it 'til you make it. Act as if you've got the confidence of a hot seductress or seducer, and before too long, you'll have it. If you think sexy, you'll *be* sexy.

Your Own Private Mood Enhancers

You can put yourself into a sexy mood before you even see your date. Here are a few tips for getting your senses—and your sensibilities—primed:

1. Since we've been talking about movies, now is a good time to suggest that you rent, and watch a few scenes from, your favorite sexy, seductive movie. Can't think of any right off the bat? Well, here's a short list to get you started. You'll notice I've already mentioned some of them, but I'll list them again here, along with a few other selections.

   ➤ *No Way Out* (the limo scene...wow)

   ➤ *Sirens* (pick a scene, any scene...let's say, the blindfold scene)

   ➤ *Don Juan de Marco* (especially the opening seduction scene)

   ➤ *Basic Instinct* (the famous interrogation scene)

   ➤ *9½ Weeks* (one long, sexy ride)

   ➤ *Last Tango in Paris* (may be a bit rough and explicit for some, but many find this one incredibly sexy)

   ➤ *Body Heat* (Kathleen Turner really heats this one up)

   ➤ *Tom Jones* (the food scene)

   ➤ *Disclosure* (office sex scene)

   ➤ *Sea of Love* (has some hot scenes with Al Pacino and Ellen Barkin)

   ➤ *Love at Large* (a quirky but sexy takeoff on the film noir genre; has a seductive soundtrack too)

   ➤ *Belle de Jour* (with Catherine Deneuve; 'nuff said!)

2. Read a few pages from your favorite erotic literature. If you're not familiar with any erotic literature, check out the Resources list in Appendix A at the back of this book for just a few ideas.

3. Eat or drink something you find deliciously seductive or sensuous—a strawberry, an orange, a chocolate truffle, a glass of champagne. Exercise moderation, of course, and be sure to brush your teeth afterwards.

Not only will these little teasers help get you *really* in the mood, they'll also provide a diversion to take the edge off any pre-game jitters you still may be experiencing.

A Lair to Lure Your Love

I can't stress enough how crucial atmosphere is. The surroundings in which your seduction occurs are almost as important as the lovemaking itself.

217

French courtesans took special care to create erotic and sensuous environments. These exquisite seductresses knew how to engulf their paramours in a seductive ambience that brought out each man's sexual best. Taking into consideration the taste of her partner, the courtesan would add or take away elements from the room, in order to create the perfect delight just for him. She took particular pains to appeal to each of her partner's senses, using, for example:

➤ Evocative paintings to stimulate his eyes

➤ Pungent oils for the nose

➤ Luscious juicy fruits and wines for the taste buds

➤ Soft fabrics such as silk for the skin

The key point to remember is that the surroundings you create must arouse your lover's senses, not just your own. After all, that's why you have been doing all that observing and planning since the first seductive date. Let's review a few sexy tricks and tips for weaving your irresistible web:

➤ *Your private gallery:* Place erotic prints or sexy photos in strategic locations in your bedroom—perhaps something that would suggest, "That position might be fun to try."

➤ *Your garden of earthly delights:* Plants and flowers appeal to the primitive romantic in all of us. Don't skimp here.

➤ *Falling softly in lust:* Throws, soft spreads, comforters and overstuffed pillows give an ambience of luxury and say, "Snuggle into me; I want you to stay."

➤ *Music to his or her ears:* In Chapter 16 I talked about the disparity between movie seductions and real life. Of course, this certainly doesn't mean you can't borrow some ideas from the movies. And let's face it: No movie seduction scene would be complete without background music. Here you have a distinct advantage that the French courtesans of centuries past didn't have. So just go to your favorite music store and pick your seduction soundtrack with your lover in mind.

➤ *Clearing the palate for the next course:* The most ardent lovers need to replenish their strength for encore performances. Chilled wine or flavored mineral water, fruits and sweet treats are perfect for those delicious in-between times.

➤ *You light up my life:* No star would be filmed in unflattering lighting, so pay attention here. Soft pink or peach light bulbs are always right. And remember, while you want lighting to be flattering, be sure it's not so dark that the costars can't see each other. (A special note for women: Remember that guys are visual. So provide enough light to give him the visual stimulation he craves.)

➤ *Sweet supplies:* Next to your bed, keep a basket of essentials such as lubricants, body oils, creams, condoms, and clean towels. Depending upon your preferences, you might want to add a couple of sexual toys, feathers, pearls, silk scarves, and the like. You want to keep things interesting.

➤ *Just for you:* Always add at least one element to the scene that is unmistakably for your lover alone. If she loves grapes or black olives, or he's driven wild by feathers, make sure these are prominently displayed. You want to send a sweet, clear message that tells your lover, "I created this love nest just for you."

The Added Seduction of the Unexpected

Lovemaking doesn't always have to take place in the bedroom. As we saw in Chapter 17 with Christy and Paul, who showed us how seductive a Jeep can be, sometimes even the first time occurs in an unconventional place. Making love in an unexpected location, or at an unexpected time, can add a thrilling dimension to your seduction.

Again, you can draw on the movies for inspiration. Think of Kevin Costner's hot limo scene in *No Way Out*, or Jessica Lange and Jack Nicholson on the kitchen table in *The Postman Always Rings Twice*, or that sexy elevator encounter between Glenn Close and Michael Douglas in *Fatal Attraction*.

Indeed, there is something highly charged and irresistibly seductive about taking it away from home, or at least away from the bedroom. Here's just a sampler of ideas:

➤ *When was the last time you had rug burns?* One of the simplest ways to create the unexpected is to make love in some other room besides the bedroom. The leather chair in the den…the island in the kitchen…the dining room floor…the bathroom counter…these can all make for a sweet, thrilling experience—and you don't even have to leave home.

➤ *Backseat drivers.* Many people still harbor fantasies about making out (and more) in the back seat. So why not hop in the car and treat yourselves to a little bit of naughty nostalgia?

➤ *Out in the wild blue yonder.* Nature adds a powerful seductive element of its own. Whether you're under the stars in the middle of the desert, or in a clearing in the deep forest, doing the wild thing out in the wild can be supremely erotic.

➤ *A little motion on the ocean.* Ever thought of making love in a small sailboat? The sky above, the ocean around you…what a wet, wild, and completely heavenly seduction scene.

Ask the Love Coach

Lindy and Sam had been dating for a couple of months. She had been putting him off, but the seduction was progressing, and they both knew it was only a little time before it was complete. They'd even covered all the issues about safe sex and birth control. It wasn't a matter of "if," just of "when." One summer evening, Lindy's boss gave a formal cocktail party. Lindy wore a long, form-fitting gown that provided a striking contrast to her tan skin. She wore silver heels and, since the weather was almost as hot as she and Sam were, she decided not to wear hose.

After dancing several dances with Sam, and whispering naughty suggestions in his ear to get him mentally as well as physically primed, Lindy led him to the guest bathroom right off the dance floor. Locking the door, she began to kiss him passionately, pressing against him and delighting in his obvious state of arousal. Then she turned around and put both of her hands against the Venus-shelled sink, lifted her skirt up, looked back over her shoulder and said, "Take me from behind."

The voices and music from the dance floor just outside the door made Sam both anxious and excited. In just a few short strokes, he exploded. He began to apologize, but Lindy put her index finger to his lips and whispered, "No need to apologize now. I know you will more than make it up to me later." She smiled and kissed him. She quickly tidied up, and then the two of them rejoined the party. Lindy mingled with her business associates as if nothing had happened, and somehow, watching her act so nonchalant excited Sam even more. He ached to show her what he could really do. They stayed at the party until he couldn't stand it anymore...and when they got back to Sam's place, he turned her every way but loose.

Clothes Encounters of the Seductive Kind

In Chapter 3, I discussed how clothing can help make you seductive. But clothes can also be props to enhance the seduction itself. Since you're going to be dressed at the beginning, you'll want to choose your clothes sensuously. When dressing for undressing, keep these pointers in mind:

➤ *Choose fabrics for sensation as well as color and fit.* Make sure what you're wearing feels good as well as looks good. You want it to feel good against your partner's skin as well as your own.

➤ *Choose something that is simple to slip out of seductively.* You want to be able to undress (or be undressed) with ease.

➤ *Be sure your underwear and accessories are sexy.* No stains, no holey socks, nothing to spoil the seductive image you've taken such care to create. And, just as the rest of your outfit, your underwear should be only items that are easily shed. Leave the control-top pantyhose or the industrial-strength body shaper for your work wardrobe.

➤ *Try surprising your partner with something delightfully unexpected beneath your outfit.* Consider wearing some sexy but totally incongruous underwear...or just your glorious, underwear-free self.

➤ *Know how to undress for success.* Practice undressing slowly and sexily in front of a mirror, so you'll be at ease doing a tantalizing striptease in front of your lover.

➤ *Take charge.* Slowly, sensuously undress your partner. Be sure to express your appreciation, in any way that seems appropriate, for the treasures being revealed to you.

➤ *Nearly naked.* Enhance your nudity by leaving on one piece of jewelry—a pearl necklace, a gold chain around your waist—or one article of clothing—perhaps your scanty bikini panties, which he can work around rather than remove entirely.

➤ *Delicious inequality.* For variety, try making love with one of you nude and the other one fully dressed. The feeling of the lover's clothes against one's naked skin (and the sense of being dominated) can be very exciting for both men and women.

For HER Eyes Only

Surprise him! Let your undies be a complete contradiction to your outerwear. Wear something classic or tailored—a business suit, or slacks and a blazer—and a scandalous red lacy bra and panties, or an incredibly feminine camisole, underneath. And you can't go wrong with a frilly garter belt and stockings.

For HIS Eyes Only

Surprise her! Let's say you're a casual kind of guy, who's into chinos and cotton shirts. Startle her with a shocking colored or patterned bikini brief...or silk boxers. Ooh, la, la!

For HER Eyes Only

Ask him to undress you—slowly. Of course, you want to be wearing clothes that will be easy for him to remove. (And don't forget to have some delightful underwear to surprise him.)

More Props for Your Passion Play

You're already familiar with the notion of using props to communicate seductively. And you know that clothing can be a prop to aid in the actual seduction. Here are some more ideas to add delight to your lovemaking. Consider:

➤ *A silk scarf.* Use it to stroke your lover on his or her most tender places, or employ it for gentle bondage.

➤ *Mirrors.* A mirror allows both of you to be both voyeur and exhibitionist at the same time. You may also enjoy the sensation of pressing your bare skin against the cool glass.

➤ *Feathers.* Tickle your lover unmercifully. (Of course, make sure he or she isn't allergic to feathers.)

➤ *Washable body paints.* Exercise your artistic skills by painting glorious designs all over each other's bodies. Then wash each other off in a sensuous bath.

➤ *Erotic oils and sensuous lotions.* These come in a delightful array of fragrances and flavors—everything from chocolate to mint to an almond-liqueur flavor. Used in moderation (you don't want to completely disguise your own natural flavors), these love potions can be lots of fun.

➤ *Edible spreadables.* Why stop at honey or whipped cream? Use your imagination. Go grocery shopping together, and shop for items to complement your lover.

Don't go overboard with the props, but don't be afraid to experiment, either. A sense of play and a lively imagination are very seductive.

So, we've set the scene for a sweet seduction, and the actors are in their places. Now it's time for some close-ups.

Kiss Me, Kiss Me, Kiss Me!

There are times when kissing is almost a more intimate act than intercourse. Kissing should be a true expression of your feelings—sometimes tender, sometimes passionate, sometimes playful, but always meaningful. Kisses are like seashells or snowflakes: No two should be exactly alike. A little creative imagination can make for some memorable lip locks.

➤ Use your tongue to tease outrageously. With your mouth, briefly, teasingly pull on your lover's bottom lip, touching softly once and then again. Then dart your tongue quickly in and out of your lover's mouth.

➤ Use variety—your tongue, your lips, even your teeth (gently, of course). Alternate between brushing softly and pressing hard. But always pay attention to your partner's reactions, and respond with sensitivity. Remember that kissing isn't something you do *to* your lover, but *with* him or her.

➤ Don't overlook the corners of the mouth, which are very sensitive. A little gentle tongue stimulation to this area can be intensely erotic.

➤ Have a playful "war of tongues." How you handle a truce is up to the two of you.

➤ Surprise your lover by giving him or her a "kiss with something extra." Have a strawberry, an ice cube, or some champagne in your mouth. The champagne can be held in your curled tongue for several seconds, enhancing the feeling of surprise, penetration, and release.

➤ Don't forget the erotic power of breath. One technique used in some Eastern traditions is to simply pause in your love play, and inhale each other's breath for awhile.

Ask the Love Coach

In some Eastern traditions, a kiss is equivalent to the commingling of souls. After all, kissing involves the exchange of breath, which signifies the life force of a person. The Japanese, Chinese, and Inuit (Eskimos) have traditionally concentrated more on the breath than on kissing as we normally think of it. Rather than a deep exploration of mouths, more emphasis is placed on nasal contact, with delicate inhalation of the breath and the scent of the skin.

...And Other Oral Delights

To some people, oral sex is strictly foreplay, just a prelude to intercourse. To others, it is every bit as pleasurable, if not more so, than intercourse. There are even some people to whom oral sex, like kissing, implies a greater level of intimacy than intercourse. And although there are a few people who are turned off by the idea of giving or receiving oral sex, most couples in our society today do consider it a normal part of lovemaking—whether it occurs before or after intercourse, or as an act in and of itself.

This book isn't the forum to go into a great deal of detail about techniques. There are plenty of good books and videos that can help you there, and I've listed some of them in the Resources list in Appendix A at the back.

I do, however, want to share a few important points about oral sex (also called *cunnilingus* and *fellatio*). Perhaps the most important is that, like the rest of lovemaking, your emphasis should be on mutual pleasure rather than on performance. Of course, everyone wants to be "good" at oral sex. And, in fact, you can be, if you remember the "three C's":

Wordplay

Cunnilingus (pronounced cun-nuh-LING-us) is the technical term for oral stimulation of a woman's vulva and clitoris (pronounced CLI-tor-iss). **Fellatio** (pronounced fuh-LAY-shee-o) is the technical term for oral stimulation of a man's penis.

1. *Craving.* Don't just like it; crave it. The more you hunger for the taste of your lover, the better you'll be.

2. *Concentration.* Concentrate on your partner's reactions, and respond accordingly. If your partner isn't giving you any indication, don't be shy about asking, "Does this feel okay? Tell me what you like...."

3. *Confidence.* If you master the first two items, you can't help but become adept at this delightful form of lovemaking. And the better you become, the more confident you'll be in your abilities.

Seductive Oral-Sex Secrets for Her

As most women know, the typical man loves it when a woman lavishes oral attention on his penis. This goes far beyond just physical sensations, however. A man's penis is a significant mark of his sexual identity and, in turn, of his being. If you show him that you think his penis is beautiful, and that you truly enjoy touching and kissing it, you will also be showing him you enjoy him.

Ask the Love Coach

Cheryl, a former client of mine, says she used to have a problem shared by many women: letting herself go enough to have an orgasm through oral sex. Though she was enchanted with her lover Doug, she couldn't quite let herself go "over the edge." One night she had a dream that she was falling, and all of a sudden Doug caught her. The next day she told him about the dream. Later, when they went to bed, he wanted to perform oral sex on her. She told him, "It's always very uncomfortable for me; I've never been able to have an orgasm that way, because I have the sensation that I'm falling."

He wisely said, "Cheryl, don't you remember that I caught you in the dream? I will now, too." Cheryl finally let herself go that night, and he did indeed "catch" her. They've been married five years now, and Cheryl always has a smile on her face.

While your attitude is infinitely more important than fancy technique, there are little things you can do while giving your man oral sex that will drive him wild. For example, men love the sensation of a woman's lips as she is taking his penis into her mouth. While moving your mouth over your man's penis, hold your lips tight against it, creating a seal to the point that your cheeks puff out slightly as you take it in deeper, and are drawn in as you withdraw it from your mouth. (Caution: Watch those teeth! A little nibble goes a long way on his most sensitive body part.)

For HER Eyes Only

A woman's tongue, flicked across the opening in the end of a man's penis as he has an orgasm, is a surefire way to send him into outer space.

Of course, every man is different, so get to know him and what he loves. Be genuinely enthusiastic, stay attentive to his responses, and you're almost sure to delight him.

Seductive Oral-Sex Secrets for Him

The main point to remember when giving oral sex to your lover is to be soft and gentle with your oral attentions. The second point: Use variety. Don't keep making the same motions over and over, even if she seems to especially like it when you do a specific thing. Entice her with a variety of sensations, making her gasp in anticipation of your occasional return to her particular favorite. Alternate direct clitoral stimulation by running your tongue along the outside of her vagina, and kissing her upper thighs from time to time.

For HIS Eyes Only

Guys, a key element in seductiveness is being reciprocal—and this definitely includes oral sex. If you want to receive it, give it. As one male client once told me, "Show me a man who refuses to give his woman oral sex, and I'll show you a woman I can take away from him!"

You can even stop altogether to look in her eyes. This builds the intense tension that transports the two of you to a profoundly erotic plateau, where you can linger before going on to what will probably be a toe-curling orgasm for her. And, if you overwhelm her with delight, she will be much more excited about giving you all the pleasure you can handle.

I Sing the Body Erotic

If you ask me, the concept of erogenous zone is almost moot. With the right stimulation, the entire body can be an erogenous zone. You can supercharge your lover by lavishing your attentions on:

➤ *Ears.* Gently sucking your lover's earlobe, or softly probing the tender inner portions of the ear with your tongue, can create shivers of delight. But remember to be gentle.

➤ *Neck.* This is another sensitive area that responds beautifully to gentle sucking and licking. (As you may know, the Japanese consider the back of a woman's neck to be intensely erotic.)

➤ *Hair and scalp.* Gentle hair-pulling can be quite erotic. Grab your lover by the hair, pull his or her head back gently, and apply your tongue to his or her neck. Scalp stimulation can be very sensual too. (Try washing your lover's hair some time.)

➤ *Nipples.* Nipple stimulation isn't just for women anymore; men can find this a delightful experience as well. However, women, do keep in mind that a man's reaction to having his nipples stimulated is more localized than yours, and too much stimulation is likely to be irritating. So be gentle.

➤ *Inner arms and inner thighs.* Like any body part that is not normally exposed very much, these areas are very sensitive. Stroking, nibbling, or licking these parts can make your lover squirm with delight.

➤ *Hands and fingertips.* These areas are rich with nerves and are very sensitive to different sensations and textures. Use your own hands and fingertips, as well as your mouth and tongue, to tease and please your partner.

➤ *Feet and toes.* Another nerve-rich area. Give an erotic foot massage. Or rub some other part of your body besides your hands against the soles of your lover's feet (use your imagination).

➤ *Navel.* Tease the perimeter by massaging and licking; then plunge your tongue in. Or pour in a little champagne or something else that's tasty, and suck or lick it out.

➤ *Tush.* You know those buns were made to be played with. So pinch them, lick them, gently bite them, or, during intercourse, massage them, or playfully slap them. Delightful!

➤ *Anus.* This is absolutely one of the most sensitive spots on the body. Obviously, you and your lover need to take care to exercise proper hygiene—this is very important—but if you've got that base covered, go for it. A moistened fingertip, gently applied, can send your lover over the edge. (And don't forget the *perineum*, that small but exquisitely sensitive area between the anus and scrotum on men, and the anus and vulva on women.)

Well, anyway, you get the idea. Under the right circumstances, virtually any part of your lover's body—and yours—can be a source of explosive sensations. Happy exploring!

Giving and receiving sexual pleasure is an art. Like seduction itself, it is an art that must be learned, and the best way to learn is by doing. In a good relationship, you both keep learning about each other's needs and desires, and the sex keeps getting better and better. It's like a movie that you want to watch again and again, and each time you see it, you notice something new—and you love it even more.

Ask the Love Coach

Ah, skin! It's the easiest thing to stimulate because, well, it's all over you. A light-as-a-feather touch with your fingernails over your lover's skin can "charge" the roots of the skin surface and body hair over his or her entire body. Keep it up until you feel your lover shudder all over.

Hair can be a marvelous stimulant on the skin, as well. Women, your long hair, brushed across his chest or wrapped around his penis, can create wonderful sensations.

Guys, if you have a beard (and it's soft, not coarse), try tickling sensitive parts of her body with it. Or tickle her with your eyelashes. Mmmmmm.

Whether you try every trick in the *Kama Sutra,* or you just stick to a few favorite techniques over the long haul, isn't important. If you both bring a playful and adventurous attitude to bed with you, your sex life will always be exciting. And the really wonderful news is that in a good relationship, the sex just keeps getting better and better!

The Least You Need to Know

➤ If you think sexy, you'll *be* sexy, and there are many things you can do to "think yourself sexy."

➤ Create your love nest with your lover's individual tastes in mind, taking care to appeal to all of his or her senses.

➤ Lovemaking in unconventional places, and/or at unexpected times, can add a thrilling dimension to seduction.

➤ Seduction can be made especially sweet by the use of props—including clothes, jewelry, mirrors, feathers, erotic oils, and lotions.

➤ Your entire body can be an erogenous zone.

➤ Remember, the wonderful news is that in a good relationship, the sex keeps getting better all the time.

Part 4
Seduction Is Forever

Is there life after seduction? Actually, that's a trick question, because the seduction doesn't have to end at all. With a little desire and a lot of creativity, you can make it last indefinitely.

In this section, I'll begin with advice on how to deal with that first morning after, whether the night before left you disappointed or longing for more. Then we'll explore some ways you can keep your new relationship intriguing (or add some zing to your old one). Next we'll take a brief journey into the steamy world of men's and women's sexual fantasies. Although this chapter is titillating, that is not its (only) purpose; I'll show you how the two of you can use fantasies and games to bring you closer together as a couple. We'll end by talking about the force that makes the world go 'round: Love. No book on seduction would be complete without an exploration of this most profound emotion. We'll explore the stages of romantic love, and I'll give you tips on how to keep passion and seduction alive indefinitely. It all comes back to the choices you make—and if you so choose, seduction can, indeed, last forever.

Chapter 19

There's Got to Be a Morning After

In This Chapter

➤ Dealing with those morning-after doubts

➤ Why buyer's remorse isn't necessarily the end of the affair

➤ What to do if you really don't want to continue the relationship

➤ What to do if you want to go on

➤ The delicate balance between closeness and smothering

➤ Setting the seduction stage for the next time

The sun is rising, the birds are chirping, and another fine morning is ready to begin. As you open your eyes to greet the day, you roll over, and lying there next to you is a complete stranger, sleeping peacefully. Well, hopefully that person's not a complete stranger, but perhaps he or she is a long way from knowing your mother's maiden name or who your favorite grade school teacher was.

Right now, at a time when your most important consideration would normally be the preparation of your morning coffee, you are faced with what can be one of the most awkward scenarios that two humans can face: waking up with a new partner for the first time.

Do you feel inclined to spring joyfully from the bed, singing show tunes, or do you find yourself wishing you'd never met this person? Equally important, if not more so: How does your new love feel about you? What emotions are lurking behind that sleepy smile—a burning desire for an encore performance of last night's seduction scene or a desperate longing to run away at the first opportunity?

Most likely, your emotions and your partner's will fall somewhere in between the extremes. This chapter is about dealing with those morning-after feelings. I'll also give you tips on how to gently nip the situation in the bud if you've decided you truly don't want to continue your relationship with this person, and how to handle your disappointment if your partner is the one who decides to say "thanks, but no thanks." And I'll show you how to keep the intrigue and maintain that delicate balance between closeness and clinging, if you do want to carry on.

Got the Morning-After Blues from My Head Down to My Shoes

In a perfect world, lovers would always wake up in a warm glow with smiles on their faces. After a leisurely morning romp, a sensuous shower together, another round of lovemaking, and perhaps a delicious brunch, they'd be ready to face the world. From start to finish, it would be all rapture, no regrets.

As most of us know, however, it usually doesn't work out quite this way. Along with those first rays of sunlight comes a dose of reality—not necessarily unpleasant reality, but hardly the stuff of which romantic movies are made. No matter how wonderful it was the night before, you may very well find yourself with a case of the morning-after blues. You might be filled with self-doubts and feelings of insecurity, and perhaps even questions about whether you really seduced the right person after all.

Ask the Love Coach

Self-doubts and insecurities are normal after you've made love with a new partner for the first time. If there's true chemistry between the two of you, your partner will help allay your fears through words and actions. But you can help yourself by practicing self-talk and affirmations. Remind yourself of your attractive features or remarkable personality traits. No matter how the affair turns out, remember that you're still the same sizzling seductress or seducer you were before you made love with this person.

Self-Doubt and Insecurities

There's no question that having sex leaves us in a state of vulnerability. This can lead to feelings of insecurity, even if you normally have a healthy sense of self-esteem. After all, you don't know exactly what that person on the pillow next to you is thinking and feeling at this moment (this is one time you'd probably give far more than a penny for someone's thoughts). No matter how great the sex was, a part of you may be wondering if your partner really thought you were wonderful, or if he or she was just being polite.

➤ *If you're a woman, you may be having renewed doubts about your attractiveness.* What if he was secretly turned off by the cellulite on your thighs? What if he was disillusioned when he saw you in the morning light, with most of your makeup gone and your hair messed up?

➤ *If you're a man, you may be particularly concerned about your performance.* What if you really didn't satisfy her, and she was just faking passion? What if you're a terrible lover? What if she thought your penis was too small?

These two concerns reflect the basic needs of women and men that we've been discussing all along: a woman's need to feel beautiful, and a man's need to feel that he was the best in bed. But women, too, may have doubts about their performance ("Was that really the best oral sex he's ever had, or was he just being diplomatic?"); and men may have doubts about their attractiveness ("I hope she wasn't too turned off by my love handles.").

And both of you may be concerned about the overall impression you made during and after lovemaking. Sometimes the silliest little details will nag at you. What if you snored too loudly? Did you steal the covers? Hog the bed? Drool in your sleep? Sleep talk about an old girlfriend or boyfriend? These are all ways of dancing around the big worry: *What if you were a huge disappointment to your partner, and he or she can't wait to leave?*

This is a time when you need to call upon your rational, left-brain mode of thinking. Here are some points that can help you work your way through this period of insecurity.

➤ *You're in good company.* Keep in mind that your partner may be experiencing feelings of insecurity, too. It's only human to have self-doubts just after making love with a new partner for the first time. If you had a wonderful time, be sure to let your partner know for his or her sake—not to fish for compliments yourself (remember what I said about sincerity earlier?). Don't discuss your anxieties and insecurities right now; early morning really isn't the best time to have a deep psychological discussion. Make the morning as tranquil and pleasant as possible for both of you.

➤ *Women: Remember our mantra, "Even Cindy Crawford…."* If you're having doubts about your attractiveness, remember that even the supermodels don't look perfectly stunning when they first wake up in the morning. You're a real woman, not a retouched photo. If there's genuine chemistry between you and that real man lying next to you, he's still going to find you much more thrilling than the pictures in the *Sports Illustrated* swimsuit issue—yes, even now, in the morning light, with your make-up gone.

Heart Brakes

Don't try to force an evaluation out of your partner by asking, "Was I good? Did you really like it last night? What could I have done better?" Just because your partner doesn't seem as certain of his or her feelings as you are doesn't necessarily mean that your excitement isn't shared. Your new lover may even be seriously considering taking the relationship further, and doesn't want to make a mistake. Give your lover the space he or she needs to make a decision without pressure from you; and trust that, wherever this new situation is meant to go, it will go without your prodding. (Meanwhile, you can find out a lot about what's going on with your partner by paying attention to those nonverbal cues we mentioned in Chapter 11. Remember, you can learn a lot from someone else's body language.)

➤ *Men: You were probably better than you thought you were.* If you're having doubts about your performance, remember what your Love Coach says: The first three games don't count. And you could be wrong about your woman faking it. Why not take her responses at face value? If she said you were good, then, by golly, you *were* good. As for your penis being too small, you know that's nonsense. As we said in Chapter 16, most women couldn't care less if you're not super-sized.

➤ *Remember, you're only human—and so is your partner.* Your lover surely knows that people (yes, even people of the opposite sex!) snore and do all those other things that are part of the package deal when you have a body. In the very unlikely case that your partner is truly turned off by the fact that you're human, I would suggest you find someone whose perspective is more realistic.

➤ *Don't assume the worst.* Give your partner the benefit of the doubt where feelings about you are concerned. Assume, unless you are given a very good reason to believe otherwise, that this person is being honest when he or she says, "You were wonderful last night." If your partner hasn't said anything, don't try to force an assessment. Take a cue from his or her actions; if the person seems warm and affectionate, you probably have nothing to worry about.

➤ *Remember who you are.* Finally, if you're still feeling insecure about your attractiveness, or your self-esteem is a little shaky in the morning light, remember the exercises you learned in Part I of this book. Recall the affirmations you created; think about your attractive features and wonderful personality traits. Focus on the beautiful, seductive you—that entire package that is so much more than the sum of all its parts.

No matter how the affair turns out, remember that you're still you: the same seductive person you were before you even met this person.

Buyer's Remorse

If there's a lot of chemistry between the two of you, it's possible you may both wake up raring to go with another round of lovemaking. Eventually, however, there's going to be a period of "coming down." No matter how attracted you are to your partner, and how passionate the lovemaking is, at some point those postcoital doubts are going to kick in. You may, to put it bluntly, experience a form of *buyer's remorse.*

This is quite normal, and, like most feelings, there is a physiological cause as well as a psychological one. Our brains and bodies simply aren't wired to sustain a sense of ecstasy indefinitely. I suppose that's nature's way of ensuring that we have the presence of mind to do something else besides have sex—you know, such as looking after the kids, getting dinner, or doing our taxes.

No matter how natural it is, that coming-down feeling can be hard to deal with when you're with a new lover. In fact, you may experience it as a sense of disappointment, at which point it's sometimes easy to do one of two things: direct your disappointment at your lover for not measuring up, or, more rarely, berate yourself for not being satisfied with such a wonderful person. (By the way, if you have a hangover to wrestle with as well, the letdown may be even more dramatic—which is another argument for moderation.)

Once the rapture has died down, both partners may be left with misgivings about the affair, based in part on the primal fears mentioned in Chapter 16. Depending on whether you're a man or a woman, you may experience these thoughts and feelings:

➤ *A woman* might have a strong sense of having made herself too vulnerable to her partner. She might fear he will abuse her vulnerability by deserting her, bragging about the conquest to his friends, or in some other way making it apparent that the act was less significant to him than it was to her.

Wordplay

After making love with a new partner, you may experience **buyer's remorse**—feelings of remorse that are very similar to the feelings you have after making a major purchase, such as a car or a home. After the exhilaration, brought on by the rush of endorphins to your brain, comes the inevitable letdown, accompanied by feelings of doubt. These feelings lead to questions about whether you did the right thing. Know that these feelings and thoughts are natural and more than likely will pass.

Heart Brakes

You've heard it before, but I'm going to say it again: The best way to prevent a nasty hangover is to drink moderately, if at all, the night before. Do yourself a favor and don't make your morning after with your new lover any more uncomfortable than it has to be.

➤ *A man* might have an irrational fear of being smothered. He may fear that having had sex with his partner will obligate him to make more of a commitment to her than he is ready to make.

Once again, you need to call upon the rational, left-brain you. Here's how you can help yourself through the period of coming down:

➤ Tell yourself your feelings are normal. Nearly everyone has second thoughts and even feelings of remorse on the morning after, whether they've made love to a new partner or just made a down payment on a house.

➤ Realize that a significant part of what you're feeling is the result of natural brain chemistry at work. It's a biological impossibility to be in a state of ecstasy all the time. This letdown feeling, too, will pass.

➤ Remind yourself that if you and your partner have been honest with each other about your expectations, most of your fears ("What if he abandons me now that we've had sex?" "What if she assumes we're engaged just because we've been to bed together?") are groundless.

➤ Be aware that your own self-doubts and insecurities also may be influencing your feelings.

Unless you have a persistent gut feeling that you've made a terrible mistake—which isn't likely if you've followed the advice in this book so far—what you probably need more than anything else is to give the new affair time to settle. Read on for information on how to decide what to do next.

Encore...or Final Curtain?

So you've had your morning shower and cup of coffee. You've worked your way through your self-doubts and remorse, and, best of all, your partner and you are still looking at each other with that gleam of lust in your eyes. You're really feeling pretty darned good about the whole seduction.

Or, alternatively, you've had your shower and coffee, you've had some time to think about your feelings, and frankly, you're thinking that maybe the whole thing was a big mistake.

Or perhaps you're vacillating between elation and regret. Or maybe you just feel sort of numb.

In any case, you may be feeling obligated, at this point, to make an intelligent decision about where you want your new relationship to go.

Well, stop right there. Remember that you're right in the middle of a new experience, and even though you have now made love with this person, in many ways the two of you still may be strangers. You don't have to, and in fact you should not, make any life-changing decisions at this moment.

This is not to say that the feelings you are having about this person right now are completely invalid. To some extent, your morning-after feelings may be a foreshadowing of the feelings you'll have if the relationship continues. But remember that if you're ambivalent at this point, it could just be a result of the natural processes we talked about earlier in this chapter. More than likely, you're going to need some time alone before you make any decisions, even for the short term.

Ask the Love Coach

Don't try to make any long-term decisions about a relationship after making love with someone just one time. If you're glad you've spent the time together, but don't know for certain how much farther you want things to go, remember there isn't a timer ticking toward a deadline for making your decision. Take enough time to figure out what you truly want. You or your partner may need some extensive time alone for introspection. If there is something special between you, it won't just disappear while you make up your mind.

Unless the person has a serious critical flaw, or there's some other reason you definitely know you don't want to see him or her anymore, you really don't have to make a decision now. Nobody is giving you a deadline for deciding whether or not this person is "the one," or even whether or not you want to go to bed together again.

What If Your Cup of Tea Isn't Your Mug of Morning Coffee?

Suppose that for some reason you've realized you truly aren't interested in seeing your partner again. This happens sometimes, even if you've carefully screened your lover beforehand. The most important thing to remember is that this isn't a failure, on your part or your partner's. Though it may have seemed the night before that the two of you had a lot to share with each other, you—or your partner— might have realized that you have simply exhausted the supply of things that you had in common.

Heart Brakes

Even though you shouldn't feel obligated to make a decision about the future of a relationship after going to bed with somebody only one time, pay attention to obvious warning signs. If there is something about your partner that is truly making you uncomfortable, heed your intuition. If you just proceed, ignoring your intuitive warnings, you are setting yourself up for real heartbreak later on. Never stay in any relationship where you don't feel safe, honored, and respected.

It's not unusual for people to be incredibly interested in something—or someone—only to find that the interest wanes rapidly. It's not so much a matter of one or the other person's shortcomings as it is that you've looked closely enough to know that you aren't well matched to each other. If you can take away the need to blame somebody for a relationship not working out, you also take away a lot of the pain and, ultimately, the bitterness that so frequently arises.

If you are able to view the situation in such a no-fault light, you will be able to tell your partner how you feel without adding to his or her discomfort. Similarly, it will be easier for you to handle your disappointment if your partner is the one who decides he or she doesn't want to continue. After all, it does you no good to attack your partner's (or your own) feelings of self-worth by implying that one or the other of you is, for whatever reason, unworthy of a relationship. Here are some pointers to remember if you've decided you definitely do not want to continue the relationship.

➤ If there are specific reasons you're no longer interested, you can tell him or her those reasons. But be careful about what you say. Be diplomatic and nonjudgmental.

➤ Even if there is no specific reason, but you just don't feel right about the relationship, you owe it to your partner, and to your own sense of integrity, to tell him or her. Don't beat around the bush and say, "Maybe we should just cool it for awhile." Let the person know this is goodbye. How much you tell your partner about the reason for your decision is up to you. But do say something. Simply avoiding contact by not calling, or returning calls from, the other person is just plain rude. It sends a negative message about you, and can cause the other person to have major self-doubts. You both deserve better.

➤ Whatever you have to say, say it now, in person. If you're certain you don't want to see your partner again, you probably won't change your mind if you wait a week or so, and you will only prolong the agony for that person (and you) if you drag it out. And please do not take the coward's way out, deciding you'll relay the news later by phone, mail, or e-mail. If this person was worth the time and effort of a lovemaking session, he or she is certainly worth the decency of a face-to-face farewell.

➤ Above all else, be kind. Don't make a disappointing situation worse than it has to be.

Heart Brakes

If you tell your soon-to-be-ex partner, "It's all my fault that things didn't work out," you will only make that person angry at you. Such an obviously patronizing statement is offensive, and insults your partner's intelligence. It's better to adopt a no-fault position. The two of you simply weren't well matched after all, and nobody is to blame.

You Don't Float Your Partner's Boat

What if the situation is reversed, and your partner is the one who decides he or she doesn't want to go on with the relationship? It's natural to be disappointed; the trick is not to think of this as a rejection of your entire being. It's certainly appropriate to ask your partner the reason for his or her decision, but if the person is evasive or gives you a generic answer, don't dig for a more specific response.

More than likely you didn't do anything wrong. It could be that your partner had sudden cold feet. It could be that (despite your careful screening) he or she has turned out to be one of those serial seducers for whom the hunt is everything, and once the deed has been done the thrill is gone. Don't waste time speculating or placing blame. The best favor you can do for yourself is to accept the short-lived affair with good grace and go on. Here's what you need to do:

➤ Thank your partner for his or her honesty, and say you are sorry it didn't work out. If you had a good time, be sure to thank him or her for that too.

➤ Allow yourself to feel your disappointment, but don't think of this as a rejection of your total being. If your partner simply isn't interested, just consider this his or her issue, not yours.

➤ Feel grateful that your partner was honest early in the relationship, instead of leading you on. Sure, it would have been better if you had known *before* you had sex, but this way is still easier than it would have been if the relationship had dragged out for weeks or months, allowing you that much more time to grow attached.

➤ Again, remember who you are. This person may have taken a few hours of your time, but did not, and cannot, take away your essence. You are the same seductive person you were before you had sex with this person.

How to Handle It If It Knocked Your Socks Off

Let's say that, upon waking, you find yourself singing those sappy show tunes we mentioned earlier, and overcome by the desire to wrap your new partner up in your arms and smother him or her with kisses? You feel exuberant, as if the world has taken on a new richness, and your life has been reborn. You are, to put it mildly, elated. What do you do?

My first recommendation is that you take a few deep breaths, count to about a thousand, and even run around the block a couple of times to let off some of that steam you're filled with right now. You feel great, and I want you to hang on to that feeling. I just want you to take a little time out, so you won't come across as some wild-eyed Jack or Jenny when you face your new partner again. After all, you want to entice this person, not scare him or her away! Just keep these points in mind:

➤ *The other person may not feel quite the same as you do.* Even though you want to give your partner the benefit of the doubt where feelings are concerned, don't assume that the object of your new-found excitement is just as giddy as you are. While the other person might well share your feelings, he or she might just as likely be feeling some doubts, and your exuberance could even add to those doubts.

➤ *Realize that the giddy stage won't last.* Even if both of you are so ecstatic that you're singing those show tunes in harmony with each other, it's a good idea to at least acknowledge to each other that you feel giddy right now, but that you want to be smart about the whole thing. You can even share a laugh or two about how the two of you feel like kids, cut loose in a toy store with your parents' credit cards. At least pay lip service to the fact that you're both acting purely on emotion, but that you need to let common sense creep in at some point.

No matter how good the sex was and how strong your mutual passion still is, it's important to know that your relationship is still rather fragile at this point. You both need to maintain the delicate balance between feeling close and being smothering. You want to sustain your newfound closeness, while allowing the relationship a little cooling-off time too so it won't burn out too soon.

Ask the Love Coach

No matter how wonderful the sex was, if you want to continue the relationship you need to have a slight "cooling-off" period. It's important to maintain a balance between being close and clinging to each other. Plan some fun, nonerotic activity, such as going to the zoo, a water park, a funny movie, or a comedy club.

This may very well be the point at which both of you need to have some alone time. But if you choose to stay together the rest of the day, plan an activity that doesn't lend itself quite so readily to physical intimacy, or that doesn't sustain and amplify such an emotionally charged atmosphere. For example, this would be a great time to consider doing something together that is purely fun, without being romantic. A good guide for selecting such a place would be to imagine that you're both adolescents, who aren't sexual with each other, and to plan your date accordingly. Some examples are:

➤ Amusement parks

➤ A funny movie

➤ A comedy club

➤ Getting together with a group of friends

➤ An organized group function, such as a church or singles mixer

Wherever you go, remember to have fun. If you're feeling giddy, enjoy the feeling but don't take it too seriously. Realize that eventually you are going to come down.

Do Unto Others...

No matter where you think the relationship is going, there are two points to keep in mind:

1. *Don't abandon rationality.* Keep your eyes open, and one foot firmly on the ground (even if your head is up in the clouds, or, ahem, momentarily under the table). Don't let your excitement blind you to things that you would normally reject.

2. *Remember the Golden Rule.* Whether you are excited about the prospect of seeing this person again, or just want to turn the page on your mutual involvement, act toward him or her in the same manner as you would want someone to act toward you. The Golden Rule really applies here, and how you behave will affect you as much as it will your partner. You wouldn't enjoy being misled by someone who didn't want to be with you, or smothered by someone who did; it doesn't feel any better if you're the one doing the misleading or the smothering.

Maintaining the Intrigue: Setting the Stage for Next Time

Okay, so you've at least feigned an attempt to keep a rein on your enthusiasm and your passion. You've convinced yourself that you're behaving in a mature manner, and that you have looked at the situation as objectively as you can at this point. Now that all the mature stuff is out of the way, you want to focus on making sure that the incredible excitement you have shared isn't a one-time thing.

At one time, the argument against premarital sex was that people "didn't buy the cow when the milk was free." Actually, this admonition was mainly directed to women, as a means of persuading them to withhold "the milk" from men until after marriage. At any rate, while this is no longer the prevalent attitude, it does highlight the validity of maintaining some mystique, even mystery, as a means of keeping a relationship interesting.

Now, I'm not talking about deceiving your partner. That kind of behavior, as I've stressed throughout this book, is inconsistent with the delicious seduction of the new millenium. But, to keep your partner interested, you will want to leave him or her with some questions, retaining a little bit of mystery about yourself.

Ask the Love Coach

If you are interested in someone, it only makes sense to express it, but you don't necessarily have to tell this individual *everything* you're feeling. Recall, for example, a time when you were absolutely fascinated and enthralled with another person, and it seemed that the interest was mutual. Remember how much energy you would put into wondering if the other person's feelings were as intense as your own? Can you remember how excited you would get when the other person gave you little hints that his or her feelings might mirror your own, yet how deeply you craved some real, concrete confirmation instead of just hints? Maintaining that air of mystery will make your relationship much more exciting, sexy, and seductive than spelling everything out for your partner.

Though you don't want to keep another person dangling in suspense by simply withholding all the minute details of what is on your mind—and in your heart—you can keep interest piqued and the object of your desire coming back for more.

For example, say that you've been seeing someone that you find exciting, interesting, and generally a lot of fun to be with. You really look forward to the next opportunity to spend time together, and wish that there weren't any limits on the time the two of you share. Over coffee one afternoon, your partner starts talking about possibly taking a weekend trip together, and you feel your heart racing with excitement at the idea.

If you were to be totally honest, you might jump out of your chair and scream, "Yes! I'd *love* to go!" And your partner would be pleased. If you chose to play a game, and be deceitful, you could respond with some noncommittal statement such as, "Well, I don't know. I'll have to check my work schedule to see if my father needs me to help with his taxes," or something of the sort. Your partner wouldn't know whether the idea sounded good to you or not, and would probably suspect that you were searching for some excuse not to go. Most likely he or she would assume that you were either not interested, or that you were playing a game. Either possibility would hardly be conducive to an issuing of subsequent invitations.

Faced with the same situation, you could smile thoughtfully, look into your partner's eyes, and respond with something such as, "Hmm. That might be kind of fun." This response is honest enough to show that you are interested, yet it will leave some mystery as to the depth of that interest. You will have been encouraging, while retaining a bit of mystique about your feelings. In essence, you will have given your partner an emotional appetizer, which will encourage his or her desire for the whole meal. This form of benign enticement is what "mystique" is all about.

Best of all, you have maintained your integrity in the relationship, because you haven't misled your partner or given any false signals. You're still seducing him or her by keeping a spark of intrigue, while simultaneously maintaining your integrity (which is an art in and of itself, within the bigger art of building a good relationship). As long as your intent is clear and your motivations are clean, it isn't quite the balancing act that it seems on the surface. When you are acting from a place that is concerned with your partner's well-being as well as your own, the easiest thing for you to do in any given situation is to act in a way that doesn't hurt either of you. And acting in such a manner is the essence of delicious seduction.

The Least You Need to Know

➤ Nearly everybody has self-doubts and insecurities after making love with a new partner for the first time, but if there's true chemistry between you, your partner will put your doubts to rest in some way. Meanwhile, you can help yourself with self-talk.

➤ Buyer's remorse isn't necessarily the end of the affair; it is a natural part of the coming-down process after making love, and it will probably pass.

➤ Don't feel obligated to make any big decisions about a relationship after you've made love with someone just one time.

➤ If you honestly feel you don't want to see the person again, be honest but tactful, and don't be condescending.

➤ If you want to continue the relationship beyond the first lovemaking, you need to strike a balance between closeness and smothering.

➤ Maintaining a slight air of mystery and intrigue is not deception; it is just a part of a delicious seduction.

Chapter 20

Keeping It Intriguing: Understanding Needs Beyond the Bedroom

In This Chapter

➤ The never-ending seduction

➤ Women's and men's most significant emotional needs

➤ Collecting souvenirs of your journey together

➤ Creating adventures together

➤ Preparing a feast for your senses

➤ More ways (besides the obvious) to get physical

You've seduced—or been seduced by—someone in the most delicious way. The two of you have had your night to remember, filled with passion and laughter and everything else that makes a new relationship so exciting and wonderful. You've even survived your morning after. Some big questions that lingered in both your minds have been answered, and you're ready to move on to what are, perhaps, even bigger questions. Maybe you haven't yet decided that you're soul mates, but you do know that whatever it is that's between the two of you is far more than a one-night stand.

So, now that you feel confident in your desire for and interest in each other, the seduction part is over, right? Well, let me tell you a secret that too many people discover only after finding themselves alone again, their once promising relationship reduced to nothing but memories: *The seduction never ends.* When it ends, so does the excitement of the relationship, and, perhaps, the relationship itself.

Admittedly, you can't forever sustain the sheer excitement that is the earmark of a brand new relationship. But you can do more than you might have ever imagined to keep the fires of interest and passion burning white-hot. How? First of all, you must meet your partner's needs outside of the bedroom as well as in it. Second, you need to continually bring new experiences into your relationship in order to keep it exciting for both partners. No relationship comes with a lifetime guarantee, but I can tell you this for certain: Whether your relationship lasts for only one summer or for several decades, you will never regret putting your all into making your time together as pleasurable as possible for both of you.

Ask the Love Coach

Like any living thing, a relationship must be nurtured and tended to constantly in order for it to stay healthy. You can't just assume the relationship will take care of itself once you've gone to bed together. That sort of complacency is a sure path to boredom and burnout. If you want the relationship to continue past those first passionate encounters (or if you want to revive a long-term relationship that has lost some of its zing), you must ensure that you and your partner meet each other's needs outside of the bedroom as well as in it. You need to keep seducing each other on all levels—physical, intellectual, and emotional.

The Laws of the Gender Jungle

Every human being has a range of intellectual and emotional needs, and no single person can meet all of those needs. Too many relationships fail because people expect their lovers or spouses to meet all of their needs. That's too heavy a burden to place on one person, or one relationship.

There are, however, certain basic emotional needs that only an intimate partner can meet. Some of these needs are different for men and women, and some are shared by both sexes. If both partners' needs aren't met within the relationship, it won't be a happy union. On the other hand, if you and your partner do fulfill all of each other's basic needs, you will set the stage for a never-ending seduction—whether your relationship is brand-new and you want the excitement to continue, or you've been married for 20 years and you wish to rekindle the flames.

Let's look at some of the top needs of women and men, and some of their shared needs. (Also see Chapter 5.)

Ask the Love Coach

You've probably heard the old saying that a woman needs love in order to have sex, and a man needs sex in order to have love. Though this wisdom comes down to us from the days of traditional sex roles, there's still a lot of truth in it. This isn't to say that sex isn't important to women, or that love isn't important to men. To truly open up sexually, however, most women do need affection and romance, and the average man is much more likely to be loving and romantic with his partner if he is sexually fulfilled. A happy relationship is one in which these basic needs are satisfied for both partners.

Women's Basic Emotional Needs

Let's face it: a man is generally happy within a relationship if his woman is happy; conversely, if she's miserable, so is he. Why is this? Well, for one thing, we women are more likely to express our relationship discontent to our partners directly via complaining; whereas a man who's unhappy is more likely to grin and bear it, or simply withdraw. When a woman expresses her unhappiness, it makes her partner unhappy in turn, mainly because you men feel it's your job to please us. If we're not pleased, you feel you've failed somehow. If we are happy, you feel that you're a success.

Men, I don't want to imply that you are completely responsible for your woman's happiness. Happiness comes from within a person; it is not something that is bestowed upon her or him by someone else. No matter how much you care for your partner, you can't make her happy if she hasn't already gotten a good start on the process. But I can tell you that if you meet her basic emotional needs, she will be happy with you, and she will bend over backwards (in a manner of speaking) to make you happy with her in return. Here are four of her most compelling requirements for happiness in an intimate relationship:

1. *Emotional security.* No matter how independent she is, a woman still looks to her intimate partner for emotional security. You don't have to make a lifelong commitment to a woman in order to meet her essential need for emotional security, but you do have to make her feel emotionally safe with you. For a woman, there are many facets to emotional security. For example, she needs to feel that:

    ➤ You find her more attractive than any other woman

    ➤ You're truly glad you are with her

➤ You will respect the confidentiality of your relationship

➤ To some degree, she is supported emotionally—for instance, by knowing that you'll be there to hold her, stroke her, or otherwise comfort her when she has a down day.

If you meet her need for emotional security, the relationship will be much more fulfilling than you might ever have imagined for both of you.

2. *Affection and romance.* For the average woman, affection is a necessary prerequisite to enjoyable sex. One obvious way to express affection is by touching her. In fact, most women need touching not just in a sexual way, but in a caring and tender way. A woman loves to be touched by her man just for the sake of being touched; not only does this give her sensual pleasure, but it adds to that all-important sense of emotional security. As for romance, well, you guys know what suckers we women are for that. Give your woman a daily dose of romance, and I bet she will be more than willing to give you all the passionate sex you could ask for.

Ask the Love Coach

Many women complain that their guys "just don't get it" about nonsexual touching. Terri, for example, would occasionally ask her husband Josh to give her a shoulder rub at the end of a long day. "But once I would start to respond to the pleasure of his touch," she said, "he'd take that as a cue that I wanted to jump into bed immediately. If I let him know I really didn't feel like having sex at the moment, he would pout and imply I was being a tease."

The solution to Terri and Josh's problem was simple once Josh learned how important nonsexual touching is to a woman. In fact, with Terri's gentle encouragement, he learned that touching just for the sake of it was also quite pleasurable to him. Now they're more affectionate than ever with each other, and, to Josh's delight, the sex is better than ever too. Paradoxical as it may seem, a woman whose man has truly learned the art of touching outside of the bedroom will be much more passionate in the bedroom.

3. *Your undivided attention.* No matter how long you've been with a woman, there are times when she needs you to focus on her completely. This isn't usually a problem for you guys in the early, pursuit stages of a relationship, particularly before you've gone to bed with her. Sadly enough, however, many men become

complacent after they've bedded a woman. It's as if they believe that once they've "gotten" her, most of their obligation to be attentive has ended. That's simply not the case. Guys, no woman expects you to give her your complete, undivided attention 24 hours a day. But you do need to let her know that her happiness and well-being are high priorities to you. And I'm not just talking about sex, though of course sexual attention is certainly part of the package. I'm also talking about the little everyday things, such as getting up to get her a blanket when you notice she seems cold, or offering to give her a neck rub when she seems tense, or just sitting down with her and asking her how her day went. Just remember that when you're focusing, focus completely on her. Turn off the TV, put down your magazine, look in her eyes, and pay attention to her. Even a little bit of concentrated, focused attention will go a long way with her. But be sure to make it a regular habit.

4. *To be listened to.* This is related to focus, and it's very important. It's so often a problem in relationships, however, because men and women have different listening styles. As I mentioned in earlier chapters, men have a tendency to want to provide solutions when someone talks to them about problems or concerns. Women, however, very often talk about their problems just to unload. They aren't necessarily seeking advice; the simple act of letting it out is therapeutic enough for them. Keep this in mind when you're listening to your woman. Give her your undivided attention, don't interrupt her, and don't offer advice unless she specifically asks for it. Simple as this may sound in theory, the man who truly knows how to listen to women is a rare man indeed. More than likely he's also a man who will never lack for female attention. If you learn how to listen to your woman, you will be fulfilling one of her most crucial relationship needs.

Men's Basic Emotional Needs

Science has made many exciting discoveries in recent years. Previously unknown species of plants and animals have been uncovered in remote corners of the world. Evidence has been found of possible life on Mars. And, most amazingly, science has discovered that men have feelings too! Men still may not be as open as women about expressing their emotions, but the feelings are there, and it's important that women be aware of what goes on in the male psyche.

We've established that in an intimate relationship, a woman needs the support of a man in order to have her emotional needs fulfilled. Ladies, the best way to ensure that he'll be there for you is for you is to be there for him. Let's take a closer look at ways you can keep the seduction alive by meeting his four most basic emotional needs.

1. *Acceptance of him just the way he is.* This is your man's number-one emotional need in your relationship. I can't count the number of times I've listened to a man complain that his female partner wants to change him. Usually this trait

doesn't show up too strongly when the relationship is new, but as time goes on, the woman finds more and more little things about him that she wishes he would change. Maybe she doesn't like the way he dresses, or the way he wears his hair, or the decor in his apartment, or the company he keeps. Whatever it is she thinks he needs to change, one message comes across loud and clear to him: He's not okay the way he is, and she knows what's best for him. This is just plain insulting. It will make your man self-conscious or resentful, or both. That's hardly the basis for a long-term seduction. If you can't accept a guy the way he is from the time you first meet him, it's not going to get any better. You're not going to be able to change him, so just move on and find someone who meets your standards. On the other hand, if you do think your man is wonderful as he is, never stop finding ways to tell him and show him how you feel.

2. *Sexual fulfillment.* If your man doesn't satisfy your needs for romance and affection, you're probably going to be a less than enthusiastic sexual partner. Similarly, if you're not satisfying his desire for hot, passionate sex, he may not be too motivated in the romance department. Sexual fulfillment is high on most guys' priority lists. As you probably know by now, when I talk about sexual fulfillment, I don't mean that a man just needs to have orgasms. He also needs to know he is satisfying you. So let him know he's a terrific lover, and let him know often.

3. *To be admired, respected, and appreciated.* A man doesn't only want acceptance; he also wants—and needs—respect, admiration, and appreciation. He needs to know you like and respect who he is. He thrives on knowing you are as proud of him as he is of you. He also has a very great need to know, through your words and actions, that you appreciate his efforts to please you.

4. *For a woman to be his companion and confidante.* A man needs you to be an intimate friend as well as a sex partner. First of all, he wants you to be someone he can have fun with outside of the bedroom as well as in it. This means you need to share at least some of his recreational needs and outside interests. But there's more to being his friend than being a great playmate. In Chapter 5, I mentioned how important it is for a man to know that his woman will keep his confidences. He absolutely must know that you aren't spilling the details of your intimate encounters to your best friend, or gossiping about his financial woes to your mom. Most men still have a difficult time opening up to their male friends the way that we women open up to our female friends. You may be the only friend to whom he feels he can reveal his true self. That's a precious gift he's giving you, so don't abuse it.

Shared Emotional Needs

As different as men and women are, in many ways we're very much alike. All of us have certain basic emotional needs in a relationship, needs that transcend gender. These include:

➤ *Trust.* You can't be happy in a relationship with someone you don't trust. But it must be a two-way street; you have to be trustworthy as well.

➤ *Respect.* In order to be truly happy in the relationship, the two of you must respect each other (and yourselves, too).

➤ *Like.* Love and lust are wonderful, but you have to *like* each other, too, in order for the relationship to be happy in the long run.

You're on a Journey Together, So Don't Forget the Souvenirs

At the very beginning of a relationship, there are little signposts that remind you of the excitement you felt on those first couple of dates. Some couples, married for decades, remember a special song that was playing the first time they were out together. For others, the place they went on their first date is forever wrapped in the special ambience they felt that first night. It is important to remember the little details, because doing so tells your partner that you continue to look upon him or her with passion and excitement. It's the little things, not the grand gestures, that tell your partner you're still interested.

While it is impossible to determine beforehand, and nearly as difficult to tell during the early part of your relationship, what those special signposts may be, you can pick up on the things that especially move your partner. All you have to do is pay attention.

For instance, men, if she especially enjoyed the flowers you brought her on your first date, you might want to place that same kind of flower on her car seat, sneak one in front of her at the restaurant, or call ahead and have the maitre d' put a single flower on her place setting. She will be touched by your thoughtfulness.

Or, women, let's say one of his great passions is playing his guitar, and you love it when he plays for you. Take note of the type of guitar he plays and then go to a music store and surprise him with a new set of strings for it. He will be moved by the gesture of encouragement and support.

Even little things, like holding onto a book of matches or a napkin you picked up on your first date, can tell your partner you remember—and value—even the earliest times you spent together. The list of souvenirs and signposts is as long as the list of people who date, so don't bother trying to follow some set formula. The simple fact that you thought enough to remember the little things will mean a lot to your partner.

Adventures Along the Way

You can make your own signposts for your relationship by planning activities that stand out from the ordinary, everyday dating experiences. These become signposts on the basis of their uniqueness.

While planning your dates, try to include activities that are surefire memory makers. Instead of going to the most popular nightspot, you might try heading to a place that reminds you of a particularly happy time in your childhood. Though an amusement park, a baseball game, or a movie that is screening an anthology of old cartoons might not normally be considered romantic, giving your date a glimpse into the awe-filled child you once were can be quite endearing, and inspire your partner to want to bring that giddy child out to play in other ways—like in the bedroom.

Or consider being tourists in your own city. Even if you've both lived in your town for 30 years, take a tour bus and gawk at all the landmarks and historic sites. See your city together through new eyes. Then, if you can afford it, check into one of your town's historic old hotels or bed-and-breakfasts, and conduct your own private tour.

Ask the Love Coach

Plan periodic little day trips or adventures with a theme that will immerse you and your lover in a whole new world. Make sure the experience you create for the two of you appeals to all of your senses: sight, sound, smell, taste, and touch. There's nothing like the sharing of new experiences to keep the seduction going strong, and the relationship full of fire.

The whole point is to look upon life—and your relationship—as a continuing adventure. Adventure is not something that just happens to you; it's something you create. As long as you are willing to create new adventures for yourself and your lover, the seduction will never end.

You Fill Up My Senses...

There are many ways you and your partner can keep the fires burning by giving each other pleasure in ways that are not necessarily sexual, but are decidedly sensual. Consider these possibilities:

> ➤ *The power of touch.* You don't have to be registered massage therapists to give each other pleasure through massage. If you and your lover haven't already discovered

the delights that can be created by a pair of loving hands and a few drops of warm, fragrant oil, you are in for an exquisite treat. There are many good books and videos that show you simple massage techniques for relaxation or stimulation. Or just try doing what feels good to both of you. Remember, however, to pay close attention to your lover's reactions, so you don't cause any pain or damage to muscles or tender tissues.

➤ *The power of smell.* It's been said that the sense of smell is the quickest route to the emotions. "Aromatherapy" has become quite a buzzword in recent years, but it is based on traditions that began in China, India, and Egypt centuries ago. The judicious use of scent can create a delicious environment for you and your lover. Using essential oils for massage, for sensual baths, or in the bedroom can have a relaxing or stimulating effect, depending on the scents used. Essential oils, and advice for using them, are available in health food stores or shops that cater to holistic lifestyles.

➤ *The power of taste.* Sharing food can be a very sensual experience in itself. Some foods are naturals for a seductive meal, due to their reputation as an aphrodisiac, or to their taste, color, texture, or shape. (For example, slice a strawberry in half lengthwise and look at the interior portion of the slice. Remind you of anything?) Furthermore, the setting in which you eat can turn an ordinary meal into an erotic banquet. Candlelight dinners and champagne brunches are wonderful, but why not prepare a light, sensuous meal together, and then have a midnight picnic in bed, in the nude? Don't forget the chocolate!

➤ *The power of sight.* We know that guys are visual, but so are women. You can delight each other's sense of sight in many ways—for example, by using warm, sexy colors and soft lights in the bedroom.

➤ *The power of sound.* Experiment with listening to different types of music, particularly in the bedroom. Whether you sample Andean flute music, Tibetan chants, Chinese classical music, or flamenco guitar doesn't matter. Just know that there is a whole wonderful world of sounds waiting to be discovered. Some of this music is unabashedly sensual and can take you and your lover to new heights of pleasure.

The whole point is to use your imagination, and never stop finding ways to appeal to all of your senses.

Heart Brakes

Don't prepare a sensuous meal for your lover without finding out if he or she has any food sensitivities or allergies. Unfortunately, many people are allergic to common foods such as chocolate or strawberries. Many others have a sensitivity to dairy products. So before you go to all the trouble of preparing that white chocolate cheesecake or strawberry-kiwi mousse, make sure your partner will be able to enjoy the treat with you.

Ask the Love Coach

Taking a bath together is a wonderful way to appeal to all of your senses. Use fragrant bath salts and flavored massage oils to delight your senses of smell and taste. Have enough lighting to bring your sense of sight into play, and have some sensuous music in the background to add to the ambiance. How you exercise your sense of touch...well, I'll leave that up to you.

Wordplay

Yoga is a system of exercising, which involves deep meditation, controlled breathing, and achieving certain postures. It's good for the body and wonderful for the soul, and doing yoga with someone you love can be very pleasurable. If you really want to make it a sensual experience, consider doing your yoga together in the nude.

Let's Get Physical

Exercising together is another way to keep your love and lust alive. Virtually any type of robust physical activity you do together—whether you're nude or not—can be very erotic (not to mention healthy).

Working out with weights, doing *yoga* or aerobics, taking a brisk walk together, riding your bicycles to the park, salsa dancing—just about any activity that gets those natural opiates fired up in your brains will be pleasurable in itself, and can lead to fireworks in the bedroom later. Heck, even doing a couple of hours of strenuous yard work, and then having a cool-off session in the shower together, can lead to some real fun.

Don't ever be afraid to try new experiences with your partner. Get out of your comfort zone, experience life together, and your relationship will be a perpetual seduction for both of you. Even if it doesn't last, you will have made the most of your time together, and you will have given each other a precious gift.

The Least You Need to Know

➤ Women's top relationship needs include emotional security; romance and affection; a man's occasional undivided attention; and his willingness to listen.

➤ Men's chief relationship needs include being accepted just the way they are; sexual fulfillment; respect and admiration; and companionship.

➤ You can strengthen your relationship by giving attention to the signposts along the way, and collecting souvenirs of the good times.

➤ You can keep your relationship strong and lively if you get in the habit of creating adventures together, such as day trips, theme excursions, and minivacations.

➤ One way to keep the seduction going is by constantly creating experiences for you and your lover that appeal to all of your senses: touch, smell, taste, sight, and hearing.

➤ Exercising and engaging in physical activity with your lover is fun and healthy, and is almost certain to have a beneficial effect on your sex life.

Chapter 21

Keeping It Spicy: Fanning the Flames with Fantasies and Games

In This Chapter

➤ How the safe use of fantasy can bring you closer together

➤ Spicing it up with men's most steamy sexual fantasies

➤ Spicing it up with women's most sultry sexual fantasies

➤ Sharing and combining your fantasies

Just about everybody has sexual fantasies. It's perfectly normal, since we humans are imaginative creatures by nature. We fantasize about many things—winning the lottery, going on a dream vacation, buying a ludicrously expensive sports car—so it would be surprising if we didn't fantasize about sex too.

The majority of us keep our most private fantasies to ourselves, and we don't act them out. But did you know that sharing your sexual fantasies with your intimate partner can be an incredible aphrodisiac (and thus a great seductive tool) or can inject some seductive spice into a relationship that's lost some of its thrill?

Sharing your fantasies (and even some harmless acting-out) can also bring the two of you closer by giving you unique insight into each other's sexual desires and emotional needs.

Ask the Love Coach

Sharing your sexual fantasies with each other can bring you closer together, and make your sex life better than ever. However, this type of sharing will be seductive, and, inevitably, bring the two of you closer, only if it takes place within the context of a trusting and intimate relationship.

The key word here is "harmless." Obviously, you don't want to do anything that will damage the relationship—whether it be with your newly seduced partner or a long-time love—or compromise the health or safety of you, your partner, or anyone else.

Furthermore, fantasy should be only a supplement to your sex life; it should never become your entire sex life. It should absolutely never be a substitute for the intimacy of good lovemaking. With these caveats in mind, let's explore the world of erotic fantasy and games a little more closely. We'll look at some of the most common fantasies of men and women, and I'll give you some suggestions on how you can incorporate them into your own sweet seduction.

Heart Brakes

Many couples resort to sexual fantasies and games out of boredom when their relationships begin to get a little stale. It's okay to use erotic fantasizing and game playing to add some occasional spice to your love play. However, if either of you reaches the point where a fantasy or sex game becomes an absolute prerequisite for sexual desire or climax, consider the possibility that the relationship is in trouble. Work on rediscovering the attraction that brought you together in the first place.

Preventing Fantasy Faux Pas

Before we go any further, let's talk more about safety. Whether the two of you decide to act upon your fantasies, talk with each other about them, or just keep them inside is a matter of personal choice based on your own comfort levels and the state of your relationship. Here are some principles to remember for safe fantasy sex:

➤ Beyond the obvious factors of physical safety (and staying out of trouble with the law!), your first concern should be the emotional safety of both partners. Do not pursue, even on an imaginary level, any fantasy that makes either of you feel insecure or uncomfortable.

➤ Make your mate the star of all the fantasies or erotic dreams you share with him or her, even if your fantasy was originally inspired by someone else. Remember, the point of fantasy and erotic games is to bring the two of you closer together. Use the energy of fantasizing to steam up your relationship, not take away from it.

➤ Remember that not every fantasy is an indication of a real desire. Her fantasy about being ravished by a swashbuckling pirate doesn't mean she has a secret rape wish. His fantasy about having his own harem for a day doesn't mean he's not a one-woman man at heart (and in practice).

➤ When in doubt about acting out—don't do it. Be especially cautious with any fantasy that involves a third person. I've coached many couples who have acted out this fantasy, and in almost every case their relationship was harmed—often irreparably—by bringing a third person into their love play. Some things are better left in the realm of fantasy.

Sustaining the Spice with Sexy Play

Remember how excited you were before the two of you first made love. Your fantasy about what it would be like to have sex with each other was a seduction in itself. The element of the unknown brought your lust to a fever pitch. Even though you may now be in familiar territory, and that initial newness has worn off, you can supplant it with a passion even more intense than before. All it takes is adding a new element or two to the comfortable familiarity that is growing between you.

Below are three seductive scenarios to stir your imagination. These reflect a few of the most common fantasies of men and women (which we'll explore in more detail in the section that immediately follows). You may want to act out one or more of these scenes, but remember, you don't have to act them out in order to derive immense pleasure from them. Just talking about them can be enough to get you both incredibly turned on. (And if you'd like some more ideas for seductive scenarios, check out the true seduction tales in Appendix C.)

Heart Brakes

Even though sharing fantasies and playing games can be a wonderful seductive enhancement to your sexual relationship, it can also be a real turn-off if one of you isn't comfortable with the fantasy or its implications. Be honest in discussing your fantasies with each other, and never, never try to coerce your partner into doing something he or she doesn't want to do.

The Show-Off

Many people are, to some extent, exhibitionists. The idea of possibly being seen while in a state of undress, or even while having sex, is one of the most common fantasies. The element of danger that you will be caught can be quite exciting.

Imagine this, then: The two of you are out for the evening, and have just arrived at your favorite club. The music is loud, the beat compelling you to move. You and your partner enter the dance floor, blending in with the other bodies gyrating and swaying. The two of you look like any other couple on the dance floor, but your woman has a secret that even you don't know about: On a lark, she "forgot" to put on panties when she was getting dressed, so underneath her skirt, she is completely naked.

The evening begins like any other evening at a club, with the two of you laughing, dancing, and generally enjoying each other's company. Then, during a slow dance, your hand wanders down the side of her hip. Your eyes widen as you realize there's absolutely nothing but her under that little dress. She responds with a giggle that is a mixture of the innocent and the vixen. You leave the club a little later, both of you admittedly titillated by this little secret you're sharing. You barely make it back to the car before you are all over each other.

The Mysterious Blond at the Anytown Grand Hotel

Let's face it: There is something very exciting about a fine hotel. It's the perfect setting for a delicious seduction.

Just imagine this: Your wife sends you an e-mail just before quitting time. It says, "Go to the front desk of the Anytown Grand Hotel, ask for the key to Room 356. I'll be waiting for you there." Your mind is racing as you wonder what she could be up to. Reserving a room at a posh hotel in the middle of the week is not something your normally conservative wife is in the habit of doing. You can hardly concentrate on work for that last hour, and at the stroke of six, you're out of there.

You race to the Anytown Grand, and as you enter Room 356, you find the room completely dark, save for the flickering candles. As you take a few curious steps inside, you notice a trail of women's clothes creating a pathway to the dimly lit bathroom. Looking more closely, you observe that these are not your wife's clothes—or at least you've never seen her wear anything remotely like the diaphanous blouse and skimpy black skirt that lie crumpled on the floor. Nor have you seen those tiny black-and-silver panties that lie nearby…or that black garter belt…or those five-inch black stilettos. Not your wife's style at all, you think.

You're truly beginning to wonder if you somehow stumbled into the wrong room, but curiosity compels you to venture into the bathroom anyway, where you are startled to see a nude blonde woman in the round sunken bath tub.

Your heart skips a beat; your wife is a brunette.

The woman is facing away from you, her body almost covered by bubbles. You try not to look, but you can't help yourself. In a throaty voice the blonde woman says, "Amy is going to be a little late, so she sent me in her place to keep you company. I'm Nicole. Would you like a martini?"

As she turns to look at you, your anxiety and arousal fight with each other. Then you look closer, and notice that you are gazing into the gorgeous eyes of your wife Amy, who is wearing a blonde wig and a very big smile.

You sigh with relief, but relief isn't all you're feeling. You undress in record time, and you and your sultry, mysterious blonde have an absolutely frenzied night together.

A Hot Time in the Hot Tub

There is something about being in a hotel that seems to bring out people's wild side. It doesn't seem to matter if the location is across town or halfway around the world. Perhaps it's the anonymity of knowing that you'll never see your neighbors again; or maybe it's the sense that, since many of your basic needs are being provided for by someone else, you don't have to be responsible for anything, even your own actions.

So picture this: You are getting away for the weekend together to an out-of-town hotel. After checking in, the two of you take the elevator to the floor where your room is located. For no apparent reason at all, your man starts kissing and fondling you passionately as the elevator ascends. You are grateful that the car is empty except for the two of you, but can't help feeling titillated by the knowledge that the doors could open at any time, and you would be caught. By the time you get to your floor, your face is flushed with your mounting desire. Once you get to your room, you naturally assume he will make love to you immediately (and you want him to), but he has other ideas.

Instead of going at each other right there, he tells you to get your swimsuit on, and the two of you go to the hotel's hot tub. The soothing jets of water feel delightful, issuing that "take me away" command to all your stress.

Then, you feel your man's fingertips on your thigh, slowly working their way upward. The bubbles in the tub hide his ministrations from view, so you lean back and let him proceed. The combination of the warm water, the bubbles flicking gently upon your skin, and his exploring fingers both soothe and excite you, and before you know it you are having a very public climax, with no one the wiser except you and your man. At that point you both realize that it's time to return to the room.

Wordplay

Talking a fantasy simply means that you or your partner tell each other about a fantasy you may have, but don't necessarily act it out. The key to both of you enjoying a shared fantasy is in being completely honest with each other, and not doing or saying anything that will diminish your or your partner's sense of safety and trust. Realize that talking a fantasy doesn't necessarily mean you want it to come true.

You can see how even entertaining the thought of doing something daring, something that you would never normally do, can maintain a sense of newness in your play. Even if you have no desire to act upon your fantasies, you would be amazed at how exciting it can be to simply *talk a fantasy* during sexual play.

Next we're going to get a little more gender specific and take a closer look at the most common fantasies of men and women. The purpose of this exploration is not mere titillation, but to examine ways in which the two of you can enrich your relationship and become closer.

Men's Most Powerful Fantasies

After talking with thousands of men, I discovered there were several fantasies most of them had in common. While they said they enjoyed thinking about their fantasies, many said they would be hesitant to live out some of the wilder ones. Here is a list of some of the most common male fantasies:

➤ Having sex with two women at the same time

➤ Watching a woman undress or masturbate without her knowing you're watching (voyeurism)

➤ Having sex outdoors or in a public place

➤ Being with a woman who is an exhibitionist

➤ Having sex in a body of water (pool, hot tub, lake, or ocean)

The type of fantasies that most men describe support the fact that they are, by their nature, very visually oriented. Women, keep this in mind if you want to spice up the sex you have with your man. Even the tamest of activities, when tied to a guy's visual nature, can turn the heat up.

Heart Brakes

The woman-on-woman sex fantasy inspires strong feelings in men; it's either powerfully erotic or completely repugnant to them. Curiously enough, very few guys are indifferent to this fantasy. Women, before you attempt to titillate your man with a fantasy about you and another woman, make sure it's really a turn on to him.

Seeing Double

The two-women fantasy, which is very common, is partially a reflection of a man's desire to be "Super Stud," pleasing two attractive women at a time. A man also likes the idea of being the center of attention for two sexy females. But there's more to it than this; most men who have the two-women fantasy really enjoy the idea of watching the women give each other pleasure too. For one thing, guys like to look at women's bodies, and picturing not one but two female bodies together can be a real turn on for many men. But there's probably another factor at work too, at least on a subconscious level. Men in our society are expected to be production- and performance-oriented, even in bed, and these expectations can weigh heavily on a guy at times. Having two female partners assume some of the "responsibility" of giving each other pleasure allows him to lie back, relax, and enjoy the show.

Of course, I don't recommend your acting this fantasy out, but if you're comfortable feeding his fantasy, you can certainly titillate him by describing to him, in detail, a sexy scene starring him and you and another attractive female. I suggest that for the purposes of the fantasy, you do not use a friend or someone you know. Instead, make this other woman a hypothetical female whose physical features match those he finds attractive, or use some anonymous face in the crowd—perhaps an attractive woman the two of you saw at the mall earlier that day.

Ask the Love Coach

Darlene and Susan had been close friends for years. Darlene was dating a man named Brian, who made no secret of the fact that he found Susan attractive, too. At first Darlene really didn't mind, because Brian limited his attention to harmless flirtation. Susan did nothing to encourage Brian, as the last thing she wanted to do was to damage her friendship with Darlene.

The sex between Brian and Darlene was passionate and loving at first, and as time went on, they began injecting fantasy into their sex play. This is when the trouble began. Brian's favorite fantasy was to have sex with Darlene and another woman. Darlene had no problem with the fantasy itself, because she knew this is very common among men. However, Brian became obsessed with having Susan as the other woman. Darlene was a little uncomfortable with a fantasy so close to home, but she played along with it on an imaginary level.

Then Brian became more insistent about bringing his fantasy to reality. He began dropping not-so-subtle hints in Susan's presence. The tension between Brian and Darlene escalated until finally Darlene ended up breaking off her relationship with Brian. Fortunately, she and Susan are still friends.

When sharing the fantasy of bringing a third party into your bed, don't make it a friend or someone else you both know or see often. Use an imaginary person, or some attractive but anonymous face in the crowd you've both seen. Remember, you want to use fantasy to bring the two of you closer together, not to put someone or something between you.

The Naked Eye

Since men are so intensely visual, most of them have at least some voyeuristic tendencies. To feed your man's voyeuristic fantasies, you might go into the bedroom or bathroom, leave the door slightly open, and slowly, seductively undress (or, if you're feeling particularly daring, begin pleasuring yourself). The idea that he can see you while you can't see him will be especially titillating to him, especially if you don't normally put on such displays. Or, if you have privacy and you're sure the neighbors or the cops won't see you and think there's something suspicious going on, try undressing in front of a window, and then pleasuring yourself, while he's looking in watching you. (Of course, you'll want to wrap up your show by "discovering" he's out there, and inviting him in for some very passionate lovemaking.)

You Want to Do It Where?

The fantasy of having sex in a public place has so much appeal simply because it is one of those forbidden acts. Be careful when acting this one out, because you can get in trouble, either with the police or with assailants. If you're sure it's safe, though, you can act it out in a modified way by having sex in the car in a parking lot, for example. A friend of mine and her boyfriend had a spontaneous session in one of those historical cemeteries in New Orleans—a place they found romantic. Find your own romantic or idyllic spot, but again, be careful when acting out this fantasy.

Exhibit This!

If your man is excited by the idea of you as an exhibitionist, you can probably act out the fantasy without ever being on display. Try making love in a darkened room with the shades opened wide. You will be able to see your fantasy audience outside, yet remain completely hidden from their view. By playing into this fantasy, you will be fulfilling his need to show off the woman he is so proud of: you.

Wet and Wild

Water can be very sensual. Combine it with sex, and you've got a recipe for a powerfully seductive fantasy. You don't have to risk getting arrested for skinny-dipping in your local pool to incorporate his desire for aquatic sex. Just walk in while he is in the bathtub, strip down, and climb in with him.

Ask the Love Coach

To fully enjoy sharing each other's fantasies without risking additional doubts and regrets, agree beforehand to this simple rule: "While we're having sex, there aren't any limits on the fantasies we share. The actual decision whether or not to live out a fantasy, however, will be made only when we both have all our clothes on, preferably after we've had sex." Remember, clear minds harbor fewer regrets.

Women's Most Powerful Fantasies

Women have just as active a fantasy mechanism as do men. Some of the most popular women's fantasies, however, differ somewhat from men's, reflecting their unique needs and desires. By being aware of his woman's needs, a man can remain sensitive and responsive to her fantasies without feeling threatened. Some of those fantasies include:

➤ Being seen by others (exhibitionism)

➤ Being ravished

➤ Being in complete control

➤ Having other male partners

➤ Bisexuality

Now You See Me...

It's no secret: a woman needs to feel beautiful. It doesn't make us any less independent or any of the other things we've been working on since the suffragettes. But there's a little bit of Venus in us all. It's not surprising, then, that many of us fantasize about being seen and admired by other men. The fact that men have historically been the aggressors sexually, combined with the very real danger of being raped, has an inhibiting effect on a woman's desire to be put on display. Yet, the desire does exist in many women. A man who is secure enough to accept this, yet sensitive enough to

For HIS Eyes Only

Be a tender ravisher. Use soft restraints that won't leave marks on her tender skin; silk neckties make wonderful erotic restraints. Once you have her bound, tickle her with feathers, trickle warm fragrant oil on her most sensitive spots, kiss her lightly all over—in short, tease her until she is crazy with desire!

accept the limitations his woman puts on the activity, may well find that he is the lucky recipient of some fantastic sex.

So indulge her in her role-playing fantasies. If she wants to pretend to be a prostitute (with you as her only "john," of course) or a topless dancer (with you as her sole audience member), sit back and enjoy it. No doubt, you'll both find the experience thrilling.

Tie Me Up, Tie Me Down

Many women are turned on by the idea of being tied up and ravished by their partner, giving themselves up totally to his control. This is partly a result of another primary female need: a woman's desire to feel emotionally safe with her man.

For HER Eyes Only

If you really want to get into the ravishment game, but don't want to ruin any clothes you care for, have a couple of throwaway dresses on hand. That way, he can literally rip your clothes off—and your wardrobe won't suffer for it.

In any case, it's important to remember that a woman's bondage or ravishment fantasy is *not* a rape fantasy. Rape is a violent and criminal act that has no place in a loving relationship. And in order for any sort of dominance fantasy to be enjoyable for your woman, she needs to feel absolute trust in you. She needs to know that, when she gives you such a great degree of control over her, you will not do anything to abuse her trust. She must know that you would never allow any harm to come to her, and that you won't do anything that makes her feel diminished in any way.

So temper your dominance with lots of tenderness. Use soft restraints that won't hurt her. Let the only instruments of torture be your tongue and fingertips, and perhaps a feather.

Ask the Love Coach

The 1998 revival and re-release of the movie *Grease* may have demonstrated our country's love of nostalgia in the late 20th century, but it also showed something else: Sandra Dee is alive and well. Most women were brought up with the notion of being "good girls": they don't drink, smoke, or rat their hair—and they definitely don't act out their sexual desires. Here's where the notion of being tied up and ravished comes in. Obviously, if the wild sex is beyond a woman's control, then she's not "guilty." (Of course, let's not forget that ol' Olivia Newton-John broke out in a pair of tight black pants and tube top at the end—but that's another fantasy!)

That's Ms. Dominatrix to You, Buddy

Other women are excited by the idea of being in complete control of their man, to the point of domination. Having been historically cast in a submissive role, some women relish the sense of power they have over a man who is forced to succumb to their desires. Even though it might seem strange or uncomfortable to some men to be so completely controlled by a woman, remember that, by allowing her the opportunity to act on this fantasy with you, you are telling her that you not only trust her completely, but that you are willing to accept the parts of her personality that don't fit within stereotypical roles. By allowing her to tie you up, tease, and tantalize you, you are encouraging her to share her deepest sexual secrets. Trust me, you will be the joyous beneficiary of her exploration.

Naturally, you must have complete trust in your woman's intent in order to feel comfortable with, much less enjoy, acting out such a fantasy. And, just as when the roles are reversed, she must respect your limits.

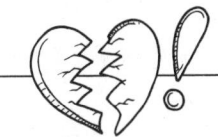

Heart Brakes

Men or women: Where the fantasy of bondage is concerned, a word of caution is needed. Don't allow yourself to be completely restrained. You want to make certain that, while you are giving your partner the illusion of control, you remain in a position of safety—where you can set and keep your limits, and, most importantly, you can get out of the restraints yourself if necessary.

Ask the Love Coach

If the two of you engage in dominance role-playing, you should establish a clear signal beforehand that says "Stop." Choose a single word or signal that you both agree will bring the play to a halt, and then honor that signal. In the heat of passion, you can say or do things that might not be inside one or both of your comfort zones, and you both need to know that you have a panic button you can push if things start to go too far.

Having Other Male Partners

It is not unusual for a woman to fantasize about being with a man—or men—other than her current one. Not unlike many men, some women crave a sense of variety and adventure, which may show up as a desire to be with another man (or even another

For HER Eyes Only

Be sure to make your man the center of the fantasies you share with him, no matter what (or who) originally set your fantasy off. If you were turned on earlier that afternoon by the handsome Greek carpet cleaner or the muscular fireman you saw at your biannual office fire drill, make up a fantasy with your lover as the carpet cleaner or fireman who ravishes you in some forbidden place. Get him involved in the fantasy by telling him about it; you can whisper an entire erotic scenario in his ear as he's making love to you. Just remember to make him the star of the fantasy; you want to excite him, not cause him to think you'd really rather be with that carpet cleaner or fireman instead of with him.

For HIS Eyes Only

Don't allow your own fantasies of two women together make you push her farther than she wants to go with her bisexual fantasies. Find a common ground with your woman, and you'll both be satisfied with the results.

woman; more on that in a moment). The fantasy partner might be one person or a room full of faceless strangers.

I want you men to realize that this is a fairly common fantasy, and it certainly doesn't mean that your woman is dissatisfied with you as a lover. More than likely, it's simply an expression of her desire for many men to appreciate her beauty. If you can allow her to talk about the fantasy, especially when the two of you are in the heat of passion, you may well find the heat is turned up considerably. Afterwards, you can reassure each other that it was, after all, just a fantasy, and smile comfortably at the extra zing it brought to your lovemaking.

Bisexuality

Throughout history, women have looked to each other for emotional support. Sometimes, we are able to share our most intimate thoughts with each other in a way that we can't with the men in our lives. I hope you men realize that this isn't a put-down, but rather a reflection of the way society has been for hundreds of years, and how we perceived things while we were growing up ("Don't disturb Dad when he comes home from work."). Add to this the fact that women have always been held up in our culture as the standard for human beauty and encouraged at every step of the way to perceive the female form as being beautiful. It's no wonder that a significant number of women wonder about—and even experiment with— each other sexually.

This doesn't mean that women who fantasize about being with another woman are really lesbians. It is simply an outgrowth of how we were raised and the society in which we live. At any rate, most men don't have problems with this fantasy, because it's one that so many of them share. All you have to do is let her know that this fantasy, like any other, is not only okay, it's perfectly normal and healthy.

Ask the Love Coach

Props, toys and sex aids can add lots of fun to your love play. Going shopping together in one of those adult toy stores can be a seduction in itself. Check out the array of vibrators and other sex toys, flavored creams and body oils, erotic books and videos, and sexy leather or lace get-ups. Just beware of becoming too dependent on any of these items for arousal or orgasm. Like fantasies and games, they should be used to bring you closer together, not distract you from each other.

Share and Share Alike

In a perfect relationship, both people would have the same fantasies, the same limits, and the same motivations. Such a relationship simply doesn't exist, and would be incredibly boring if it did. The real magic of a relationship with another person is in discovering his or her unique qualities and being willing and able to integrate that uniqueness with your own. The real challenge in the relationship is to see that both your needs are met, that both of you feel secure with each other, and that you are filled with hope and excitement when you think of each other. This isn't something that comes later on, after you've been seeing each other for a long time. It begins with your first meeting, and everything you do from that point either adds to or diminishes it.

You can add to your partner's good feelings by being alert and sensitive to his or her needs, by allowing your partner's uniqueness to shine through—including his or her fantasies—without judgment, and by encouraging an exploration of those needs openly with you. Making your partner feel safe and accepted, even when you know his or her secret hopes, fears, and fantasies, is the surest path to a delicious seduction. And by allowing your partner a safe place, where limits are respected, he or she will want to share even more with you. If that doesn't constitute a delicious seduction, I don't know what does.

The Least You Need to Know

➤ Sexual fantasies and games have a place in seduction and a lively sex life, but they should never become a substitute for the intimacy of good lovemaking.

➤ When sharing fantasies or indulging in sex games, know your own limits and respect those of your partner. The emotional safety of both people should be your paramount concern at all times.

➤ When in doubt about acting out a fantasy, don't do it, particularly if it involves a third person.

➤ Men's and women's sexual fantasies are an exaggerated reflection of their different sexual and emotional needs.

➤ Sharing your sexual fantasies can bring the two of you closer together by helping you explore each other's sexual desires and emotional needs—and can be deliciously seductive.

Chapter 22

What's Love Got to Do with It?

In This Chapter

➤ The stages of a romantic relationship

➤ What love has to do with seduction (and vice versa)

➤ Dancing around the "C" word: commitment

➤ Staying seductive forever

No book on seduction would be complete without talking about love. After all, for the majority of us, sex is most fulfilling in the context of a loving relationship—and most people, at some point, do fall in love. No doubt, many of you who are reading this book are in the process of falling in love, are already in love, or simply have a future goal of finding the Big L, but aren't quite there yet. Perhaps you're even already in a committed relationship.

That's why I'm going to devote this chapter to taking a closer look at this phenomenon we call love. While it is beyond the scope of this book to delve into the details of compatibility and commitment, I will share some insights into love: the different kinds of love, the phases of a love relationship, and—because I haven't forgotten why you came to this book in the first place—the role that seduction plays as the relationship progresses. And I'll end the chapter—and the book—by talking about how you can make seduction last forever.

When Love Is on the Agenda (Whether You Planned It or Not)

Men's and women's roles are changing as we approach the new millennium. Many of you guys are becoming more relationship-oriented, and many of you women are becoming more independent. It's no longer true, if it ever was, that men are just out for "one thing" (sex) and that women are interested only in marriage. Even so, it is true that many people enter into the process of seduction with agendas that would seem to be more consistent with traditional sex roles:

➤ To some men, seduction is simply a means to getting a woman into bed.

➤ To some women, seduction is a means to getting a man to fall in love and propose marriage.

Obviously, there is enormous potential for trouble if either one of these agendas clashes with the partner's plans for the relationship. In a perfect world, both parties would have no agenda other than to enrich each other's lives with the experience. They would be open to whatever happened, without being unduly attached to the outcome. In reality, most people are rarely that detached. At the very least, partners should have compatible expectations for the relationship.

Sometimes, however, expectations change. One or the other partner in the couple who was in it only for the sex may find him- or herself falling in love. The partner who is marriage-minded may decide he or she would rather wait awhile longer before jumping into such a serious commitment. No matter how careful we are, and how well we think we know ourselves or our partners, the human heart is often unpredictable. Lust is bewildering enough, but when love enters into the picture too, it can really throw us for a loop.

So what do you do when love calls you by your name, as the old Leonard Cohen song puts it? For that matter, how do you know it's really love calling, as opposed to infatuation? Let's start by exploring what love is.

Just What the Heck Is True Love, Anyway?

Love is an emotion that nearly everyone has experienced at some time in his or her life. You would think, then, that we'd all be able to agree on just what it is. But this hasn't been the case. After all, there are different kinds of love. Furthermore, the experience of love is different for everybody; there are as many definitions of true love as there are people to define it. For centuries, philosophers, poets, and novelists have tried to capture it in words, and artists and sculptors have attempted to capture it in forms and images. In more recent decades, social scientists and biologists have tried in various ways to quantify it. So far, there's no real consensus about what *real love* is. The only point on which we all seem to agree is that it exists.

It should come as no surprise that I don't have the ultimate definition of love, either. But I will offer you the best indicator I know of the *presence* of real love: It is when you put the other person's needs on an equal basis with your own—not below them (that's selfishness), nor above (that's martyrdom).

As many of you have probably already learned the hard way, the road to real love is often rocky. How do you know when you're on that road, and what can you do to keep love alive and exciting once you've reached your destination? We can begin solving this mystery by taking a look at how a romantic relationship develops.

Wordplay

Real love means putting your partner's needs on the same level as your own needs, rather than above or below.

Love Means Never Having to Say You're Static

One thing most of us can agree on is that love never remains in a static condition. The love between two people grows and changes; like the people themselves, it either gets better or it fades, but it never stays the same. Even though the experience of love is different for everybody, however, most romantic relationships go through fairly predictable stages: passionate love and mature love.

In the Beginning: Passionate Love

Some call it infatuation, some call it insanity, but most of us agree that it's glorious. I'm talking, of course, about that fevered state known as passionate love. *Passionate love* is a state of fierce longing for your partner. At this early stage in your romantic relationship, the two of you are completely absorbed in each other, and it's often difficult to tell where lust ends and love begins. Perhaps that point is moot—unless, of course, you're thinking of making a long-term commitment when you're still at this stage.

You absolutely should not make any crucial life decisions while under the influence of passionate love. That's because during this time of wondrous highs (and devastating lows, when things don't go right), the two of you really are not in your right minds. Let's face it: Passionate love makes most of us a little crazy—crazy in a good way, but crazy nonetheless. And, much as we may wish it, that delicious high just doesn't last. Eventually the endorphin levels drop off, and things get more or less back to normal. We're simply not wired for perpetual ecstasy.

Wordplay

Passionate love is a state of intense longing for union with another. It is usually expressed by kissing, hugging, gazing intently at each other, frequent touching, and, of course, making love.

Of course, this doesn't stop some people from trying to maintain a state of constant rapture. Since it's almost impossible to sustain the passionate high with one person, people who are hooked on that new-love feeling will go from partner to partner, ending the relationship as soon as the newness wears off. These "love addicts" may leave the proverbial trail of broken hearts behind them, but in the end, they're the ones who suffer the biggest heartbreak.

For those who stick it out past the infatuation stage, what comes next? Is it all boredom and stagnation from there on out? Unfortunately, this is true with some couples. However, in the best-case scenario, people who continue to nurture their relationships can reap the rewards of a deeper kind of love.

As Time Goes By: Mature Love

No matter how hot passionate love is, eventually and inevitably it simmers down. For most couples, the passion begins fading within two to four years. People have different ways of coping with this loss of "paradise," but there are certain discernible patterns. Studies have shown, for example, that couples don't express affection to each other as frequently after about two years. Furthermore, in cultures worldwide, the divorce rate peaks after about four years of marriage.

What gives? As mentioned previously, the fading of passionate love is partly a biochemical phenomenon; endorphin production returns to normal levels with the passage of time. Then there's the emotional reality of getting to know somebody; any illusions you may have had in the beginning about your partner's perfection are inevitably replaced with the day-to-day actuality of being with someone who is, after all, only human—just like you.

The result of reality setting in is that the highs in the relationship aren't as high. The good news is that the lows aren't as low either, but that may be small comfort for those who are hooked on the thrill.

If love is to last, it must settle into a steadier, but still warm, state known variously as mature love or *companionate love.* This type of love is characterized by true bonding and emotional intimacy. Other factors besides physical attraction, such as shared values and shared experiences, become increasingly important. And while love in its more mature stages may be more low-key than passionate love, it is deeper and, some would say, in many ways it is sweeter.

The important thing to know is that companionate love does not preclude passion. It's not a complete trade-off, where you give up passion and get endurance in exchange. You may have to work harder at keeping the passion alive, but you can keep it alive for as long as you both wish.

Wordplay

Companionate love is characterized by true bonding and emotional intimacy. Shared values and shared experiences become increasingly important.

As a matter of fact, I believe that a lasting relationship must include passion in order to be truly satisfying. The other two components for a successful long-term relationship are compatibility and commitment. (We'll talk about the latter in just a little while.)

Ask the Love Coach

Although many people believe that the demise of passion is inevitable in a long-term relationship, it's possible to keep passion alive indefinitely if you work at it. In fact, passion is a necessary component for a truly satisfying long-term romantic relationship.

You don't believe it's possible? Many of the seduction scenes in this book have been shared with me by clients or friends, some of whom have been married for years or even decades. (Remember the story of the octogenarians Seth and Sara in Chapter 17?) A former client of mine named Dan is yet another case in point. Dan and his wife Catherine recently celebrated their 20th wedding anniversary, and their passion for each other is stronger than ever. What's their secret?

"We never forget that no matter how well we know each other, there is always something new to learn," Dan says. Catherine adds, "We try very hard not to take each other for granted, and we always make it a point to experience new things together—whether it's a camping trip in New Mexico, or learning another language together. So far we've studied French and Italian, and we're thinking of tackling Russian next. Doing new things keeps us excited about life, which translates into excitement for each other." (Oh, and those classes in Tantric yoga that they've been taking together certainly haven't hurt their sex life.)

So...Where Does Seduction Fit into This?

If we're to accept the idea that seduction is a never-ending process, we need to be aware of how it fits into our lives as the relationship grows and changes. Let's take a closer look at the role seduction plays in the different phases of a romantic relationship.

➤ *Infatuation phase.* This is where seduction plays the most obvious part—the starring role, if you will. In the beginning of your relationship, everything is new and enchanting; there is magic in the air around you. You're in the throes of passionate love, and virtually everything about your relationship is seductive. Seduction is what makes you both keep coming back for more.

➤ *Middle phase.* At this point, some of the newness is wearing off, but seduction continues to play a pretty strong part. It just requires a little prodding once the initial excitement wanes. This is why it is so important that you continue to seduce each other on all levels, and that you create adventures together, so your relationship doesn't become stagnant. (See Chapter 20.)

➤ *Decision/commitment phase.* Sooner or later, if your love lasts long enough, and you are both so inclined, you will reach a point where you're considering taking your relationship to the next level. For some couples this means moving in together; for others it means marriage. In any case, when you are making a decision to commit to someone, seduction should not play a major role. This doesn't mean you suspend seduction and passion altogether, but for a major decision such as commitment, you need to let your head and your heart be your guide, rather than your libido. That's why it's extremely important that you don't attempt to make any long-term commitments while you are still in that wild-and-crazy infatuation stage.

Heart Brakes

Seduction plays a major part in keeping the passion alive once you have decided to make a commitment to someone, but it should never be the sole factor in the decision-making process. When making such an important decision, use your head as well as your heart.

➤ *Postcommitment phase.* Now is the time for you to haul seduction out from wherever you temporarily placed it while you were making your big decision to commit to each other. Once you've made your commitment, seduction is not only desirable, it is necessary to keep the passion alive. Many people think that after the initial passion fades—an average of two to four years into the relationship—this is the beginning of the end of passion. That is emphatically not true. You can make the passion last indefinitely. This may take some work, but the rewards are worth it.

Ask the Love Coach

Just because a romantic relationship does not end in a long-term commitment, this doesn't mean the love wasn't real, and it certainly doesn't mean the relationship was a waste of time.

Deanna and Brad were together for nearly three years. They were passionately in love and extremely compatible in many areas, not the least of which was sex. In fact, they came very close to getting married. In the end, however, they concluded that they wanted radically different things in life and could never truly be happy as husband and wife. Brad wanted very much to settle down and raise a family in the small town in which he'd grown up. Deanna had a wanderlust, however, and wanted to spend the next 10 years or so traveling. She was also quite sure she did not want to have children.

When Deanna and Brad said goodbye, many of their friends and family members expressed disappointment. "You two were such a perfect match!" they heard over and over. Or, "You were soul mates! You guys really blew it." Many people, particularly Deanna's friends, ventured the opinion that Deanna had wasted nearly three years of her life.

"That's ridiculous," Deanna says. "Brad and I taught each other so much, and we truly helped each other grow. I wouldn't trade my time with him for anything in the world." Brad feels the same way. "No, it didn't end in 'happily ever after,'" he says. "But Deanna is the most beautiful, most seductive woman I have ever known, and I know I'm a better person because of the time I spent with her."

Brad's and Deanna's was truly "an affair to remember," and they remember it fondly because they did not become too attached to the outcome of their relationship. Like Deanna and Brad, we should all learn to appreciate the people in our lives for the gifts they truly are, whether or not the relationship lasts forever.

Can We Talk About Commitment?

What if it looks as if your love is going to be much more than just another "affair to remember"? What if you want it to be "an affair to continue"? What if you're thinking about that "C" word: commitment? Well, first of all, I don't believe you can, or should, make a commitment to somebody until you have been with that person long enough to determine whether you are truly compatible. As I said at the beginning of this chapter, it is beyond the scope of this book to go into the details of compatibility. In *Cracking The Love Code*, I have several lengthy questionnaires that can help you determine whether or not you and your partner are compatible. But I do want to touch on the subject of commitment here, because it is important, and because questions about commitment are almost certain to come up between you and your partner if you stay together past the infatuation stage.

Commitment means different things to different people. Or rather, different people express their commitment in different ways. For most people in our society, marriage is the ultimate expression of commitment. Unfortunately, it is possible to be married and not committed. The act of getting married is, after all, an outward expression of intent.

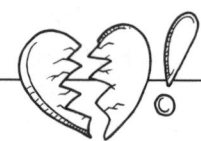

Heart Brakes

Never try to coerce someone into making a commitment, and don't allow yourself to be coerced. Whether its outward expression is marriage or living together, commitment is first and foremost an internal pledge each person must make in his or her heart. You may be able to manipulate someone into marrying you, but you cannot force that internal pledge—and if the pledge isn't there, the two of you will not be happy together.

If, however, it is not backed up by true commitment—an internal pledge both partners must make in their hearts—it will be nothing more than an act.

You cannot force anybody to commit to you. My files are full of stories of people who tried to coerce a commitment, and not one of these tales has a happy ending. Granted, some of the couples in question did get married, but these were not happily-ever-after marriages.

So, no matter how passionately in love (and in lust) you are, there are two principles to remember when you're trying to make up your mind about commitment:

1. *Take your time.* I recommend not making a decision until you've been together at least a year.

2. *Use your head.* Passion and seduction play major roles in getting the relationship underway, and in keeping it intriguing over the long haul. But they should not be the major factors in making the all-important decision to commit to somebody.

Seduction Can Be Forever—Make It So!

If I didn't believe that seduction can be forever, I wouldn't have devoted an entire book to this topic. I hope by now you're convinced that seduction is a process, and that it's up to you to choose how long that process lasts.

Of course, there's only one first time with your partner, but that doesn't mean that the two of you can't continue to discover thrilling new things about each other—and yourselves, and the world around you—for as long as your relationship lasts. So how do you make seduction last forever? You do it by making conscious choices about the relationship and yourselves. As you'll see, these choices reinforce each other.

Choose to Stay in Love with the Relationship

In order for a relationship to continue to be fulfilling, you need to continue to focus on its positive traits. Too often relationships begin a slow (or fast) decline once the passion wears off. Eventually not only the passion is gone, but so is the love. In most cases, this is because the partners have forgotten to focus on what worked about the relationship. It has somehow become easier for them to concentrate on what's not working. If you find this happening to you, you both need to go back to Square One and rediscover the magic that first drew you to each other.

One way to do this is to keep doing romantic and fun things together (or start doing them again, if you've quit). If the relationship is to survive, both of you must continue to associate it with good times. Some psychologists call this the "liking by association" principle. Whatever you call it, it works.

Choose to Keep Seducing Your Partner

In order to stay in love with the relationship, and keep the passion alive, you need to continue to seduce your partner on all levels (see Chapter 20). Of course, you must be motivated to do this, and in order to be so motivated, you have to continue to focus on your partner's positive traits. This can sometimes be a challenge in long-term relationships; in fact, it's inevitable that intimate partners are going to find fault with each other sooner or later. When faultfinding becomes a habit, however, you need to take a few steps back and remember why you were so attracted to your lover in the first place. And then you need to choose to keep seducing that attractive person.

Choose to Keep Seducing Yourself

In order to be able to focus on the positive traits in your partner, you must also continue to focus on the positive traits in you. In other words, you have to keep seducing yourself.

How do you do this? First, you take care of yourself—physically, intellectually, emotionally, and spiritually. Continue your personal growth—and never stop growing. Change is a characteristic of life, and since you're going to change anyway, for better or worse, why not make it for better? Go back to the beginning of this book as often as you need to; do the exercises that focus on developing your seductiveness on all levels. Continue to be seduced by life, and you, in turn, will continue to be seductive—to yourself and to your partner. It's inevitable.

Ask the Love Coach

Life is all about change; nothing alive is static. We are always either getting better or getting worse, but no matter what we do (or don't do), we cannot stay the same. It's up to you to make the choice for positive change in your life. Whether you're in a relationship or you're flying solo, get out there and grow. Remember, part of being seductive is being interesting and interested!

Let Love and Seduction Feed on Each Other

When you think about it, love and seduction are natural partners. And if you can remain in love with yourself, your partner, the relationship, and life, there's no reason you can't make seduction last forever—or, as they sometimes say these days in wedding vows: *for as long as you both shall love.*

The Least You Need to Know

➤ Sex is most fulfilling in the context of a loving relationship.

➤ Real love exists when you put your partner's needs on the same level as your own (as opposed to above or below).

➤ Although the experience of love is different for everybody, most romantic relationships go through fairly predictable stages—beginning with passionate love and, if they last, evolving into a steadier but still warm state sometimes known as companionate love.

➤ Although the initial passion inevitably fades somewhat with time, it is not only possible but desirable to keep passion alive in a romantic relationship.

➤ Commitment is an internal pledge both parties must make to themselves and to each other; you cannot coerce someone into making a commitment to you.

➤ Seduction can be a never-ending process if you make the conscious choice to stay in love with the relationship, with yourself, with your partner, and with life.

Resources

Books

Below are just a few of the many books on sexuality and relationships. The list is by necessity incomplete; there are many other excellent books and tapes as well. Take your lover on a leisurely browse through your local bookstore, and...happy reading!

Nonfiction

Anne Hooper's Pocket Sex Guide by Anne Hooper, DK Publishing, 1994.

Aphrodite: A Memoir of the Senses by Isabel Allende, HarperCollins, 1998.

The Art of Sexual Ecstasy by Margo Anand, J.P. Tarcher, 1991.

The Best Love, The Best Sex: Creating Sensual, Soulful, Supersatisfying Relationships by Suzi Landolphi, Putnam Publishers Group, 1996.

Body Language by Julius Fast, Pocket Books, 1970.

Cracking the Love Code: Six Proven Principles to Find and Keep Real Love With the Right Person by Janet O'Neal, Broadway Books, 1998.

The Eastern Way of Love: Tantric Sex and Erotic Mysticism by Kamala Devi, Simon and Schuster, 1977.

For Each Other: Sharing Sensual Intimacy by Lonnie Barbach, Ph.D., New American Library, 1984.

The Great Sex Weekend: A 48-Hour Guide to Rekindling Sparks for Bold, Busy or Bored Lovers by Pepper Schwartz, Ph.D. and Janet Lever, Ph.D., Putnam, 1998.

The Guide to Getting It On!: A New and Mostly Wonderful Book About Sex for Adults of All Ages by The Goofy Foot Press, 1997.

Hot Monogamy: Essential Steps to More Passionate, Intimate Lovemaking by Dr. Patricia Love and Jo Robinson, Penguin, 1995.

How to Drive Your Man Wild in Bed by Graham Masterson, Signet, 1975.

How to Make a Man Fall in Love With You by Tracy Cabot, Dell, 1984.

How to Satisfy a Woman Every Time and Have Her Beg For More by Naura Hayden, Dutton, 1983.

Intercourses: An Aphrodisiac Cookbook by Martha Hopkins and Randall T. Lockridge, Terrace Publishing, 1997.

Just Between Us Girls: Secrets About Men From the Madam Who Knows by Sydney Biddle Barrows, St. Martin's Press, 1997.

The Kinsey Institute New Report on Sex by June M. Reinish, Ph.D., St. Martin's Press, 1990.

Men in Love by Nancy Friday, Delacorte Press, 1980 (explores male sexual fantasies).

Mindblowing Sex in the Real World by Sari Locker, HarperPerennial, 1995.

The New Joy of Sex: A Gourmet Guide to Lovemaking for the Nineties by Alex Comfort, Crown (compact edition), 1994.

The One-Hour Orgasm: The Ultimate Guide to Totally Satisfying Any Man or Woman Every Time by Dr. Bob Schwartz, Breakthru Publishing, 1995.

101 Nights of Grrreat Sex by Laura Corn, Park Avenue Publishing, 1995.

Secrets About Men Every Woman Should Know by Barbara DeAngelis, Dell, 1991.

Sex in America: A Definitive Survey by Robert Michael, et al., Warner, 1994.

Sex on Campus: The Naked Truth About the Real Sex Lives of College Students by Leland Elliott, Cynthia Brantley Johnson, Random House, 1997.

203 Ways to Drive a Man Wild in Bed by Olivia St. Claire, Harmony Books, 1993.

365 Ways to Improve Your Sex Life by James R. Petersen, Plume, 1996.

What Men Really Want: Straight Talk From Men About Sex by Susan Crain Bakos, St. Martin's Press, 1991.

What Men Won't Tell You But Women Need to Know by Bob Berkowitz with Roger Gittines, Avon, 1990.

Women on Top by Nancy Friday, Pocket Books, 1991 (one of several works by this author that explore female sexual fantasies).

Zone Therapy by Anika Bergson and Vladimir Tuchack, Pinnacle Books, 1974.

Fiction

Delta of Venus by Anaïs Nin, Harcourt Brace Jovanovich, 1977.

Emmanuelle by Emmanuelle Arsan, Dell, 1971.

Little Birds by Anaïs Nin, Harcourt Brace Jovanovich, 1979.

A Man With a Maid by Anonymous, Ballantine, 1974.

Memoirs of a Geisha by Arthur Golden, Alfred A. Knopf, 1997.

The Olympia Reader, edited by Maurice Girodias, Grove Press, 1965.

Pleasures: Women Write Erotica edited by Lonnie Barbach, Ph.D., Perennial, 1985.

Instructional Videos

The Venus Butterfly for Men by Dr. Bob Schwartz, Breakthru Publishing, 1998.

The Venus Butterfly for Women by Dr. Bob Schwartz, Breakthru Publishing, 1998.

The Language of Seduction: A Wordplay Glossary

AIDS   Acronym for acquired immune deficiency syndrome, a fatal disorder that cripples the body's disease-fighting mechanisms. AIDS is caused by a virus called HIV. So far there is no cure for AIDS, so prevention is the best policy. Check with your health care professional, or local public health organizations, for more information.

Attraction   Being drawn to someone. A manifestation of attraction is the need to please and impress the object of your attention. This does not necessarily imply sexual attraction.

Auditory   One of the three principal ways in which people process information, according to neuro-linguistic programming (NLP) theory. If your partner is an auditory person, he or she is especially likely to be captivated by the sound of your voice and by what you say.

Aura   The dictionary defines an aura as (1) the atmosphere surrounding and radiating from a person or thing, and (2) a luminous radiation. While many people associate the concept of the aura with New Age beliefs, the idea is actually quite old. It's possible the halos surrounding holy figures in many of the Old Masters' paintings were actually supposed to represent auras.

Buyer's remorse   Feelings of remorse that sometimes occur after making love with a new partner. These are very similar to the feelings people have after making a major purchase, such as a car or a house. After the exhilaration brought on by the rush of endorphins to your brain, comes the inevitable letdown accompanied by feelings of doubt. These feelings lead to questions about whether you did the right thing. It's helpful to realize such feelings and thoughts are natural, and more than likely they will pass.

Charisma   Originally a theological term meaning "free gift of God's grace." It is derived from the Greek *kharisma*, meaning "to show favor or grace." Though the word still has religious meanings, it is most commonly used these days to describe a person's power to inspire devotion and enthusiasm.

Chat room An online communication forum that allows you to have real-time "conversations" with many people at once, or just one person. There are chat groups for every conceivable interest. If someone in the chat room captures your interest, the two of you can transfer to a *private chat room* and continue your exchange one-on-one. Online chat is as safe as you want it to be; since you use a nickname to identify yourself for the duration of your chat, you don't have to reveal your real name or even your e-mail address.

Companionate love A mature form of love, characterized by true bonding and emotional intimacy rather than intense passion or infatuation.

Courtesan A courtesan was, for all practical purposes, a prostitute, but one who was highly trained and educated, and catered only to the most wealthy and powerful men. In many cases she wielded considerable power herself.

Cunnilingus (pronounced cun-nuh-LING-us) The technical term for oral stimulation of a woman's vulva and clitoris.

Delicious seduction Seduction that has a beneficial outcome for both people.

Endorphins Substances produced in the brain that block or reduce sensations of pain, and can also cause a sense of euphoria. Endorphins are produced not only in response to pain but to excitement, and are partially responsible for the feeling of ecstasy that accompanies falling in love (or in lust).

Fellatio (pronounced fuh-LAY-shee-o) The technical term for oral stimulation of a man's penis.

Flirting The dictionary defines flirting as "acting amorously without serious intention." Flirting can, however, be destructive, or it can merely be a harmless way of testing your attractiveness to another individual. It can also be a prelude to a sweet seduction.

Foreplay For most people, the word foreplay means certain acts that lead to sexual intercourse. Foreplay generally implies a greater level of intimacy than just kissing or holding hands, such as fondling each other's genitals or having oral sex. However, passionate kissing or even flirting can be considered foreplay. There's really no set script to follow, and even if your foreplay doesn't end in intercourse—or if it occurs some time after intercourse—what's important is that it is a mutually pleasurable experience.

Frigidity An obsolete term for *female sexual dysfunction*, such as difficulty reaching orgasm, inability to have an orgasm, or a general disinterest in sex. Any number of physiological or psychological factors may be responsible, but with qualified professional help and/or an understanding partner, a woman can conquer this problem.

Geisha A Geisha is a professional female entertainer trained in singing, dancing, playing a musical instrument, and the art of conversation. In fact, the word Geisha means, "art person." This profession began in Japan in the 18th century and still exists today.

Golden Rule   "Do unto others as you would have others do unto you" is a good rule to follow in all areas of your life, including dating and seduction. Treat your partner with the same consideration and respect with which you want to be treated.

HIV   The human immunodeficiency virus, the retrovirus that causes AIDS. There are several ways HIV can be spread: through transfusions with contaminated blood (currently less of a likelihood in the U.S., as the nation's blood supply has been screened for HIV since 1985); use of contaminated needles (as with intravenous drug users); or through unprotected sexual contact. Though years may elapse between infection with HIV and the onset of AIDS, AIDS is incurable and fatal, so prevention is the best policy. Check with your health care professional or local public health organizations for more information.

HIV test result—negative   A negative HIV test result simply means that no HIV antibodies were found in your blood, which usually means you are not infected. Even so, this does not mean you are immune to HIV; nobody is. You still need to practice safe sex.

HIV test result—positive   A positive HIV test result does not necessarily mean you have AIDS, but it does mean that it's likely that you will develop AIDS.

Image consultant   A professional who advises clients on hair color, hairstyle, make-up, and clothing and accessories, and may advise on posture and general appearance and demeanor. Some offer both personal and corporate image consulting services. *Make-up consultants* advise clients on type, color, and application of make-up. *Color consultants* advise clients on choice of colors for clothing that will complement their appearance. Many consultants offer a combination of the above services. Look in the Yellow Pages under "Image Consultants."

Impotence   A misleading term for *erectile dysfunction*, or a man's inability to have an erection. This can be an isolated incident or a chronic occurrence. There are numerous physiological or psychological causes; the good news is that plenty of treatments are available today, including the much-touted virility pill, Viagra.

Kinesthetic   One of the three principal ways in which people process information, according to neuro-linguistic programming (NLP) theory. A kinesthetic, or tactile, person is especially likely to be warmed or turned on by touching.

Malicious seduction   Seduction that has harmful or negative results to the person being seduced and possibly to the seducer as well.

Meridians   Pathways in the body along which life energy (which the Chinese call "qi" or "chi") flows. Used in zone therapies such as acupuncture, acupressure, and reflexology.

Millennium   This word has several definitions in the dictionary. The first is simply "a period of one thousand years." The term also refers to the thousand-year reign of Christ on Earth, as prophesied in the Bible. The third meaning (and more to our point here) is a period of general happiness and good living. No matter what your frame of reference, there's something about this approaching new millennium that is genuinely exciting, much more so than just any old New Year.

Mixers   Get-togethers that usually are geared for specific groups of people—singles, MENSA members, computer enthusiasts, and the like. Mixers can take place virtually anywhere—in hotel ballrooms, fellowship halls in places of worship, restaurants, bookstores, even grocery stores. These events provide a wonderful opportunity to meet other people in a fun and non-threatening environment. Particularly if you're newly single, keep a lookout for announcements about singles mixers that appeal to your particular interests.

Neuro-linguistic programming (NLP)   The study of how language, both verbal and nonverbal, affects our nervous system. The name is derived from "neuro," referring to the brain, and "linguistic," referring to language. According to NLP, there are three principal ways in which people process information. Everyone uses all three modes, but most people have one that is dominant. Some people are predominantly *visual*, some are *auditory*, and some are *kinesthetic*, or tactile (see individual definitions in this Appendix). Knowing which mode is dominant in your partner can help you plan a delicious seduction.

Nutritionist   A dietary counselor; not to be confused with a registered dietician. In many states in the U.S., anyone can call him- or herself a nutritionist and can set up a dietary counseling practice. When seeking advice from a nutritionist, it's always a good idea to ask about his or her credentials, and ask for references as well.

Passion   In the context of "passionate love," a state of intense longing for union with another. It is usually expressed by kissing, hugging, gazing intently at each other, frequent touching, and, of course, making love.

Real love   Putting your partner's needs on the same level as your own needs, rather than above or below.

Resonance   Originally, resonance was a scientific term describing the action of sympathetic frequencies. In human terms, it simply means that when you describe a feeling, experience, or idea, the person to whom you are describing it fully comprehends, and to a degree, shares, that feeling, experience, or idea.

Seduce   From the Latin *seducere*, which is made up of the prefix *se* (without, apart) and *ducere* (to lead)—in other words, "to lead apart (or away)." In its earliest uses, "seduce" meant "to divert from allegiance or service," or "to induce [a woman] to surrender her chastity." The negative connotation lingers today, but the "new" seduction we've focused on in this book is a positive, exhilarating, and sensual experience for both parties.

Self-confidence   Trust in your abilities and belief in your competence. Often confused with *self-worth*, self-confidence is fed by your accomplishments, such as learning a new procedure or solving a problem.

Self-talk The little voice in your head that, for better or worse, is constantly making judgments about you and the world around you. Much of the time you're probably not even consciously aware of it, but that doesn't mean it isn't affecting you. Constant negative self-talk eats away at your self-esteem. With conscious effort, however, you can redirect your negative thoughts into glowing affirmations of your wonderful qualities.

Self-worth Your perception of your value as a human being. It is often confused with *self-confidence*, but it is a more intrinsic factor than confidence.

Sexual peak The point in a person's life when he or she has the most intense sexual responses. Generally speaking, a man's sexual peak is from late adolescence through the mid to late twenties. It was formerly thought that women didn't reach their peak until their mid to late thirties, though experts now disagree on whether or not there even is such a thing as a woman's sexual peak. Nevertheless, many women report that it takes years of experience for them to really come into their own sexually. In any case, age is not the only determinant of a person's sexual response; many other factors, such as physical health, the state of a person's relationships, and cultural conditions also play a part.

Spirit The word *spirit* has several definitions in the dictionary, the first one being, "a person's mind or feelings, or animating principle, as distinct from his body." A more holistic way of looking at spirit is to think of it as encompassing the physical presence, rather than being distinct from it. Of course, "spirit" includes much more than the physical; it's the sum total of who you are.

Talking a fantasy When you or your partner tell each other about a fantasy you may have, without acting it out. This, in fact, can be every bit as exciting as acting it out.

Trust Confidence in each other's integrity. Trust is an essential element of a truly delicious seduction, and trustworthiness is a mark of the delicious seducer or seductress.

Viagra The so-called virility pill. Men of all ages who have experienced erectile difficulties have found this prescription drug makes a remarkable difference. In fact, some doctors are even recommending Viagra to help alleviate problems that may merely be a result of those "pre-game jitters." Viagra works not by producing sexual desire, but by amplifying signals at the nerve endings, thereby easing the pathways for normal sexual stimulation. Ask your doctor for more information.

Visual One of the three principal ways in which people process information, according to neuro-linguistic programming (NLP) theory. A visual person is likely to be especially attentive to your looks and to other visual cues.

Yoga A system of physical exercise, controlled breathing, and (depending on the type of yoga) meditation. Yoga is good for the body and wonderful for the soul, and doing yoga with someone you love can be very pleasurable and even erotic.

Zone therapies . Generic term referring to techniques such as acupuncture, acupressure, and hand or foot reflexology, that treat pain, tension, or even some types of illness by applying direct pressure (by a needle or fingers, for example) on key parts of the body. Most of these techniques are based on the concept of meridians, which are pathways along which life energy is said to flow through the human body. (By the way, if you know a little bit about reflexology, you can give your partner an extremely seductive foot massage.)

Steamy Seduction Tales

Following are true tales of seduction that have created some glorious memories for the couples involved. I hope you enjoy reading these stories, and I hope they will give you some terrific ideas about how to set up your own unforgettable seduction scenes.

Seductresses at Work

Calling all temptresses: Here are a few smoky tales of lust to get those creative seductress juices flowing. Read on!

Easy in the Big Easy

Stacy and her boyfriend Ralph were spending the weekend in New Orleans. The police happened to be on strike, and one noticeable effect was that the prostitutes had emerged from hiding and were openly offering their services everywhere. As you might imagine, there were many willing customers.

Stacy was a woman whose Christy-Brinkley-type, girl-next-door good looks made men do a double take wherever she went. She was really attracting attention today, for in place of her usual conservative garb she was dressed in a slightly daring but classy outfit of black Lycra pants, with a skimpy gold metallic top, black jacket and gold high heels. The contrast between her clean, innocent beauty and that sizzling, seductive outfit was stunning, and as she walked down the sidewalk with Ralph, Stacy attracted more than one lustful glance from male passers-by.

At one point Ralph stopped to look in a store window, and Stacy walked on ahead a few feet. Almost immediately, she was propositioned by a man, somewhat warily, for he wasn't truly sure if she was a prostitute or not. When she told him she wasn't, he turned red and apologized profusely, but she laughed and told him not to worry about it.

The incident sparked an idea in Stacy's mind. She waited for Ralph to catch up to her, and said, "Let's play a little game." She told him to follow her at a discreet distance for about six blocks, whereupon she would stop at a lamp post. "Let's see how many men proposition me."

"Well, okay," Ralph said, a little uncertain but somehow excited at the prospect. As Stacy began to walk confidently and seductively down the street, she could feel the men's eyes on her. Briefly making eye contact, she smiled at them, giving the more promising-looking ones a more encouraging smile. By doing this, she was able to single out the men whom she wanted to approach her. When they did approach, of course, she smiled but told them she wasn't a "working girl." Most went away disappointed, though several asked her if she wanted to have a drink anyway, which she politely declined.

From his discreet distance, Ralph observed this with mixed emotions: anxiety for Stacy's safety, admiration for the way she attracted the men and then politely turned them away, and pride that this striking woman, hungered after by so many other men, was his. As he watched, he realized he had never wanted her so much. And when she finally stopped and leaned against the street light, attracting a small crowd of eager men, Ralph was seized with an overwhelming desire to "claim" his woman.

Why not present Stacy with a little surprise of his own, he thought. He waited until she had turned away several disappointed men, and then brashly walked up to her, as if introducing himself. "Hi, I'm Ralph," he said. Gently tugging her hair and tipping her face up to his, he kissed her passionately and then took her by the arm, saying, "You're coming to my hotel room now."

As they left the scene, Stacy and Ralph could barely contain their laughter at the disbelieving stares and gasps from the rejected suitors, who wondered how some unknown man could just walk up and steal this stunning woman from their midst. The excitement and confidence this incident inspired in both Ralph and Stacy resulted in some of the sexiest lovemaking they had ever experienced.

Jersey Girl

Jennifer had been dating Max for a little over two months, and recently they had begun a sexual relationship. One evening Max called from his cell phone and asked if he could stop by her place for awhile. "I thought maybe we could watch a video," he said. "I rented the new Steven Seagal movie." He added, "I'm about ten minutes away."

Jennifer had only recently arrived home after a long, grueling day at work, and had just finished shedding her clothes, preparing for a relaxing evening alone. But she didn't want to turn Max away, so she said, "Sure, come on."

She raced around the apartment, straightening the place as much as she could and frantically searching for something to wear. Unfortunately, just about all of her decent-looking casual clothes were in the hamper, and there was no way she was going to get back into her work clothes. She quickly slipped into Max's football jersey. Max, who had once played pro football, had given her the jersey when she asked for one of his shirts to sleep in. Jennifer also put on a pair of little white cotton panties, and then, on impulse, snapped a red belt around her waist, and put on a pair of red high heels.

When he was greeted at the door by this All-American seductress, Max was blown away. He laughed, then grabbed her up in his arms and began kissing her passionately.

They didn't watch the Steven Seagal video that night.

There's a post script to this story. Months later, Max and Jennifer separated after a disagreement. They were both miserable, but neither one wanted to be the one to make the first move to come back. Finally Max did come back to Jennifer, saying the whole disagreement was his fault. He also confessed that during their separation he had been fixated on that vision of her answering the door in his jersey and her high heels. The vision left him laughing, thinking of how much fun they'd had; crying, thinking of how much he missed her; and lustful, thinking of the hot sex they always had (particularly on that night). "Not just any woman could make me forgo a Steven Seagal movie," he said, laughing. Because of her quick thinking and flair for spontaneous fun, Jennifer had truly left him with a seduction to remember.

The Apartment

Audrey and Philip were successful trial lawyers who had been married for 10 years. Though their careers were soaring, their private life wasn't faring so well. Audrey felt Philip was taking her for granted, and to make matters worse, they scarcely saw each other anymore. On many nights, they both worked late in the city, so they often ended up spending the night in their respective offices rather than take the long train ride home. Slowly but surely they were drifting apart. Audrey thought, "I've got to do something." And so she began hatching a plan.

First she leased a small one-bedroom apartment in town and hired a decorator to furnish it in a style that was just this side of decadent (or, as Audrey described it, "like a call girl who almost has good taste"). The apartment was only about 800 square feet, so mirrors were placed everywhere to create a feeling of space. A chaise longue and an overstuffed pink chair graced the living room. The focal point of the bedroom was a large bed draped in green gauzy material and reminiscent of a harem.

Then Audrey planned the night. A complete scrumptious meal from the local takeout gourmet place was in the refrigerator, and a bottle of very expensive champagne was chilling in the ice bucket. She called Philip at his office and told him to meet her, giving him the address.

When Philip knocked on the door, he was greeted by a very attractive woman in a belly dancing costume—a woman who was not Audrey. "Where's my wife?" he asked, puzzled and somewhat wary. "She'll be with you shortly," the woman answered as she pulled him into the room and asked him to lie down on the chaise longue. She poured him a glass of champagne, and then began to do a most audacious belly dance, complete with bells. By the time she had finished, Philip felt quite aroused.

The belly dancer then led him into the bedroom, which was lit with flickering candles. The fragrance of spices was in the air, and there was exotic music—some jazzy Mediterranean/Middle-Eastern fusion he couldn't quite identify—playing softly in the background. The belly dancer led Philip to the bed and pulled the curtain back, and there he beheld his wife, who was nude and was receiving a massage from another woman dressed in harem attire like the belly dancer. Audrey beckoned Philip to join her in the bed. He took off his shirt and shoes, but chose to keep his pants on to hide his obvious state of arousal.

When he got into bed, the harem-clad masseuse began to knead his shoulders, rubbing aromatic oils into his skin as Audrey poured him another glass of champagne. Audrey then proceeded to join the belly dancer in a well choreographed, erotically charged dance, during which Audrey wore nothing but a large feathered fan.

Just when Philip thought he couldn't stand it anymore, Audrey dismissed the two women, whom she had paid in advance. Then Audrey and Philip began making love more passionately than they had in a long time. Somewhere around midnight, they took a break to enjoy the gourmet dinner Audrey had ordered, and then they went right back to a night of love play that lasted through the next day. It was the first day they'd missed at the office in years.

Suffice it to say that Philip has not taken his wife for granted since then. And these days, they're spending less time at the office, and a lot more time in each other's arms.

Seducers' Success Stories

Okay all of you Don Juan's in waiting, here are a few tales of temptation for you, too, to help you woo that beautiful woman with a little creative seduction.

I'm a Little Tied Up Right Now

When Katy arrived at Rod's for dinner, she could smell all sorts of delicious aromas coming from the kitchen—not surprising, because Rod was a gourmet cook. Rod called out to her from the kitchen, saying he was running a little behind. "I've drawn a bath for you," he said. "Oh, and I bought you a little present; it's in the bedroom."

Wondering what was in store for her, Katy went into the bedroom, where she found a note on the bed, telling her to remove all her clothes immediately and get into the tub. "Leave your clothes on the bed," the note said, "and when you get out of your bath, you will have a new outfit, which you must wear to dinner."

Katy took a leisurely bath and when she returned to the bed, she found a red empire nightgown and a black blindfold. There was another note, instructing her to put on the nightgown (no underwear allowed) as well as the blindfold, and call Rod when she was ready.

Katy put on the red gown, a little uneasy by how sheer and short it was. Then she glanced in the mirror and saw how beautiful she looked; the vivid red was a startling contrast to her black hair and white skin. Almost reluctantly, she put on the blindfold, and then called out to Rod.

Rod came into the room and kissed her, telling her she was in for a real treat. He checked her blindfold to make sure she couldn't see, and then he asked her to put her hands together and hold them out, palms up, so he could put a "surprise" in them. She obeyed, and before she knew it he had tied them together with a velvet cord, leaving a long lead for him to pull her gently in the direction where he wanted her to go.

At once Katy felt a little anxious, and yet at the same time very excited. She trusted Rod and knew she was in no danger; all the same, there is something scary as well as exciting about the unknown.

Rod led her to the dining room, had her sit down in a chair, and told her to make herself comfortable. It was then that she realized he was putting a sash around her waist, tying her to the chair. Sitting there blindfolded, with her hands bound and tied, she realized she was completely at his mercy.

"Open your mouth," Rod commanded. And so she did…but wait, it wasn't at all what she expected. It was a luscious, juicy, ripe strawberry, and it exploded in her mouth. Just as it dawned on her that this reminded her of a scene from the movie *9½ Weeks*, she noticed the soundtrack from that very movie playing in the background. A thrill of excitement raced through her body.

Rod pulled down the bodice of the empire gown, exposing her breasts. Then he pulled up the gown's skirt, leaving her completely exposed below the waist as well. And then he began his relentless but delightful assault on her senses—alternately placing warm food, cold food, and ice cubes in her mouth, compelling her to savor the varying tastes and textures.

Next he turned his attention to her breasts, first applying something cold to her nipples, then something creamy to her breasts. She was never quite sure what was being rubbed on her body, but it all smelled delightful and felt exquisite on her naked skin. Finally he pulled her legs apart, took a handful of warm spun honey, and spread it between her thighs. "I'm making you a real honey pot," he said. And as Katy tugged at her restraints, he began to lick off the honey and cream and everything else he had applied to her body. Working at first leisurely, and then furiously, his tongue lapped mercilessly at her crevices until she let out an involuntary scream and her body began to convulse.

When she was finally quiet again, Rod calmly untied her, wiped his mouth delicately on a napkin, and then, holding her chin in his hand, said, "Did you enjoy dinner? I sure did!"

The Wicked Queen

Lisa and James had been dating for a few months when, one weekend, James told Lisa he wanted to give her a gift. "You've given me so much, without asking for much in return," he said. "I can't afford to take you away for a weekend right now, but I would like to fulfill one of your secret fantasies. Just name it; I'll do anything you want."

Lisa was a sweet and rather passive person, so James was somewhat surprised when she requested to play "Wicked Queen." She explained that James was to be her slave, and must fulfill her every wish or his whole village would be executed. Lisa was an amateur actress, so details were important to her. She left the room and returned in a regal but sexy outfit, and a totally new demeanor.

Immediately, Queen Lisa began giving James orders. First, he was to remove his clothes—slowly. "And you're going to remain naked until I tell you otherwise," she commanded imperiously.

Then Lisa began ordering James to do very specific things to pleasure her, directing him at every turn: "Slower. Lighter. Harder. Softer. More to the left." The comfort and confidence with which Lisa had slipped into this role struck James as humorous, and at one point he chuckled. Whereupon Lisa slapped him and told him slaves weren't allowed to laugh, only to follow orders. James really got into his slave role after that, and went on to pleasure his queen for hours until they both fell into a deep, sweet sleep.

The next morning when James woke up, he reached over and, gently and playfully, he pushed Lisa out of bed. Then he carefully put his foot on her throat and said, "The Wicked Queen is dead!" She looked up demurely at him, smiled, and said, "Of course, James."

Two things were different after that night. One, James really knew how to make love to Lisa now; the Wicked Queen had taught him many things that sweet Lisa had been too shy to communicate. And two, whenever he looked at his sweet, good-natured Lisa, he knew there was a woman with a backbone of steel. He also saw a woman with the imagination and creativity to surprise *him* with a sublime seduction.

This one was definitely going to keep him on his toes.

Pier Pressure

Bill took Madison to his lake house for the weekend. As it began to get dark, Bill grilled some fresh salmon and vegetables for dinner. Madison started to set the table, but Bill stopped her, pulling out a picnic basket. "Put the utensils and plates in here," he said. "It's such a beautiful night I thought we'd eat out on the pier tonight. Let's go." They took the short walk down to the pier, with Madison carrying the basket while Bill brought the food. He also carried a plush clean comforter.

When they reached their destination, Madison was quite surprised to see a mattress lying on the pier. "Hmmm, where did that come from?" she asked. Bill just smiled, feigning innocence as he spread the comforter on the mattress and began laying out the dinner.

Darkness had fallen by then. There was no moon, but the stars were out and a cool breeze was blowing off the lake; the night felt magical. "Wait, I forgot the champagne," Bill said, and Madison offered to go back and get it. As she walked back up to the house, she looked around and realized how dark it was; she couldn't see Bill or the pier from the house.

After they finished the delicious dinner, Bill began to kiss Madison and remove her clothes, pushing her gently back onto the soft comforter. She protested mildly, saying, "What about your neighbors?" Bill reassured her, confirming what she'd already seen for herself: Even though they could see into the neighbors' homes, they themselves were shrouded in darkness. No one would be able to see their nakedness except each other. So there, under the stars, they made love. Afterwards they talked and had more champagne, and then made love again.

Madison says that now whenever she closes her eyes, she can recapture that evening; she can smell the water, see the stars, hear the waves, and feel the breeze. She swears this is the night she fell in love with Bill. The man she thought she had known was logical, analytical, and really quite conventional—almost to the point of being stuffy. That one night under the stars changed her assessment of him from good old dependable Bill to the most deliciously seductive man she has ever known.

Index

V

vacations, taking for self-improvement, 48

vaginal orgasms, 211

Venus Butterfly for Men, The, 283

Venus Butterfly for Women, The, 283

Viagra, 289

videos (instructional), 283

visual people, 118

visualization, 211, 253, 289

voice
    attractiveness of, 36-38
    characteristics and impressions, 36
    self-evaluation, 37

voyeurism, 264

vulnerability, 55

W

wardrobes, improving, 34-36

What Men Really Want: Straight Talk From Men About Sex, 282

What Men Won't Tell You But Women Need to Know, 282

wine, as a prop for seduction, 218

Women on Top, 282

X-Y-Z

X-rated movies, *see* pornography

yoga, 289

zone therapies, 290

Zone Therapy, 282

When You're **Smart** Enough to **Know** That **You** Don't Know It All!

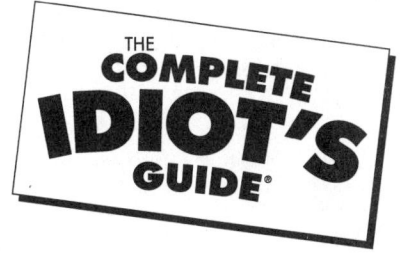

*For all the ups and downs you're sure to encounter in life,
The Complete Idiot's Guides give you
down-to-earth answers and practical solutions.*

Lifestyle

The Complete Idiot's Guide to Etiquette
ISBN0-02-861094-6
$16.95

The Complete Idiot's Guide to Dating
ISBN: 0-02-861052-0
$14.95

The Complete Idiot's Guide to Trouble-Free Car Care
ISBN: 0-02-861041-5
$16.95

The Complete Idiot's Guide to the Perfect Wedding
ISBN: 0-02-861963-3
$16.95

The Complete Idiot's Guide to the Perfect Vacation
ISBN: 1-56761-531-7
$14.99

The Complete Idiot's Guide to Trouble-Free Home Repair
ISBN: 0-02-861042-3
$16.95

The Complete Idiot's Guide to Getting Into College
ISBN: 1-56761-508-2
$14.95

The Complete Idiot's Guide to a Healthy Relationship
ISBN: 0-02-861087-3
$17.95

The Complete Idiot's Guide to Dealing with In-Laws
ISBN: 0-02-862107-7
$16.95

The Complete Idiot's Guide to Choosing, Training, and Raising a Dog
ISBN: 0-02-861098-9
$16.95

The Complete Idiot's Guide to Fun and Tricks with Your Dog
ISBN: 0-87605-083-6
$14.95

The Complete Idiot's Guide to Living with a Cat
ISBN: 0-02-861278-7
$16.95

The Complete Idiot's Guide to Turtles and Tortoises
ISBN: 0-87605-143-3
$16.95

Leisure/Hobbies

The Complete Idiot's Guide to Baking
ISBN: 0-02-861954-4
$16.95

The Complete Idiot's Guide to Beer
ISBN: 0-02-861717-7
$16.95

The Complete Idiot's Guide to Cooking Basics
ISBN: 0-02-861974-9
$18.95

The Complete Idiot's Guide to Entertaining
ISBN: 0-02-861095-4
$16.95

The Complete Idiot's Guide to Mixing Drinks
ISBN: 0-02-861941-2
$16.95

The Complete Idiot's Guide to Wine
ISBN: 0-02-861273-6
$16.95

The Complete Idiot's Guide to Antiques and Collectibles
ISBN: 0-02-861595-6
$16.95

The Complete Idiot's Guide to Boating and Sailing
ISBN: 0-02-862124-7
$18.95

The Complete Idiot's Guide to Bridge
ISBN: 0-02-861735-5
$16.95

The Complete Idiot's Guide to Chess
ISBN: 0-02-861736-3
$16.95

The Complete Idiot's Guide to Cigars
ISBN: 0-02-861975-7
$17.95

The Complete Idiot's Guide to Crafts with Kids
ISBN: 0-02-862406-8
$16.95

The Complete Idiot's Guide to
Fishing Basics
ISBN: 0-02-861598-0
$16.95

The Complete Idiot's Guide to
Gambling Like a Pro
ISBN: 0-02-861102-0
$16.95

The Complete Idiot's Guide to
Hiking and Camping
ISBN: 0-02-861100-4
$16.95

The Complete Idiot's Guide to
Needlecrafts
ISBN: 0-02-862123-9
$16.95

The Complete Idiot's Guide to
Photography
ISBN: 0-02-861092-X
$16.95

The Complete Idiot's Guide to
Quilting
ISBN: 0-02-862411-4
$16.95

The Complete Idiot's Guide to
Yoga
ISBN: 0-02-861949-8
$16.95

The Complete Idiot's Guide to
the Beatles
ISBN: 0-02-862130-1
$18.95

The Complete Idiot's Guide to
Elvis
ISBN: 0-02-861873-4
$18.95

The Complete Idiot's Guide to
Understanding Football Like a
Pro
ISBN:0-02-861743-6
$16.95

The Complete Idiot's Guide to
Golf
ISBN: 0-02-861760-6
$16.95

The Complete Idiot's Guide to
Motorcycles
ISBN: 0-02-862416-5
$17.95

The Complete Idiot's Guide to
Pro Wrestling
ISBN: 0-02-862395-9
$17.95

The Complete Idiot's Guide to
Extra-Terrestrial Intelligence
ISBN: 0-02-862387-8
$16.95

Health and Fitness

The Complete Idiot's Guide to
Managed Health Care
ISBN: 0-02-862165-4
$17.95

The Complete Idiot's Guide to
First Aid Basics
ISBN: 0-02-861099-7
$16.95

The Complete Idiot's Guide to
Vitamins
ISBN: 0-02-862116-6
$16.95

The Complete Idiot's Guide to
Losing Weight
ISBN: 0-02-862113-1
$17.95

The Complete Idiot's Guide to
Tennis
ISBN: 0-02-861746-0
$18.95

The Complete Idiot's Guide to
Tae Kwon Do
ISBN: 0-02-862389-4
$17.95

The Complete Idiot's Guide to
Breaking Bad Habits
ISBN: 0-02-862110-7
$16.95

The Complete Idiot's Guide to
Healthy Stretching
ISBN: 0-02-862127-1
$16.95

The Complete Idiot's Guide to
Beautiful Skin
ISBN: 0-02-862408-4
$16.95

The Complete Idiot's Guide to
Eating Smart
ISBN: 0-02-861276-0
$16.95

The Complete Idiot's Guide to
First Aid
ISBN: 0-02-861099-7
$16.95

The Complete Idiot's Guide to
Getting a Good Night's Sleep
ISBN: 0-02-862394-0
$16.95

The Complete Idiot's Guide to
a Happy, Healthy Heart
ISBN: 0-02-862393-2
$16.95

The Complete Idiot's Guide to
Stress
ISBN: 0-02-861086-5
$16.95

The Complete Idiot's Guide to
Jogging and Running
ISBN: 0-02-862386-X
$17.95

The Complete Idiot's Guide to
Adoption
ISBN: 0-02-862108-5
$18.95

The Complete Idiot's Guide to
Bringing Up Baby
ISBN: 0-02-861957-9
$16.95

The Complete Idiot's Guide to
Grandparenting
ISBN: 0-02-861976-5
$16.95

The Complete Idiot's Guide to
Parenting a Preschooler and
Toddler
ISBN: 0-02-861733-9
$16.95

The Complete Idiot's Guide to
Raising a Teenager
ISBN: 0-02-861277-9
$16.95

The Complete Idiot's Guide to
Single Parenting
ISBN: 0-02-862409-2
$16.95

The Complete Idiot's Guide to
Stepparenting
ISBN: 0-02-862407-6
$16.95